A SECOND FLOWERING

Malcolm Cowley was born near Belsano, Pennsylvania, in 1898, grew up in Pittsburgh, and was graduated from Harvard, where he interrupted his undergraduate career to drive an ambulance during the First World War. In Paris during the 1920s he worked on the magazines *Broom* and *Secession,* encountering that "lost generation" whose outstanding chronicler he was to become. He was literary editor of *The New Republic* from 1929 to 1944, succeeding Edmund Wilson, and he has been a frequent contributor to magazines and literary journals as well as a visiting professor of English at various universities in the United States and in England. President of the National Institute of Arts and Letters from 1956 to 1959 and from 1962 to 1965, he was Chancellor of the American Academy of Arts and Letters from 1966 to 1976. His most recent book, published in 1980, is *The Dream of the Golden Mountains: Remembering the 1930s.* Penguin Books also publishes Malcolm Cowley's *Exile's Return: A Literary Odyssey of the 1920s, The Faulkner-Cowley File: Letters and Memories, 1944–1962,* and *—And I Worked at the Writer's Trade: Chapters of Literary History, 1918–1978.*

A SECOND FLOWERING

Works and Days of the
Lost Generation

MALCOLM COWLEY

PENGUIN BOOKS

Penguin Books Ltd, Harmondsworth, Middlesex, England
Penguin Books, 625 Madison Avenue, New York, New York 10022, U.S.A.
Penguin Books Australia Ltd, Ringwood, Victoria, Australia
Penguin Books Canada Limited, 2801 John Street, Markham, Ontario, Canada L3R 1B4
Penguin Books (N.Z.) Ltd, 182–190 Wairau Road, Auckland 10, New Zealand

First published in the United States of America by The Viking Press 1973
Viking Compass Edition published 1974
Reprinted 1974
Published in Penguin Books 1980

LIBRARY OF CONGRESS CATALOGING IN PUBLICATION DATA
Cowley, Malcolm, 1898–
  A second flowering.
  Reprint of the 1973 ed. published by Viking Press, New York.
  1. American literature—20th century—History and
criticism. 2. Authors, American—20th century—
Biography. I. Title.
[PS221.C68 1980]   813'.5'209   79-25844
ISBN 0 14 00.5498 7

Printed in the United States of America by
Offset Paperback Mfrs., Inc., Dallas, Pennsylvania
Set in Fairfield

ACKNOWLEDGMENTS
Leo Feist, Inc.: Lyrics from "Over There," on page 8, w/m George M. Cohan,
copyright 1917, 1945 by Leo Feist, Inc. Harcourt Brace Jovanovich, Inc.: From
Collected Poems by E. E. Cummings; from The Country of Marriage by Wendell
Berry. Harvard University Press: From i: Six Nonlectures by E. E. Cummings.
Charles Scribner's Sons and William Heinemann Ltd: From The Letters of Thomas
Wolfe (in England, Selected Letters of Thomas Wolfe). Charles Scribner's Sons
and Constable & Co. Ltd: From "I Have a Rendezvous with Death" by Alan Seeger.
Charles Scribner's Sons: From the Introduction by Malcolm Cowley to The Stories
of F. Scott Fitzgerald, copyright 1951 by Charles Scribner's Sons; from the Introduc-
tion by Malcolm Cowley to The Great Gatsby, in Three Novels by F. Scott Fitz-
gerald, copyright 1953 by Charles Scribner's Sons; from the Introduction by Malcolm
Cowley to The Sun Also Rises, in Three Novels by Ernest Hemingway, copyright
© Charles Scribner's Sons, 1962.

Some of these articles originally appeared in The Atlantic Monthly, Horizon, The
New Republic, Saturday Review, The Southern Review, and The Yale Review.

to Allen Tate / Poet and Companion

A Foreword

⚡ This is a study of what is still called for convenience the Lost Generation, one that has grandly played out its part in American life and letters. The World War I generation would be a more accurate name for it. The war, as I have tried to show in an introductory chapter, was a watershed that young writers crossed in their education, and it gave them the feeling of having lived in two eras, almost on two different planets. The second era seemed tawdrier in many ways, when they judged it by standards retained from an earlier time, but still it had become their own world or century. It smiled at them like the heroine of *The Great Gatsby*, as if to promise "that there were gay, exciting things hovering in the next hour." Suspecting that the promise might be delusive, they still pressed forward to enjoy and truthfully portray the era.

I have told their story in terms of eight representative figures: Fitzgerald, Hemingway, Dos Passos, Cummings, Wilder, Faulkner, Wolfe, and Hart Crane, all born between 1894 and 1900. That particular age group had more experiences in common and was more conscious of possessing shared purposes than the groups that preceded or followed it, and this gives coherence to the story. With attention to the salient traits of each writer—and they were all extraordinary persons—I have dealt with their early dreams of the literary life, their subsequent careers at home and abroad, and the works they produced during a period that now seems to have been a second flowering of American literature. The period having ended, a final chapter passes judgments and tries to set the generation in perspective.

The generation is my own, and I have been writing about it at intervals almost since I started to write. In paging through a scrapbook not long ago, I came across my first literary essay, written in 1921 after two years of doing book reviews. "This Youngest Generation" it was called, and it appeared in Dr. Canby's new weekly *The Literary Review,* then printed as a supplement to *The New York Evening Post.* The essay described some characteristics of still mostly unpublished writers, as notably their interest in form and Flaubert, and it brashly predicted that they would earn a place in American letters. It also mentioned names, a hard thing to do at the time, but at least I knew Cummings, Dos Passos, Kenneth Burke, and S. Foster Damon, a college friend who afterward displayed a peculiar gift for doing quite original work at the wrong times, when it was almost certain to be overlooked. The essay didn't mention Fitzgerald, but that must have been because *This Side of Paradise,* published the year before, had been too popular for what was then my rarefied taste. Hemingway, Faulkner, and the others it couldn't mention, since their work had not been printed anywhere.

Later, though, as the work appeared, I followed it with the warm feeling that those authors were speaking for all of us. Since I had predicted the books, after a fashion, it was now my task to define and defend them, or sometimes to explain why one of them had fallen short of the author's intention. In 1934 I published *Exile's Return,* an account of how my contemporaries had lived in Greenwich Village and Paris. The book received a few very friendly notices, all by younger men, but it was howled down by older reviewers. Almost unanimously they ridiculed my notion that the men of the 1920s had special characteristics and that their adventures in Paris were a story worth telling. Lewis Gannett, usually a tolerant critic, said in *The New York Herald Tribune* that the writers I dealt with were sentimental drunks who "felt there was something superb in starving three days while waiting for papa's next check." "Nobody wrote great books in the past decade," said William Soskin of *The New York American.* "Mr. Hemingway is growing dim. So are his colleagues."

In the 1940s, when Hemingway and his colleagues had proved that Mr. Soskin was shortsighted, I began writing longer studies of their work. By then the work was being widely praised, except in the universities, but I was trying to show that it had more depth and broader implications than critics had found in it. Also there was Faulkner, whose books were scandalously neglected, and there was still the task of presenting the generation as a whole. I was delighted to find that the studies, as they continued, were helping to set in motion whole battalions of scholars, including gifted ones.

Most of the chapters that follow were written at different times, for different immediate purposes, though always with the notion that they were part of the same undertaking. Some of them were introductions to anthologies or to republished works by various authors (*The Portable Faulkner, The Stories of F. Scott Fitzgerald, A Thornton Wilder Trio*). Others were lectures or magazine articles, or the two combined. I usually wrote far too much for the occasion, then chopped the manuscript down to size, or sawed it into fireplace lengths, with the result that some of the studies had a complicated publishing history. One of them started as a simple book review when *The Letters of Thomas Wolfe* appeared in 1956. I became fascinated by the personality revealed in the letters and wrote not quite a book about it, but something much too long for magazine publication. Scissored into pieces it appeared in three magazines, *The New Republic, The Reporter,* and *The Atlantic Monthly.* Here the whole study, in a lately revised version, appears for the first time.

It has been a pleasure to bring the studies together, to supply interconnections, to have second thoughts, to bridge various gaps with fresh material, and in short to produce what I hope is a book, not a mere collection. It has also been a pleasure to write new chapters for the book, including those on Dos Passos, Cummings, Hemingway's later years, and of course the final chapter with its effort to establish perspectives. On the other hand, it has been no pleasure at all to find that some older studies had to be omitted as a result of their having been reprinted in too many anthologies. Once I was proud of them for laying bare new beds of ore, but now the ore has been mined and smelted by others. Rereading those studies before filing them away, I felt myself sinking back into the magma of history. I wonder if anyone else has had the experience of writing about the same group of authors at intervals during half a century.

The subject approaches and recedes like a landscape seen from a raft as the river sweeps by. Future appears before present, which fades into past. One starts by trying to predict the nature of books that are still to be written—continues by talking about actual books and listening to their authors—ends with a retrospect of amazing careers that assume new shapes and meanings. One starts by speaking *for* the youngest writers and ends by speaking *to* them, from a point one hopes is not too distant for the voice to carry. That final chapter might prove to be my last word on the generation. Its story is almost ended and I have other things to write about while there is time.

Contents

a second flowering

I The Other War

They were in their late teens or early twenties, the right age for soldiering, when Congress declared war on Germany in April 1917. Most of them served in uniform, but only for a brief period, usually not more than a year. American losses in the war were modest ones when judged by the standards imposed on us by World War II; some fifty-three thousand men were killed in action. Among those who would be the prominent writers of the generation, only Hemingway and the dramatist Robert E. Sherwood, both serving with foreign armies, were seriously wounded; the others got home unscathed. Still, more than anything else it was the First World War that made them a generation, by changing their world and by giving them shares, as it were, in a rich fund of common emotions.

Questions that strike us now are what the emotions were, why writers felt them so deeply, and what effects they were to have. The answers, of which there are many, must be looked for partly in military and social history, partly in the special field of literary folkways and the literary imagination. Several paths might be explored. In this first chapter I shall confine myself to three topics that more or less suggest the others: "Casualties," "The Theater of War," and "The Big Words."

1 CASUALTIES

In 1917 it seemed to Americans of many opinions, pacifistic or patriotic, that the war in Europe was becoming an enormous carnival of death. Nothing else in the history of the continent, not even the Black Death, had produced such an extravagance of corpses. Looking at statistics compiled after the Armistice, we find that 1.8 million German soldiers died, most of them on the Western Front; that the French had 1.35 million killed out of a much smaller population—with total losses, which include the wounded and missing, of six million, or almost exactly three-fourths of the Frenchmen under arms; and that the British Empire, with fewer divisions on the front, still had nine hundred thousand killed in action. It was death on the production line, with the output of corpses planned in advance for each operation, but almost always exceeding the plan.

And it was not death for outcasts, for *Untermenschen,* as Hitler would call the Jews in the second war as an excuse for having them butchered—along with lesser numbers of Polish and Russian peasants and Gypsies, whom he also regarded as belonging to infra-human stocks; on the contrary, it was death for young men socially and physically attested as the flower of the nation. Called up by age groups, they were stripped naked, weighed, measured, auscultated; they were examined for gonorrhea, fallen arches, defects of vision; and finally, after passing the tests, they were given identity disks like cattle government-stamped as being fit for slaughter. The tallest and most robust would be among the first to die, since they made better targets, but moral qualities could also be fatal, as, for example, enterprise, bravery, leadership, idealism, and self-sacrifice. It was the extinction of the fittest—and for what discernible purpose? Through 1917 the battles in which they died month after month, year after year, had never ended in decisive victories or defeats, but had merely subsided in exhaustion.

Verdun, the greatest battle of all, had been started by the Germans with no strategic purpose and merely in the hope—as General von Falkenhayn later confessed in his memoirs—that the French would "bleed to death." From the first attack in February 1916, it lasted six months without remission. There has never been an accurate count of the dead and wounded, but the usual estimate is that a million men were lost on the two sides, with the French losses heavier by a few scores of thousands. The battle was several times renewed, and it ended with both sides almost exactly where they began. That summer the British attacked on the Somme and lost sixty thousand men on July 1 without gaining any ground whatever. The highest death rate was among lieutenants from universities and great public schools, who led their platoons over the top in tailored uniforms and Sam Browne belts. Fighting on the Somme continued past the middle of November, by which time the British had suffered four hundred thousand casualties, "including," as a recent author says, "the men who in the normal way would have been leaders in politics, the arts, the sciences, commerce and industry."

Those enormous butcheries of 1916 produced a change in the moral atmosphere of the war. From that time it was death more than victory that obsessed the minds of soldiers on both sides. "After the war is over," the Tommies sang to the tune of that melancholy waltz "After the Ball"; and they added a second line, *"Après la guerre finit,"* under the illusion that it was a French echo of the first. Many of the singers, however, had by then abandoned their hope of surviving into the *après-guerre,* as had many Frenchmen and Germans. Even Blackjack Pershing was to catch the contagion. When he placed his forces at the disposal of the Allied High Command after the German breakthrough of March 1918, he said—as if he were stating the soldier's highest purpose—"We are here to be killed."

Looking back after half a century, one is tempted to postulate a death wish in an entire culture, perhaps engendered by the tranquillity and comfort of middle-class European life in the years before 1914. Tokens of that wish might be found in the tangled series of stupidities—rather than villainies, except in a few cases—that made the war inevitable while everyone claimed he was trying to prevent it; or again in the folly of generals who ordered attacks that they must have known would fail disastrously. Statesmen and generals may have felt an obscure need for self-destruction—or was it rather a sense of guilt that involved whole nations? They had been too rich and happy for too many years; they had incurred a debt to the gods; and now they must repay the debt by offering the most cherished of their young men as a human sacrifice. Cheered, almost worshiped, their faces smeared with kisses and their rifles garlanded with flowers, the young men went out to die in a ritual that exactly recalls the Aztecs and how they offered the annual sacrifice of their handsomest captive to Tezcatlipoca, the god of gods. In the months before his death, the victim feasted and played the flute; he was given the loveliest maidens as his wives; and he was worshiped by crowds when he appeared in the street wreathed in flowers.

Those blood sacrifices of the Great War had this to distinguish them, that the young soldiers were often willing victims. "Men go voluntarily to their death," said *The New Statesman*, "in a manner that has amazed all who hold that the European races had grown decadent and had lost their courage." Some proclaimed their eagerness to be killed. Said Rupert Brooke in a letter to his friend John Drinkwater, "Come and die. It'll be great fun." One of Brooke's sonnets about death, "The Soldier," became the most popular English poem of the war:

> *If I should die, think only this of me:*
>   *That there's some corner of a foreign field*
> *That is for ever England. . . .*

The most popular American poem was "I Have a Rendezvous with Death," in which the poet looks forward to being killed as if he were planning an assignation with a strange new mistress:

> *I have a rendezvous with Death*
> *At some disputed barricade,*
> *When Spring comes back with rustling shade*
> *And apple-blossoms fill the air—*
> *I have a rendezvous with Death*
> *When Spring brings back blue days and fair.*

The author of the poem was Alan Seeger, a young man who had been at Harvard with the famous class of 1910; some of his classmates were Walter Lippmann, John Reed, Heywood Broun, Robert Edmond Jones, and T. S. Eliot. In his college years he was everybody's image of a young poet in the romantic tradition: intense, frail, mannered, shy, and touch-me-not. After graduation he went to Greenwich Village with other apprentice writers, and there he wandered through the streets in a long black opera cloak, borrowed for the winter; Jack Reed described him as "the eager / Keats-Shelley-Swinburne mediaeval Seeger." He had moved on to Paris and was living in the Latin Quarter when the war started. Full of enthusiasm for everything French, he enlisted in the Foreign Legion, then the most dangerous branch of the French Army, and the spindly aesthete became a brave and robust soldier.

The poem is easy to criticize for its conventional metaphors, its poetic inversions, and its echoes of the English 1890s. At the time it was published, however, it spoke effectively for many thousands of young men. It still casts light on one of the reasons why so many of them consented to be sacrificed, even volunteering for service under foreign flags, like Seeger, and, if they wore the uniform of their own country, taking risks beyond the call of duty. Of course there were other reasons, including pride, idealism, a thirst for experience, and the fear of being called a slacker; but in those days death itself exerted a curious magnetism on young men. The possibility, almost the certainty, of being killed lent meaning and glamour to what might have been aimless lives. Death was a blind date, the chance of meeting a beautiful woman; and in Seeger's poem it is contrasted but at the same time compared with the silken beds,

> *Where Love throbs out in blissful sleep,*
> *Pulse nigh to pulse, and breath to breath,*
> *Where hushed awakenings are dear . . .*
> *But I've a rendezvous with Death*
> *At midnight in some flaming town,*
> *When Spring trips north again this year.*

Although he survived the massacres of that spring, Seeger kept his rendezvous on July 4, 1916, during an attack by the Foreign Legion designed to support the Somme offensive. His collected poems, published that fall, were widely admired, and not a few American magazines celebrated his life and talents. The same magazines were likely to praise the English war poets, most of whom were infantry officers and some of whom had been killed along the Somme. Thus, even before we entered the war, death had become a familiar and compelling subject for the new generation of American writers. The notion spread that death was the invariable fate of men in the trenches and that it was something to be courted like a woman. Writers then in college learned to regard it as a sort of final examination for which one should prepare by living intensely in the little time that remained. Scott Fitzgerald, for example, believed that he was marked for death as soon as he put on an infantry officer's uniform. Years later he explained to a reporter why he had spent his army weekends slaving away at a novel. "I was certain that all the young people were going to be killed in the war," he said, "and I wanted to put on paper a record of the strange life they had lived in their time."

2 THE THEATER OF WAR
For Americans in 1917, the war was something that you "went to," as Archibald MacLeish has pointed out. It was not a condition but a place, and the place was far away in Europe—"over there," as we should soon be singing:

> Over there, over there,
> Send a word, send a prayer over there.
> Say the Yanks are coming,
> The Yanks are coming,
> They're drum, drum, drumming everywhere.

As a matter of record, the Yanks in those days were singing, not drumming, and their songs were not of a memorable sort, lacking as they did the direct feeling of Union Army songs in the Civil War. The best of our World War songs, such as "Mademoiselle from Armenteers," were borrowed from the English, who had been fighting long enough to find expression for the sadness and bawdiness and cynicism of veterans. The American songs were usually concocted in Tin Pan Alley, though Irving Berlin wrote some lively ones when he was a sergeant at Camp Upton. Most of the songs by others apostrophized Joan of Arc or "the girl I left behind," on whom the singer promised to pin his medal—

> She deserves it more than I
> For the way she didn't cry.

Still, a few of them were good songs to sing on marches, and they added a theatrical note to the war, transforming it into a melodrama with sound effects and a musical setting.

There was indeed a theater of war, and it did not sprawl over Europe as at the end of World War II, or share attention with other theaters in East Asia and Oceania. In 1917 the Eastern Front was crumbling away. The Western Front was a narrow stage, that is, a double line of trenches from the North Sea to the Vosges Mountains, with a zone of defense that extended only a few miles to the rear. Paris, sixty miles to the rear, had remained a peacetime city, and it was still the capital of world culture. Plays, concerts, the Russian Ballet, restaurants, and houses of convenience all were packed to capacity; even the bookstores did a good-enough business. If you had been lucky enough to be given leave in Paris, you went to the Folies Bergère, where the little ladies clustered round you during the intermission; then you rose late and enjoyed a superb luncheon. After draining the last glass of wine, you took a train back to the front as if setting out for a weekend in the country. The train was slow, often stopping for more soldiers returning from their leaves, but it hadn't many miles to travel. Three or four hours later you were at the railhead, picking a louse from your tunic and listening to the rumble of artillery. There were great flashes of light against the evening clouds. You went to the war and it was like going to a theater that advertised the greatest spectacle in history.

Something that I long ago called the spectatorial attitude was especially prevalent among soldiers who were also young American writers, and this for reasons that are not impossible to explain.

In 1917 there happened to be a larger than usual number of apprentice writers, including some of exceptional talent, who were still in American colleges or had lately been graduated. They were in most respects like other young Americans of the middle classes, but they also had characteristics, good and bad, that set them somewhat apart. They had more imagination than most of their contemporaries. They had more vanity—why else should they try so hard to be published?—more initiative and curiosity, more sympathy with foreign cultures—especially French culture at the time, owing to their literary admirations—and more eagerness for experience. They wanted to see everything so they could write about everything. They had—or they expressed, since they were men of words—stronger opinions than most people, and their attitudes to the war ran the full gamut from pacifism to jingoism. Whatever the attitudes, almost all of them wanted to get over and see what the war was like. In the words of a song,

> Oh, I don't know what this war's about,
> But I bet, by gosh, I'll soon find out.

When I looked up their service records, I found that very few of them, proportionately, had waited to be drafted. Two or three, including Michael Gold, were among the radicals who escaped the draft by fleeing to Mexico. Jack Reed, the best reporter of his time, went to Russia and fought in the revolution as well as reporting it. Most of the others volunteered, if they were of military age, and most of the volunteers "got over" to France. There were exceptions like William Faulkner, who began and ended as a cadet in the Royal Canadian Air Force, and Scott Fitzgerald, who marched on board a transport with full equipment, helmet banging at his side, and was then marched off because the Germans had begged for an armistice. With his lively imagination, Fitzgerald had already suffered the wounds of an infantry officer in combat, and Faulkner, still more imaginative, was to write vivid and persuasive stories that ended with dogfights over the German lines. Those who did "get over" served in a variety of military employments; among them were airmen, artillery officers such as Archibald MacLeish, captains in the Marine Corps such as Laurence Stallings, and sergeants there such as Thomas Boyd (who was to write a first realistic novel about the Marines, *Through the Wheat*). But what impressed me in looking at the records was to find again how many of them had enlisted in the French, the British, or the Canadian Army and had thus remained foreigners in uniform. While facing death they were still, to some extent, the spectators of somebody else's war.

One service under foreign command that attracted a considerable number of writers was ambulance driving on the French or the Italian front. It offered an expeditious means of getting to the front—a fact that young writers, with their curiosity and initiative, were quicker than others to grasp—and it also offered a panorama of the battlefields only a little less extensive than that enjoyed by airmen. The ambulance drivers were gentlemen volunteers, detached in spirit from the armies with which they served, as also from the wounded Frenchmen or Italians they carried back from dressing stations to base hospitals. To the end they remained observers, if helpful ones, and the spectatorial attitude is revealed in much of their writing about the war. Hemingway, for example, might be reading from a laboratory notebook when he tells us how the corpses looked after an Italian counterattack.

A naturalist [he says], to obtain accuracy of observation, may confine himself in his observations to one limited period, and I will take first that following the Austrian offensive of June, 1918, in Italy as one in which the dead were present in their greatest numbers, a withdrawal having been forced and an advance later made to recover the ground lost so that the positions after the battle were the same as before except for the presence of the dead.

Dos Passos tells of watching from a village schoolmaster's parlor while Frenchmen by truckloads went jolting past on their way to death in still another useless attack. "Faces merged into a blur," he writes. "All we could see in the dim light was the desperation in their eyes." His tone is more compassionate than Hemingway's, but still it is that of a foreign observer. E. E. Cummings, in a few of his early poems, writes about the war in a fashion that would have seemed unthinkable to infantry officers, describing it not as a shared experience, but as something "i have seen," a spectacle of death with aesthetic properties. Thus, he says in "La Guerre":

> the bigness of cannon
> is skilful,
>
> but i have seen
> death's clever enormous voice
> which hides in a fragility
> of poppies. . . .
>
> at Roupy
> i have seen
> between barrages,
>
> the night utter ripe unspeaking girls.

Cummings, Dos Passos, and Hemingway: those three ambulance drivers, more than Fitzgerald, were the writers most admired and emulated by their younger colleagues during the postwar years, so that their special perceptions set a stamp on a whole period in American literature. What lessons did they learn from the ambulance corps?

They learned that the French Army was sullen and mutinous after the butchery at Verdun and the disastrous April 1917 offensive on the Chemin des Dames, just as the Italians would be mutinous the following winter, after Caporetto. *"Finie la guerre!"* they heard soldiers growling over their wine. With some of their comrades they learned that revolution was in the air and that people were being arrested on the vague suspicion of their being disloyal. Cummings was one of the victims; he spent three months in a detention station, "the Enormous Room," merely because a friend of his had written letters to the anarchist Emma Goldman. With others he learned to hate authority as personified in the stupid older men who had ordered the arrests and planned the butcheries. "The fellows in this section are frightfully decent," Dos Passos wrote to a classmate in the prep-school idiom of those days, "—all young men are frightfully decent. If we only governed the world instead of the swagbellied old fogies that do. . . . Down with the middle-aged!" That sentiment, expressed more forcefully in many English war poems, would lead to a bloodless but bitter conflict between the young and the middle-aged that continued through the 1920s and that, after subsiding for thirty years, would be spectacularly revived in the 1960s.

Meanwhile the ambulance drivers learned other lessons, especially if they served in France. Although their pay was that of a French private—five cents a day and a quart of sour wine—they had the privilege denied to American soldiers in the ranks of spending their leaves in Paris. Most of them fell in love with the city, and many were fascinated by its little ladies, of whom Cummings was to write:

> *little ladies more*
> *than dead exactly dance*
> *in my head, precisely*
> *dance where danced la guerre.*

After he was released from the Enormous Room, Cummings exclaimed in a letter to Dos Passos, *"Que je m'ennuie pour la Ville Immense, la Femme superbe et subtile qui s'appelle—tu le sais— Paris."* Like many others he dreamed that the war would be over soon and that Paris would be his home.

Still another lesson learned by ambulance drivers was one I have mentioned already, that the risk of death exerts a magnetic attraction on young men. Dos Passos, though a convinced pacifist, wrote that "the winey thought of death sings in the spring blood."

Later he was to write, looking back at those days, that the immediate presence of death "sharpened the senses. The sweetness of white roses, the shape and striping of a snail shell, the taste of an omelet, the most casual sight or sound appeared desperately intense against the background of the great massacres." Since there was not a sufficient likelihood of death in the ambulance corps, its members took unnecessary risks—as Hemingway, for example, who insisted on visiting a listening post in the front lines, where he was blown up by a bomb from an Austrian trench mortar. Several of the frightfully decent fellows in Dos Passos' ambulance section—as others in my camion section, where the atmosphere was much the same—had themselves transferred into other services, usually French or American aviation, in which they had a better chance of being killed.

Then suddenly the war ended, and most of them were still alive.

The war ended too soon for many Americans—not for those who had fought at Belleau Wood or in the Argonne, but for others who had only marched and countermarched behind the lines; now they would never know whether or not they were brave men. Some were ashamed of being unmedaled and unwounded. Others, especially the airmen, had lived more intensely than they would ever live again and began to feel vaguely, at intervals, that something in them had died on the eleventh of November 1918. All the young men had been exposed to a variety of strong emotions. Their individualities had been affirmed, even in the anonymous disguise of a uniform, and they had dreamed of peacetime careers in which they would play the part of heroes. Now the war had ended without giving them a chance, as Fitzgerald was to say, of expending all that accumulated nervous energy. Many of them—with Hemingway the most conspicuous example among writers—were to spend the next ten years looking for another stage on which they could re-enact the dangers and recapture the winey taste of war.

3 THE BIG WORDS

For a few months after the Armistice—only a few—young American writers were full of hope for themselves and the world. The democracies were triumphant, all the great tyrannies were overthrown, and perhaps young men could play their part in an old American dream, that of building a new order of the ages—"Novus Ordo Seclorum," as we still read on the backs of depreciated dollar bills. The hope faded away in 1919. Among the events of that disastrous year in American history were the Treaty of Versailles, which the Senate would refuse to ratify for the wrong reasons; the May Day riots of servicemen against Socialists; the general strike in Seattle, followed by strikes in major industries that were broken one after another; the Volstead Act, passed over the veto of a crippled President; the rescinding by Congress of all the progressive measures adopted during the war; the preaching of hundred-percent Americanism; and the fear of revolution that set good people to screaming, "Ship the Reds or shoot them." Together those events were a sort of counterrevolution, one that affirmed the moral dictatorship of congressmen from rural districts and left political power in the hands of businessmen with narrow aims: they wanted profits and very soon would have bigger profits than ever before, at an exorbitant cost to the world. Young writers were unhappy in that time of salesmanship and suspicion. Cummings spoke for many when he said:

> the season 'tis, my lovely lambs,
>
> of Sumner Volstead Christ and Co.
> the epoch of Mann's righteousness
> the age of dollars and no sense.[1]

The notion began to spread among writers that they were an oppressed minority, orphans and strangers in their own country, and that they had better leave it as soon as possible.

A word then frequently applied to the younger men was "disillusioned." It was a word imported from England, where it was being used more accurately. After their years in the trenches, after

---

1. In another age the names have to be identified. John S. Sumner was secretary of the New York Society for Suppression of Vice, and most of the "vice" he suppressed was books or plays. Andrew J. Volstead, congressman from Minnesota, was author of an act that went far beyond the Prohibition Amendment in its severity. James R. Mann, a standpat congressman from Illinois, gave his name to an act designed to abolish the white-slave traffic. The Mann Act was so broad in its provisions that, if a New Yorker escorted his girl to Hoboken or to Westport, Connecticut, he might be guilty of a federal offense if he paid her fare.

losing most of their comrades, and after a treaty of peace that promised to breed new wars, the English survivors had a right to be tired and cynical. The Americans still had that accumulated nervous energy, and their disillusionment was chiefly an attitude to be proclaimed in a style full of bounce. In truth they were not so much disillusioned as disaffiliated, and not so much by the war itself as by the events that followed it. Their capacity for illusion had not been destroyed, but merely displaced.

One dream they had been forced to surrender was that of governing the world—to use Dos Passos' phrase—"instead of the swagbellied old fogies that do." With the old swagbellies still in power, young men turned away from social aims and from any type of public service. Here I am thinking not only of the writers but of the whole wartime generation; there would never be many gifted politicians among its members. The new illusion into which it retreated was that young men could achieve success in their individual lives without any thought of society, or merely by seizing upon the opportunities for making money that society was soon to offer in abundance. For the next ten years, until the crash in Wall Street, the aims that young men would cherish were the self-directed ones of making money, of becoming famous—it was the age of very young celebrities—of living intensely, of having a grand time, and, for a larger number of Americans than before, of creating works of art.

In the literary art there would be a new selection of heroes and ancestors. The admired figures of the years before 1914 had been novelists and dramatists of social vision, as notably Shaw, Wells, Anatole France, and Romain Rolland. Not the ideals of such men, but rather the hope of attaining them through any sort of collective undertaking, had fallen into discredit. Edmund Wilson says at the end of *Axel's Castle*:

> . . . when the prodigious concerted efforts of the War had ended only in impoverishment and exhaustion for all the European peoples concerned, and in a general feeling of hopelessness about politics, about all attempts to organize men into social units— armies, parties, nations—in the service of some common ideal, for the accomplishment of some particular purpose, the Western mind became peculiarly hospitable to a literature indifferent to action and unconcerned with the group.

The new heroes were men who had maintained their personal integrity by sacrificing life to art; some of them were Flaubert, Mallarmé, Proust, and Eliot. The paramount hero of the age was Joyce, and his *Ulysses* came to be revered by the new writers almost as the Bible was by Primitive Methodists. I suspect, however, that *A Portrait of the Artist* exerted a deeper influence at the time, since many writers identified themselves with Stephen Dedalus in his proud revolt from church and family, in his resort to "silence, exile, and cunning," and in his dream of forging "in the smithy of my soul the uncreated conscience of my race."

That last was a social purpose, reappearing at the end of the novel as if by stealth, and Joyce himself was an Irish patriot in the fashion that many younger exiles of the time were American patriots: they had fled in despair from their own country, but still they wanted to redeem it. The younger exiles also had another purpose that was social rather than personal. They wanted to redeem the language by getting rid of what they often called "the big words."

To understand what they meant by the phrase, one has to remember that the disasters of wartime were always disguised by lofty words. Many sorts of people had taken part in that verbal effort to mislead. Politicians arriving from Paris or Rome to exhort the troops, generals publishing their orders of the day, journalists inventing legends of heroism to inspire the stay-at-homes, all found words to conceal the fact that men were being driven to slaughter like cattle. In this country the Liberty Bond campaigns engulfed us in oratory as in a sea covered with oil, and Woodrow Wilson tried to make the world safe for democracy by proclaiming ideals not for people, but for Mankind presented as a gray abstraction. Wilson had become the archvillain of several writers, including Dos Passos, while many others felt that the deceptive phrases of wartime, and even the habit of coining deceptive phrases, would have to be expunged from the language.

Hemingway made the classical statement of their revolt against the big words in *A Farewell to Arms*. "I did not say anything," the hero tells us after listening to the high sentiments of an Italian comrade. "I was always embarrassed by the words sacred, glorious, and sacrifice and the expression in vain. We had heard them, sometimes standing in the rain almost out of earshot, so that only the shouted words came through, and had read them, on proclamations that were slapped up by billposters over other proclamations, now for a long time, and I had seen nothing sacred, and the things that were glorious had no glory and the sacrifices were like the stockyards at Chicago if nothing was done with the meat except to bury it." Those familiar lines were written in 1929, and Hemingway was by no means first to express the sentiment. It can be found, for example, in a 1926 poem by Archibald MacLeish about an ambassador's big words at the dedication of a cemetery for the American war dead, the one in which MacLeish's brother was buried. It can be found in still earlier poems by E. E. Cummings, including his address to the press officers of the American Expeditionary Force:

> my little darlings, let us now
> passionately remember how—
> braving the worst, of peril heedless,
> each braver than the other, each
> (a typewriter within his reach)
> upon his fearless derrière
> sturdily seated—Colonel Needless
> To Name and General You know who
> a string of pretty medals drew
>
> (while messrs jack james john and jim
> in token of their country's love
> received my dears the order of
> The Artificial Arm and Limb)

Literary scholars might easily track down the theme in other poets and novelists of the wartime generation. I think they would also find it in the work of younger writers who merely read about the war, but who pictured themselves as turning rebellious like Dos Passos, as prisoners in the Enormous Room with Cummings, or as being wounded and making a separate peace like Hemingway. A theme once brilliantly stated is likely to be echoed for a long time.

What I wanted to suggest, however, is that the revolt against big words and noble sentiments was much more than a subject for poems and paragraphs. It also helped to shape the prose style of a generation which, as a rule, preferred the colloquial tone even in critical essays—for example, in those of Edmund Wilson—and distrusted any phrase that begged for an emotional response. The style, in turn, revealed a habit of mind and a widely shared purpose in writing. Outraged by the fake sentiments expressed in wartime, as by their sequels in 1919, the generation was trying to learn what it really felt, no matter how simple or shameful, and then, in Hemingway's words, "to put down what really happened in action . . . the sequence of motion and fact which made the emotion." That search for concrete words to express "what really happened in action" became a distinguishing feature of the new literary age. One might add that the effort to redeem the language was often combined with an attack on the politicians and generals who, as Dos Passos wrote, "have turned our language inside out . . . have taken the clean words our fathers spoke and made them slimy and foul." What seemed at first a quarrel over style was thus to develop by natural stages into the radical pacifism of the 1930s, and this in turn was to find big words of its own. But that story and all the others have to be traced in the works and careers of individual writers.

II FITZGERALD
The Romance
of Money

1 🖋 Those who were lucky enough to be born a little before the end of the last century, in any of the years from 1895 to 1900, went through much of their lives with a feeling that the new century was about to be placed in their charge; it was like a business in financial straits that could be rescued by a timely change in management. As Americans and optimists, they believed that the business was fundamentally sound. They identified themselves with the century; its teens were their teens, troubled but confident; its World War, not yet known as the First, was theirs to fight on the winning side; its reckless twenties were their twenties. As they launched into their careers, they looked about for spokesmen, and the first one they found—though soon they would have doubts about him—was F. Scott Fitzgerald.

Among his qualifications for the role was the sort of background that his generation regarded as typical. Scott was a Midwestern boy, born in St. Paul on September 24, 1896, to a family of Irish descent that had some social standing and a very small fortune inherited by the mother. The fortune kept diminishing year by year, and the Fitzgeralds, like all families in their situation, had to think a lot about money. When the only son was eleven they were living in Buffalo, where the father was working for Procter and Gamble. "One afternoon," Fitzgerald told a reporter thirty years later, ". . . the phone rang and my mother answered it. I didn't understand what she said, but I felt that disaster had come to us. My mother, a little while before, had given me a quarter to go swimming. I gave the money back to her. I knew something terrible had happened and I thought she couldn't spare the money now. 'Dear God,' I prayed, 'please don't let us go to the poorhouse.'

"A little later my father came home. I had been right. He had lost his job." More than that, as Fitzgerald said, "He had lost his essential drive, his immaculateness of purpose." The family moved back to St. Paul, where the father worked as a wholesale grocery salesman, earning hardly enough to pay for his desk space. It was help from a pious aunt that enabled Scott to fulfill his early ambition of going to an Eastern preparatory school, then going to Princeton.

In 1917 practically the whole student body went off to war. Fitzgerald went off in style, having received a provisional commission as second lieutenant in the regular army. Before leaving Princeton in November, he ordered his uniform at Brooks Brothers and gave the manuscript of a first novel to his faculty mentor, Christian Gauss, not yet dean of the college, but a most persuasive teacher of European literature. Gauss, honest as always, told him that it wasn't good enough to publish. Not at all discouraged, Fitzgerald reworked it completely, writing twelve hours a day during his weekends at training camp and his first furlough. When the second draft was finished, he sent it to Shane Leslie, the Irish man of letters, who had shown some interest in his work. Leslie spent ten days correcting and punctuating the script, then sent it to Scribners, his own publishers. "Really if Scribner takes it," Fitzgerald said in a letter to Edmund Wilson, "I know I'll wake some morning and find that the debutantes have made me famous overnight. I really believe that no one else could have written so searchingly the story of the youth of our generation."

Fitzgerald in his Brooks Brothers uniform before he went off (1917) to officers' training camp. WERNER WOLFF, BLACK STAR

Scribners sent back the novel, rightly called *The Romantic Egotist,* while expressing some regret, and Maxwell Perkins, who was still too young to be the senior editor, suggested revisions that might make it acceptable. Fitzgerald tried to follow the suggestions and resubmitted the manuscript that summer. In August it was definitely rejected, and Fitzgerald then asked Perkins as a favor to submit it to two other publishers, one radical and one conservative. His letter was dated from Camp Sheridan, in Alabama, where he was soon to be named aide-de-camp to Major General J. A. Ryan. It was at a dance in Montgomery that he fell in love with a judge's daughter, Zelda Sayre, whom he described to his friends as "the most beautiful girl in Alabama *and* Georgia"; one state wasn't big enough to encompass his admiration. "I didn't have the two top things: great animal magnetism or money," he wrote years afterward in his notebook. "I had the two second things, though: good looks and intelligence. So I always got the top girl."

He was engaged to the judge's daughter, but they couldn't marry until he was able to support her. After being discharged from the army—without getting overseas, as I noted—he went to New York and looked for a job. Neither the radical nor the conservative publisher had shown interest in his novel. All his stories were coming back from the magazines, and at one time he had 122 rejection slips pinned in a frieze around his cheap bedroom on Morningside Heights. The job he found was with an advertising agency and his pay started at $90 a month, with not much chance of rapid advancement; the only praise he received was for a slogan written for a steam laundry in Muscatine, Iowa: "We keep you clean in Muscatine." He was trying to save money, but the girl in Alabama saw that the effort was hopeless and broke off the engagement on the score of common sense. Fitzgerald borrowed from his classmates, stayed drunk for three weeks, and then went home to St. Paul to write the novel once again, this time with another ending and a new title, *This Side of Paradise.* Scribners accepted it on that third submission. The book was so different from other novels of the time, Max Perkins wrote him, "that it is hard to prophesy how it will sell, but we are all for taking a chance and supporting it with vigor."

This Side of Paradise, published at the end of March 1920, is a very young man's novel and memory book. The author put into it samples of everything he had written until that time—short stories, essays, poems, prose poems, sketches, and dialogues—and he also put himself into it, after taking a promotion in social rank. The hero, Amory Blaine, instead of being a poor relative has been reared as the heir of millions, but he looks and talks like Fitzgerald, besides reading the same books (listed in one passage after another) and falling in love with the same girls. The story told in the novel, with many digressions, is how Amory struggles for self-knowledge and for less provincial standards than those of the Princeton eating clubs. "I know myself," he says at the end, "but that is all." Fitzgerald passed a final judgment on the novel in 1938, when he said in a letter to Max Perkins, "I think it is now one of the funniest books since *Dorian Gray* in its utter spuriousness—and then, here and there, I find a page that is very real and living."

Some of the living pages are the ones that recount the eating-club elections, the quarrel between Amory and his first flame, Isabelle—Fitzgerald would always be good on quarrels—the courting of Rosalind Connage, and Amory's three-weeks drunk when Rosalind throws him over. Besides having a spurious and imitative side, the novel proved that Fitzgerald had started with gifts of his own, which included an easy narrative style rich with images, a sense of comedy, and a natural ear for dialogue. Its memorable feature, however, was that it announced a change in standards. "Here was a new genera-.tion," Fitzgerald or his hero, it isn't clear which, says in the last chapter, "shouting the old cries, learning the old creeds, through a revery of long days and nights; destined finally to go out into that dirty gray turmoil to follow love and pride; a new generation dedicated more than the last to the fear of poverty and the worship of success; grown up to find all gods dead, all wars fought, all faiths in man shaken." With energy, candor, and a sort of innocence, Fitzgerald (or the hero) was speaking for his contemporaries. They recognized the voice as their own, and his elders listened.

Suddenly the magazines were eager to print Fitzgerald's stories and willing to pay high prices for them. The result shows in his big ledger: in 1919 he earned $879 by his writing; in 1920 he earned $18,850—and managed to end the year in debt.[1] Early success

---

1. Those sums of money should be multiplied by three to give a notion of their equivalents half a century later. Income taxes were low in the 1920s. By the end of the decade Fitzgerald would be spending as much—but not for the same things—as the presidents of small corporations.

and princely spending had been added to everything else that made him stand out as a representative of his generation; and Fitzgerald was beginning to believe in his representative quality. He was learning that when he wrote truly about his dreams and misadventures and discoveries, other people recognized themselves in the picture.

The point has to be made that Fitzgerald wasn't "typical" of his own period or any other. He lived harder than most people have ever lived and acted out his dreams with an extraordinary intensity of emotion. The dreams themselves were not at all unusual: in the beginning they were dreams of becoming a football star and a big man in college, of being a hero on the battlefield, of winning through to financial success, and of getting the top girl. They were the commonplace visions shared by almost all the young men of his age and background, especially by those who were forging ahead in the business world; in many ways Fitzgerald was closer to them than he was to the other serious writers of his generation. It was the emotion he put into his dreams, and the honesty with which he expressed the emotion, that made them seem distinguished. By feeling intensely he made his readers believe in the unique value of the world in which they lived. He was to say later, writing in the third person, that he continued to feel grateful to the Jazz Age because "It bore him up, flattered him and gave him more money than he had dreamed of, simply for telling people that he felt as they did."

At the beginning of April 1920, Zelda came to New York and they were married in the rectory of St. Patrick's Cathedral—although Zelda's family was Episcopalian and Scott had ceased to be a good Catholic. They set up housekeeping at the Biltmore. To their bewilderment they found themselves adopted not as a Midwesterner and a Southerner respectively, not even as detached observers, but—Scott afterward wrote—"as the arch type of what New York wanted." A new age was beginning, and Scott and Zelda were venturing into it innocently, hand in hand. Zelda said, "It was always tea-time or late at night." Scott said, "We felt like children in a great bright unexplored barn."

2 ⚗ Scott also said, "America was going on the greatest, gaudiest spree in history and there was going to be plenty to tell about it." There is still plenty to tell about it, in the light of a new age that continues to be curious about the 1920s and usually misjudges them. The gaudiest spree in history was also a moral revolt, and beneath the revolt were social transformations. The 1920s were the age when puritanism was under attack, with the Protestant churches losing their dominant position. They were the age when the country ceased to be English and Scottish and when the children of later immigrations moved forward to take their places in the national life. Theodore Dreiser, whom Fitzgerald regarded as the greatest living American writer, was South German Catholic by descent, H. L. Mencken, the most influential critic, was North German Protestant, and Fitzgerald did not forget for a moment that one side of his own family was "straight potato-famine Irish." Most of his heroes have Irish names and all except Gatsby are city-bred, thus reflecting another social change. The 1920s were the age when American culture became urban instead of rural and when New York set the social and intellectual standards of the country, while its own standards were being set by transplanted Southerners and Midwesterners like Zelda and Scott.

More essentially the 1920s were the age when a production ethic—of saving and self-denial in order to accumulate capital for new enterprises—gave way to a consumption ethic that was needed to provide markets for the new commodities that streamed from the production lines. Instead of being exhorted to save money, more and more of it, people were being exhorted in a thousand ways to buy, enjoy, use once and throw away, in order to buy a later and more expensive model. They followed the instructions, with the result that more goods were produced and consumed or wasted and money was easier to earn or borrow than ever in the past. Foresight went out of fashion. "The Jazz Age," Fitzgerald was to say, "now raced along under its own power, served by great filling stations full of money. . . . Even when you were broke you didn't worry about money, because it was in such profusion around you."

Young men and women in the 1920s had a sense of reckless confidence not only about money but about life in general. It was part of their background: they had grown up in the years when middle-class Americans read Herbert Spencer and believed in the doctrine of automatic social evolution. The early twentieth century seemed to confirm the doctrine. Things were getting better each year: more grain was reaped, more iron was smelted, more rails were laid, more profits earned, more records broken, as new cities were founded and all cities grew, as the country grew, as the world apparently grew in wealth and wisdom toward the goal of universal peace— and those magical results were obtained, so it seemed, by each man's seeking his private interest. After 1914 the notion of automatic progress lost most of its support in events, but retained its place in the public mind. Young men and women of Fitzgerald's time, no matter how rebellious and cynical they thought of themselves as being, still clung to their childhood notion that the world would improve without their help; that was one of the reasons why most of them felt excused from seeking the common good. Plunging into their personal adventures, they took risks that didn't impress them as being risks because, in their hearts, they believed in the happy ending.

They were truly rebellious, however, and were determined to make an absolute break with the standards of the prewar generation. The distinction between highbrow and lowbrow (or liberal and conservative) was not yet sharp enough to divide American society; the gulf was between the young and the old. The younger set paid few visits to their parents' homes and some of them hardly exchanged a social word with men or women over forty. The elders were straitlaced or stuffy, and besides they had made a mess of the world; they were discredited in younger eyes not only by the war and what followed it—especially Prohibition—but also, after 1923, by the scandals that clustered round Teapot Dome and the little green house on K Street, in Washington, where members of President Harding's Cabinet, and sometimes the President himself, played their cozy games of poker with the oil barons. So let the discredited elders keep to themselves; the youngsters would then have a free field in which to test their standards of the good life.

Those standards were elementary and close to being savage. Rejecting almost everything else, the spokesmen for the new generation celebrated the value of simple experiences such as love, foreign travel, good food, and drunkenness. "Immortal drunkenness!" Thomas Wolfe was to exclaim in a novel,[2] interrupting the adventures of his hero. "What tribute can we ever pay, what song can we ever sing, what swelling praise can ever be sufficient to express the joy, the gratefulness and love which we, who have known youth and hunger in America, have owed to alcohol? . . . You came to us with music, poetry, and wild joy when we were twenty, when we reeled home at night through the old moon-whitened streets of Boston and heard our friend, our comrade and our dead companion, shout through the silence of the moonwhite square: 'You are a poet and the world is yours.'" Others besides Wolfe heard the voice repeating "You are a poet!" and they hastened to enjoy their birthday-present world by loving, traveling, eating, drinking, dancing all night, and writing truthfully about their mornings after. They all recognized the value of being truthful, even if it hurt their families or their friends and most of all if it hurt themselves; almost any action seemed excusable and even admirable in those days if one simply told the truth about it, without boasting, without shame.

They liked to say yes to every proposal that suggested excitement. Will you take a new job, throw up the job, go to Paris and starve, travel round the world in a freighter? Will you get married, leave your husband, spend a weekend for two in Biarritz? Will you ride through Manhattan on the roof of a taxi and then go bathing in the Plaza fountain? "W Y B M A D I I T Y ?" read a sign on the mirror behind the bar of a popular speakeasy, the Dizzy Club. Late at night you asked the bartender what it meant, and he answered, "Will You Buy Me A Drink If I Tell You?" The answer was yes, always yes, and the fictional heroine of the 1920s was Serena Blandish, the girl who couldn't say no. Or the heroine was Joyce's Molly Bloom as she dreamed about the days when she was being courted: ". . . and I thought as well him as another and then I asked him with my eyes to ask again yes and then he asked me would I yes to say yes my mountain flower and first I put my arms around him yes and drew him down to me so he could feel my breasts all

---

2. For the complete invocation to drunkenness, see *Of Time and the River*, pp. 281–82. The novel is in the third person, but here, in celebrating what he regarded as a generational experience, Wolfe shifts to the first person plural.

perfume yes and his heart was going like mad and yes I said yes I will Yes."

The masculine ideal of the 1920s was what Fitzgerald called "the old dream of being an entire man in the Goethe-Byron-Shaw tradition, with an opulent American touch, a sort of combination of J. P. Morgan, Topham Beauclerk and St. Francis of Assisi." The entire man would be one who "did everything," good and bad, who realized all the potentialities of his nature and thereby acquired wisdom. The entire man, in the 1920s, was one who followed the Rule of the Thelemites as revealed by Rabelais: *Fais ce que vouldras,* "Do what you will!" But that rule implied a second imperative like an echo: "Will!" To be admired by the 1920s young men had to will all sorts of actions and had to possess enough energy and boldness to carry out even momentary wishes. They lived in the moment with what they liked to call "an utter disregard of consequences." In spirit they all made pilgrimages to the abbey of the Thelemites, where they consulted the Oracle of the Divine Bottle and received for answer the one word *Trinc.* They obeyed the oracle and drank, in those days of the Volstead Act when drinking was a rite of comradeship and an act of rebellion. As Fitzgerald said at the time, they drank "cocktails before meals like Americans, wines and brandies like Frenchmen, beer like Germans, whiskey-and-soda like the English . . . this preposterous mélange that was like a gigantic cocktail in a nightmare."

But the 1920s were not so much a drinking as a dancing age—the Jazz Age, in the phrase that Fitzgerald made his own. In those days one heard jazz everywhere—from orchestras in ballrooms, from wind-up phonographs in the parlor, from loudspeakers blaring in variety stores, lunch wagons, even machine shops—and jazz wasn't regarded as something to listen to and be cool about, without even tapping one's feet; jazz was music with a purpose, *Gebrauchsmusik*; it was music to which you danced:

> *I met her in Chicago and she was married.*
> *   Dance all day,*
> *leave your man, Sweet Mamma, and come away;*
> *manicured smiles and kisses, to dance all day, all day.*
> *   How it was sad.*
>
> *Please, Mr. Orchestra, play us another tune.*

My daddy went and left me and left the cupboard bare.
Who will pay the butcher bill now Daddy isn't there?
   Shuffle your feet.
Found another daddy and he taught me not to care,
   and how to care.
Found another daddy that I'll follow anywhere.
   Shuffle your feet, dance,

dance among the tables, dance across the floor,
slip your arm around me, we'll go dancing out the door,
Sweet Mamma, anywhere, through any door.
Wherever the banjos play is Tennessee.

Jazz carried with it a constant message of change, excitement, violent escape, with an undertone of sadness, but with a promise of enjoyment somewhere around the corner of next week, perhaps at midnight in a distant country. The young men heard the message and followed it anywhere, through any door, even the one that led into what was then, for Americans, the new world of difficult art. They danced too much, they drank too much, but they also worked, with something of the same desperation; they worked to rise, to earn social rank, to sell, to advertise, to organize, to invent gadgets, and to create enduring works of literature. In ten years, before losing their first vitality, they gave a new tempo to American life.

Fitzgerald not only represented the age but came to suspect that he had helped to create it, by setting forth a pattern of conduct that would be followed by persons a little younger than himself. That it was a dangerous pattern was something he recognized almost from the beginning. "If I had anything to do with creating the manners of the contemporary American girl I certainly made a botch of the job," he said in a 1925 letter. In a notebook he observed that one of his relatives was still a flapper in the 1930s. "There is no doubt," he added, "that she originally patterned herself upon certain immature and unfortunate writings of mine, so that I have a special fondness for —— as for one who has lost an arm or a leg in one's service." When he was living at La Paix, a brown wooden late-Victorian lodge on a thirty-acre estate near Baltimore, a drunken young man teetered up to his door and said, "I had to see you. I feel I owe you more than I can say. I feel that you formed my life." It was not the young man—later a widely read novelist and an alcoholic—but Fitzgerald himself who became the principal victim of his capacity for creating fictional types in life. "Sometimes," he told another visitor to La Paix, late at night, "I don't know whether Zelda and I are real or whether we are characters in one of my novels."

That was in the spring of 1933, a few weeks after the banks had closed all over the country. It seemed then that the whole generation of the 1920s had been defeated by life, and yet, in their own defeat, Scott and Zelda were still its representative figures.

3   Fitzgerald never lost a quality that very few writers are able to acquire: a sense of living in history. Manners and morals were changing all through his life and he set himself the task of recording the changes. These were revealed to him, not by statistics or news reports, but in terms of living characters, and the characters were revealed by gestures, each appropriate to a certain year. He wrote: "One day in 1926 we"—meaning the members of his generation— "looked down and found we had flabby arms and a fat pot and we couldn't say boop-boop-a-doop to a Sicilian. . . . By 1927 a widespread neurosis began to be evident, faintly signaled, like a nervous beating of the feet, by the popularity of cross-word puzzles. . . . By this time"—also in 1927—"contemporaries of mine had begun to disappear into the dark maw of violence. . . . By 1928 Paris had grown suffocating. With each new shipment of Americans spewed up by the boom the quality fell off, until towards the end there was something sinister about the crazy boatloads."

He tried to find the visible act that revealed the moral quality inherent in a certain moment of time. He was haunted by time, as if he wrote in a room full of clocks and calendars. He made lists by the hundred, including lists of the popular songs, the football players, the top debutantes (with the types of beauty they cultivated), the hobbies, and the slang expressions of a given year; he felt that all those names and phrases belonged to the year and helped to reveal its momentary color. "After all," he said in an otherwise undistinguished magazine story, "any given moment has its value; it can be questioned in the light of after-events, but the moment remains. The young prince in velvet gathered in lovely domesticity around the queen amid the hush of rich draperies may presently grow up to be Pedro the Cruel or Charles the Mad, but the moment of beauty was there."

Fitzgerald lived in his great moments, and lived in them again when he reproduced their drama, but he also stood apart from them and coldly reckoned their causes and consequences. That is his doubleness or irony, and it is one of his distinguishing marks as a writer. He took part in the ritual orgies of his time, but he kept a secretly detached position, regarding himself as a pauper living among millionaires, a Celt among Sassenachs, and a sullen peasant among the nobility; he said that his point of vantage "was the dividing line between two generations," prewar and postwar. Always he cultivated a double vision. In his novels and stories he was trying to intensify the glitter of life in the Princeton eating clubs, on the north shore of Long Island, in Hollywood, and on the Riviera; he surrounded his characters with a mist of admiration, and at the same time he kept driving the mist away. He liked to know "where the milk is watered and the sugar sanded, the rhinestone passed for the diamond and the stucco for stone." It was as if all his fiction described a big dance to which he had taken, as he once wrote, the prettiest girl:

> There was an orchestra—Bingo-Bango
> Playing for us to dance the tango
> And the people all clapped as we arose
> For her sweet face and my new clothes—

and as if he stood at the same time outside the ballroom, a little Midwestern boy with his nose to the glass, wondering how much the tickets cost and who paid for the music. But it was not a dance he was watching so much as it was a drama of conflicting manners and aspirations in which he was both the audience and the leading actor. As audience he kept a cold eye on the actor's performance. He wrote of himself when he was twenty, "I knew that at bottom I lacked the essentials. At the last crisis, I knew that I had no real courage, perseverance or self-respect." Sixteen years later he was just as critical, and he said to a visitor at La Paix, "I've got a very limited talent. I'm a workman of letters, a professional. I know when to write and when to stop writing." It was the maximum of critical detachment, but it was combined with the maximum of immersion in the drama. He said in his notebook, and without the least exaggeration, "Taking things hard, from Ginevra to Joe Mankiewicz," mentioning the names of his first unhappy love and of the Hollywood producer who, so he thought, had ruined one of his best scripts: "That's the stamp that goes into my books so that people read it blind like Braille."

The drama he watched and in which he overplayed a leading part was a moral drama leading to rewards and punishments. "Sometimes I wish I had gone along with that gang," he said in a letter that discussed musical comedies and mentioned Cole Porter and Rodgers and Hart; "but I guess I am too much a moralist at heart and want to preach at people in some acceptable form, rather than to entertain them." The morality he wanted to preach was a simple one, in the midst of the prevailing confusion. Its four cardinal virtues were Industry, Discipline, Responsibility (in the sense of meeting one's social and financial obligations), and Maturity (in the sense of learning to expect little from life while continuing to make one's best efforts). Thus, his stories had a way of becoming fables. For virtues they displayed or failed to display, the characters were rewarded or punished in the end.

The handle by which he took hold of the characters was their dreams. These, as I said, might be commonplace or even cheap, but usually Fitzgerald managed to surround them with an atmosphere of the mysterious and illimitable or of the pitifully doomed. His great scenes were, so to speak, played to music: sometimes the music from a distant ballroom, sometimes that of a phonograph braying out a German tango, sometimes the wind in the leaves, sometimes the stark music of the heart. When there was no music, at least there were pounding rhythms: "The city's quick metropolitan rhythm of love and birth and death that supplied dreams to the unimaginative"; "The rhythm of the week-end, with its birth, its planned gaieties and its announced end"; "New York's flashing, dynamic good looks, its tall man's quick-step." Fitzgerald's dream of his mature years, after he had outgrown the notion of becoming a big man in college, was also set to music, perhaps to the *Unfinished Symphony;* it was the dream of becoming a great writer, specifically a great novelist who would do for American society in his time what Turgenev, for example, had done for the old regime in Russia.

It was not his dream to be a poet, yet that was how he started and in some ways he remained a poet primarily. He noted, "The talent that matures early is usually of the poetic type, which mine was in large part." His favorite author was Keats, not Turgenev or Flaubert. "I suppose I've read it a hundred times," he said of the "Ode on a Grecian Urn." "About the tenth time I began to know what it was about, and caught the chime in it and the exquisite inner mechanics. Likewise with the 'Nightingale,' which I can never read without tears in my eyes; likewise 'The Pot of Basil,' with its great stanzas about the two brothers. . . . Knowing these things very young and granted an ear, one could scarcely ever afterwards be unable to distinguish between gold and dross in what one read." When his daughter was learning to be a writer he advised her to read Keats and Browning and try her hand at a sonnet. He added, "The only thing that will help you is poetry, which is the most concentrated form of style."

Fitzgerald himself was a poet who never learned some of the elementary rules for writing prose. His grammar was shaky and his spelling definitely bad: for example, he wrote "ect." more often than "etc." and misspelled the name of his friend Monsignor Fay on the dedication page of *This Side of Paradise*. In his letters he always misspelled the given names of his first and last loves. He was not a student, for all the books he read; not a theoretician and perhaps one should flatly say, not a thinker. He counted on his friends to do much of his thinking for him; at Princeton it was John Peale Bishop who, he said, "made me see, in the course of a couple of months, the difference between poetry and non-poetry." Twenty years later, at the time of his crack-up, he re-examined his scale of values and found thinking incredibly difficult; he compared it to "the moving about of great secret trunks." He was then forced to the conclusion "That I had done very little thinking, save within the problems of my craft. For twenty years a certain man had been my intellectual conscience. That man was Edmund Wilson." Another contemporary "had been an artistic conscience to me. I had not imitated his infectious style, because my own style, such as it is, was formed before he published anything, but there was an awful pull towards him when I was on the spot."

Fitzgerald was making the confession in order to keep straight with himself, not to forestall any revelation that might have been made by his critics. The critics would have said that there was little of Wilson's influence perceptible in his work and still less of Hemingway's, although he once wrote a story about two dogs, "Shaggy's Morning," that is a delicate and deliberate pastiche of the Hemingway manner. By listening hard one can overhear a few, a very few suggestions of Hemingway in the dialogue of other stories, especially the later ones, but Fitzgerald was faithful to his own vision of the world and his way of expressing it. His debt to Wilson and Hemingway is real, but hard to define. In essence they were two older-brother figures (though Hemingway was younger than Fitzgerald); two different models of literary conduct. Though his style of life bore no resemblance to either of theirs, he used them to test and define his moral attitude toward the problems of his craft.

4 ✍ There was one respect in which Fitzgerald, much as he regarded himself as a representative figure of the age, was completely different from most of its serious writers. In that respect he was, as I said, much closer to the men of his college year who were trying to get ahead in the business world; like them he was fascinated by the process of earning and spending money. The young businessmen of his time, much more than those of a later generation, had been taught to measure success, failure, and even virtue in pecuniary terms. They had learned in school and Sunday school that virtue was rewarded with money and vice punished by the loss of money; apparently their one aim should be to earn lots of it fast. Yet money was only a convenient and inadequate symbol for what they dreamed of earning. The best of them were like Jay Gatsby in having "some heightened sensitivity to the promise of life"; or they were like another Fitzgerald hero, Dexter Green of "Winter Dreams," who "wanted not association with glittering things and glittering people —he wanted the glittering things themselves." Their real dream was that of achieving a new status and a new essence, of rising to a loftier place in the mysterious hierarchy of human worth.

The serious writers also dreamed of rising to a loftier status, but—except for Fitzgerald—they felt that moneymaking was the wrong way to rise. They liked money if it reached them in the form of gifts or legacies or publishers' advances; they would have liked it in the form of prizes or fellowships, though there were few of these to be had in the 1920s; but they were afraid of high earned incomes because of what the incomes stood for: obligations, respectability, time lost from their essential work, expensive habits that would drive them to seek still higher incomes—in short, a series of involvements in the commercial culture that was hostile to art. "If you want to ruin a writer," I used to hear some of them saying, "just give him a big magazine contract or a job at ten thousand a year." Many of them tried to preserve their independence by earning only enough to keep them alive while writing; a few regarded themselves as heroes of poverty and failure. "Now I can write," Faulkner said when his third novel was turned down and he thought he would never be published again.

A disdainful attitude toward money went into the texture of Faulkner's work, as into that of many others. The work was non-commercial in the sense of being written in various new styles that the public was slow to accept. It was an age of literary experiment when young writers were moving in all directions simultaneously. They were showing the same spirit of adventure and exploration in fiction that their contemporaries were showing in the business world. That spirit made them part of the age, but at the same time they were trying to stand apart from it, and some of them looked back longingly to other ages when, so they liked to think, artists had wealthy patrons and hence were able to live outside the economic system.

Fitzgerald immersed himself in the age and always remained close to the business world which they were trying to evade. That world was the background of his stories, and these performed a business function in themselves, by supplying the narrative that readers followed like a thread through the labyrinth of advertising in the slick-paper magazines. He did not divorce himself from readers by writing experimental prose or refusing to tell a story. His very real originality was a matter of mood and subject and image rather than of structure, and it was more evident in his novels than in his stories, good as the stories often were. Although he despised the trade of writing for magazines—or despised it with part of his mind —he worked at it honestly. It yielded him a large income that he couldn't have earned in any other fashion, and the income was necessary to his self-respect.

Fitzgerald kept an accurate record of his earnings—in the big ledger in which he also kept a record of his deeds and misdeeds, as if to strike a bookkeeper's balance between them—but he was vague about his expenditures and usually vague about his possessions, including his balance in the bank. Once he asked a cashier, "How much money have I got?" The cashier looked in a big book and answered without even scowling, "None." Fitzgerald resolved to be more thrifty, knowing he would break the resolution. "All big men have spent money freely," he explained in a letter to his mother. "I hate avarice or even caution." He had little interest in the physical objects that money could buy. On the other hand, he had a great interest in earning money, lots of it fast, because that was a gold medal offered with the blue ribbon for competitive achievement. Once the money was earned, he and Zelda liked to spend lots of it fast, usually for impermanent things: not for real estate, fine motor-cars, or furniture, but for traveling expenses, the rent of furnished houses, the wages of nurses and servants; for parties, party dresses, and feather fans of five colors. Zelda was as proudly careless about money as an eighteenth-century nobleman's heir. Scott was more practical and had his penny-pinching moments, as if in memory of his childhood, but at other times he liked to spend without counting in order to enjoy a proud sense of potency.

In his attitude toward money he revealed the new spirit of an age when conspicuous accumulation was giving way to conspicuous earning and spending. It was an age when gold was melted down and became fluid; when wealth was no longer measured in possessions—land, houses, livestock, machinery—but rather in dollars per year, as a stream is measured by its flow; when for the first time the expenses of government were being met by income taxes more than by property and excise taxes; and when the new tax structure was making it somewhat more difficult to accumulate a stable and lasting fortune. Such fortunes still existed at the hardly accessible peak of the social system, which young men dreamed of reaching like Alpinists, but the romantic figures of the age were not capitalists properly speaking. They were salaried executives and advertising men, they were promoters, salesmen, stock gamblers, or racketeers, and they were millionaires in a new sense—not men each of whom owned a million dollars' worth of property, but men who lived in rented apartments and had nothing but stock certificates and insurance policies (or nothing but credit and the right connections), while spending more than the income of the old millionaires.

The change went deep into the texture of American society and deep into the feelings of Americans as individuals. Fitzgerald is its most faithful recorder, not only in the stories that earned him a place in the new high-income class, but also in his personal confessions. He liked to describe his vitality and his talent in pecuniary terms. When both of them temporarily disappeared, in his crack-up of the years 1935–36, he pictured the event as a sort of financial bankruptcy. He wrote (but without my italics), "I began to realize that for two years my life had been a *drawing on resources* that I did not possess, that I had been *mortgaging myself* physically and spiritually up to the hilt." Again he wrote, "When a new sky cut off the sun last spring, I didn't at first relate it to what had happened fifteen or twenty years ago. Only gradually did a certain family resemblance come through—an over-extension of the flank, a burning of the candle at both ends; a call upon physical resources that I did not command, *like a man overdrawing at his bank.* . . . There were plenty of *counterfeit coins* around that I could pass off instead of these"—that is, in spite of the honest emotions he had lost—"and I knew where I could get them at *a nickel on the dollar.*"

"Where was the leak," Fitzgerald asked, "through which, unknown to myself, my enthusiasm and my vitality had been steadily and prematurely trickling away?" Vitality was something liquid and it was equated with money, which was also liquid. The attitude was different from that which prevailed before World War I, when people spoke of saving money as "piling up the rocks," instead of filling the reservoir, and when the millionaire in the funny papers was "Mr. Gotrocks." In Freud's great system, which is based on his observation of nineteenth-century types, money is something solid, gold or silver, and the bodily product it suggests is excrement. Thus, the pursuit of money for its own sake develops from anal eroticism, and Freud maintains that the miser is almost always a constipated man. I doubt whether recent analysts have observed how money is losing its old symbolic value and how, in the American subconscious, it tends to be identified with other bodily products such as urine ("I just pee'd it away"), blood, sperm, or milk.

Fitzgerald was more closely involved with contemporary values than most of the professional analysts. He uses the new imagery in much of his confessional writing, and it becomes especially clear in a free-verse poem, "Our April Letter," which he wrote during his crack-up. Three lines of the poem read:

> I have asked a lot of my emotions—one hundred and twenty stories. The price was high, right up with Kipling, because there was one little drop of something—not blood, not a tear, not my seed, but me more intimately than these, in every story, it was the extra I had. Now it has gone and I am just like you now.
>
> Once the phial was full—here is the bottle it came in.
>
> Hold on, there's a drop left there. . . . No, it was just the way the light fell.

Note that the something more intimate than blood or tears or sperm—though suggested by all of these—had a monetary value and was being sold to the magazines at a price right up with what Kipling had been paid. Note also that in its absence Fitzgerald was no longer able to write salable stories, so that he came to identify emotional with financial bankruptcy. In that black year 1936 he was earning very little money and owed more than forty thousand dollars, but he kept a careful record of his debts and later paid off most of them, by living in a modest fashion even during the months when he was earning a big salary in Hollywood. He never became solvent, but his financial obligations were not so pressing at the end of his life, and he was doing some of his best work.

In writing about the romance of money, as he did in most of his earlier novels and stories, he was dealing not only with an intimate truth but also with what seemed to him the central truth of his American age. "Americans," he liked to say, "should be born with fins and perhaps they were—perhaps money was a form of fin."

5⟡ One of his remarks about himself has often puzzled his critics. "D. H. Lawrence's great attempt to synthesize animal and emotional—things he left out," Fitzgerald wrote in his notebook, then added the comment, "Essential pre-Marxian. Just as I am essentially Marxian." He was never Marxian in any sense of the word that Marxians of whatever school would be willing to accept. It is true that he finally read well into *Das Kapital* and was impressed by "the terrible chapter," as he called it, "on 'The Working Day' "; but it left in him no trace of Marx's belief in the mission of the proletariat.

His picture of proletarian life was of something alien to his own background, mysterious and even criminal. It seems to have been symbolized in some of his stories—notably in "Winter Dreams" and "A Short Trip Home"—by the riverfront strip in St. Paul that languished in the shadow of the big houses on Summit Avenue; he described the strip as a gridiron of mean streets where consumptive or pugilistic youths lounged in front of poolrooms, their skins turned livid by the neon lights. In *The Great Gatsby* he must have been thinking about the lower levels of American society when he described the valley of ashes between West Egg and New York—"A fantastic farm," he calls it, "where ashes grow like wheat into ridges and hills and grotesque gardens; where ashes take the forms of houses and chimneys and rising smoke and, finally, with a transcendent effort, of men who move dimly and always crumbling through the powdery air." One of his early titles for the novel was "Among Ash Heaps and Millionaires"—as if he were setting the two against each other while suggesting a vague affinity between them. Tom Buchanan, the brutalized millionaire, finds a mistress in the valley of ashes.

In Fitzgerald's stories there can be no real struggle between this dimly pictured ash-gray proletariat and the bourgeoisie. On the other hand, there can be a different struggle that the author must have regarded, for a time, as essentially Marxian. It is the struggle I have already suggested, between wealth as fluid income and wealth as an inherited and solid possession—or rather, since Fitzgerald is not an essayist but a storyteller, it is between a man and a woman as representatives of the new and the old moneyed classes.

We are not allowed to forget that they are representatives. The man comes from a family with little or no money, but he manages to attend an Eastern university—most often Yale, to set a distance between the hero and the Princeton author. He then sets out to earn a fortune equal to that of his wealthy classmates. Usually what he earns is not a fortune but an impressively large income, after he has risen to the top of his chosen profession—which may be engineering or architecture or advertising or the laundry business or bootlegging or real estate or even, in one story, frozen fish; the heroes are never novelists, although one of them is said to be a successful playwright. When the heroes are halfway to the top, they fall in love.

The woman—or rather the girl—in a Fitzgerald story is as alluring as the youngest princess in a fairy tale. "In children's books," he says when presenting one heroine, "forests are sometimes made out of all-day suckers, boulders out of peppermints and rivers out of gently flowing, rippling molasses taffy. Such . . . localities exist, and one day a girl, herself little more than a child, sat dejected in the middle of one. It was all hers, she owned it; she owned Candy Town." Another heroine "was a stalk of ripe corn, but bound not as cereals are but as a rare first edition, with all the binder's art. She was lovely and expensive and about nineteen." Of still another heroine Fitzgerald says when she first appears that "Her childish beauty was wistful and sad about being so rich and sixteen." Later, when her father loses his money, the hero pays her a visit in London. "All around her," Fitzgerald says, "he could feel the vast Mortmain fortune melting down, seeping back into the matrix whence it had come." The hero thinks she might marry him, now that she has fallen almost to his financial level; but he finds that the Mortmain (or dead-hand) fortune, even though lost, is still a barrier between them. Note that the man is not attracted by the fortune in itself. He is not seeking money so much as position at the peak of the social hierarchy, and the girl becomes the symbol of that position, the incarnation of its mysterious power. That is Daisy Buchanan's charm for the great Gatsby and the reason why he directs his whole life toward winning back her love.

"She's got an indiscreet voice," Nick Carraway says of her. "It's full of—" and he hesitates.

"Her voice is full of money," Gatsby says.

And Nick, the narrator, thinks to himself, "That was it. I'd never understood before. It was full of money—that was the inexhaustible charm that rose and fell in it, the cymbals' song of it. . . . High in a white palace the king's daughter, the golden girl."

In Fitzgerald's stories a love affair is like secret negotiations between the diplomats of two countries which are not at peace and not quite at war. For a moment they forget their hostility, find it transformed into mutual inspection, attraction, even passion (though the passion is not physical); but the hostility will survive even in marriage, if marriage is to be their future. I called the lovers diplomats, ambassadors, and that is another way of saying that they are representatives. When they meet it is as if they were leaning toward each other from separate high platforms—the man from a platform built up of his former poverty, his ambition, his competitive triumphs, his ability to earn and spend always more, more; the girl from another platform covered with cloth of gold and feather fans of many colors, but beneath them a sturdy pile of stock certificates testifying to the ownership of mines, forests, factories, villages—all of Candy Town.

She is ownership embodied, as can be seen in one of the best of Fitzgerald's early stories, "Winter Dreams." A rising young man named Dexter Green takes home the daughter of a millionaire for whom he used to be a caddy. She is Judy Jones, "a slender enamelled doll in cloth of gold: gold in a band at her head, gold in two slipper points at her dress's hem." The rising young man stops his coupé "in front of the great white bulk of the Mortimer Jones house, somnolent, gorgeous, drenched with the splendor of the damp moonlight. Its solidity startled him. The strong walls, the steel of the girders, the breadth and beam and pomp of it were there only to bring out the contrast with the young beauty beside him. It was sturdy to accentuate her slightness—as if to show what a breeze could be generated by a butterfly's wing." In legends butterflies are symbols of the soul. The inference is clear that, holding Judy in his arms, Dexter Green is embracing the spirit of a great fortune.

Nicole Warren, the heroine of *Tender Is the Night*, embodies the spirit of an even greater fortune. Fitzgerald says of her, in a familiar passage:

> Nicole was the product of much ingenuity and toil. For her sake trains began their run at Chicago and traversed the round belly of the continent to California; chicle factories fumed and link belts grew link by link in factories; men mixed toothpaste in vats and drew mouthwash out of copper hogsheads; girls canned tomatoes quickly in August or worked rudely

at the Five-and-Tens on Christmas Eve; half-breed Indians toiled on Brazilian coffee plantations and dreamers were muscled out of patent rights in new tractors—these were some of the people who gave a tithe to Nicole, and as the whole system swayed and thundered onward it lent a feverish bloom to such processes of hers as wholesale buying [of luxuries], like the flush of a fireman's face holding his post before a spreading blaze.

Sometimes Fitzgerald's heroines are candid, even brutal, about class relations. "Let's start right," Judy Jones says to Dexter Green on the first evening they spend alone together. "Who are you?"

"I'm nobody," Dexter tells her, without adding that he had been her father's caddy. "My career is largely a matter of futures."

"Are you poor?"

"No," he says frankly, "I'm probably making more money than any man my age in the Northwest. I know that's an obnoxious remark, but you advised me to start right."

"There was a pause," Fitzgerald adds. "Then she smiled and the corners of her mouth drooped and an almost imperceptible sway brought her closer to him, looking up into his eyes." Money brings them together, but later they are separated by something undefined— a mere whim of Judy's, it would seem, though one comes to suspect that the whim was based on her feeling that she should marry a man of her own caste. Dexter, as he goes East to earn a still larger income, is filled with regret for "the country of illusions, of youth, of the richness of life, where his winter dreams had flourished." It seems likely that Judy Jones, like Josephine Perry in a series of later stories, was a character suggested by a Chicago debutante with whom Fitzgerald was desperately in love during his first years at Princeton; afterward she made a more sensible marriage. As for the general attitude toward the rich that began to be expressed in "Winter Dreams," it is perhaps connected with his experience in 1919, when he was not earning enough to support a wife and Zelda broke off their engagement. Later he said of the time:

> During a long summer of despair I wrote a novel instead of letters, so it came out all right; but it came out all right for a

different person. The man with the jingle of money in his pocket who married the girl a year later would always cherish an abiding distrust, an animosity, toward the leisure class—not the conviction of a revolutionist but the smoldering hatred of a peasant.

His mixture of feelings toward the very rich, which included curiosity and admiration as well as distrust, is revealed in his treatment of a basic situation that reappears in many of his stories. Of course he presented other situations that were not directly concerned with the relation between social classes. He wrote about the problem of adjusting oneself to life, which he thought was especially difficult for self-indulgent American women. He wrote about the manners of flappers, slickers, and jelly beans. He wrote engagingly about his own boyhood. He wrote about the patching-up of broken marriages, about the contrast between Northern and Southern life, about Americans going to pieces in Europe, about the self-tortures of gifted alcoholics, and in much of his later work—as notably in *The Last Tycoon*—he was expressing admiration for inspired technicians, such as brain surgeons and movie directors. But a great number of his stories, especially the early ones, start with the basic situation I have mentioned: a rising young man of the middle classes in love with the daughter of a very rich family. (Sometimes the family is Southern, in which case it needn't be so rich, since a high social status could still exist in the South without great wealth.)

From that beginning the story may take any one of several turns. The hero may marry the girl, but only after she loses her fortune or (as in "Presumption" and "'The Sensible Thing'") he gains an income greater than hers. He may lose the girl (as in "Winter Dreams") and always remember her with longing for his early aspirations. In "The Bridal Party" he resigns himself to the loss after being forced to recognize the moral superiority of the rich man she has married. In "More Than Just a House" he learns that the girl is empty and selfish and ends by marrying her good sister; in "The Rubber Check" he marries Ellen Mortmain's quiet cousin. There is, however, still another development out of the Fitzgerald situation that comes closer to revealing his ambiguous feelings toward the very rich. To state it simply—too simply—the rising young man wins the rich girl and then is destroyed by her wealth or her relatives.

It is the ballad of young Lochinvar come out of the West, but with a tragic ending—as if fair Ellen's kinsmen, armed and vengeful, had overtaken the pair or as if Ellen herself had betrayed the hero. Fitzgerald used it for the first time in a fantasy, "The Diamond As Big As the Ritz," which he wrote in St. Paul during the winter of 1921–22. In the fashion of many fantasies, it reveals the author's cast of mind more clearly than his realistic stories. It deals with the adventures of a boy named John T. Unger (we might read "Hunger"), who was born in a town on the Mississippi called Hades, though it also might be called St. Paul. He is sent away to St. Midas', which is "the most expensive and most exclusive boys' preparatory school in the world," and there he meets Percy Washington, who invites him to spend the summer at his home in the West. On the train Percy confides to him that his father is the richest man alive and owns a diamond bigger than the Ritz-Carlton Hotel.

The description of the Washington mansion, in its hidden valley that wasn't even shown on maps of the U.S. Geodetic Survey, is fantasy mingled with burlesque, but then the familiar Fitzgerald note appears. John falls in love with Percy's younger sister, Kismine. After an idyllic summer Kismine tells him accidentally—she had meant to keep the secret—that he will very soon be murdered, like all the former guests of the Washingtons. "It was done very nicely," she explains to him. "They were drugged while they were asleep—and their families were always told that they died of scarlet fever in Butte. . . . I shall probably have visitors too—I'll harden up to it. We can't let such an inevitable thing as death stand in the way of enjoying life while we have it. Think how lonesome it would be out here if we never had *any*one. Why, father and mother have sacrificed some of their best friends just as we have."

In *The Great Gatsby*, Tom and Daisy Buchanan would also sacrifice some of their best friends. "They were careless people, Tom and Daisy—they smashed up things and creatures and then retreated back into their money or their vast carelessness, or whatever it was that kept them together, and let other people clean up the mess they had made." "The Diamond As Big As the Ritz" can have a happy ending for the two lovers because it is a fantasy; but the same plot reappears in *The Great Gatsby*, where for the first time it is surrounded by the real world of the 1920s and for the first time is carried through to what Fitzgerald regarded as its logical conclusion.[3]

There is a time in any true author's career when he suddenly becomes capable of doing his best work. He has found a fable that expresses his central truth and everything falls into place around it, so that his whole experience of life is available for use in his fiction. Something like that happened to Fitzgerald when he invented the story of Jimmy Gatz, otherwise known as Jay Gatsby, and it explains the richness and scope of what is in fact a short novel.

To put facts on record, *The Great Gatsby* is a book of about fifty thousand words, a comparatively small structure built of nine chapters like big blocks. The fifth chapter—Gatsby's meeting after many years with Daisy Buchanan—is the center of the narrative, as is proper; the seventh chapter is its climax. Each chapter consists of one or more dramatic scenes, sometimes with intervening passages of narration. The scenic method is one that Fitzgerald possibly learned from Edith Wharton, who had learned it from Henry James; at any rate, the book is technically in the Jamesian tradition (and Daisy Buchanan is named for James's Daisy Miller).

Part of the tradition is the device of having events observed by a "central consciousness," often a character who stands somewhat apart from the action and whose vision frames it for the reader. In this instance the observer plays a special role. Although Nick Carraway does not save or ruin Gatsby, his personality in itself provides an essential comment on all the other characters. Nick stands for the older values that prevailed in the Midwest before the First World War. His family is not tremendously rich like the Buchanans, but it has a long-established and sufficient fortune, so that Nick is the only person in the book who has not been corrupted by seeking or spending money. He is so certain of his own values that he hesitates to criticize others, but when he does pass judgment—on Gatsby,

---

3. The plot appears for the last time in *Tender Is the Night*. "The novel should do this," Fitzgerald said in a memorandum to himself written early in 1932, after several false starts on the book and before setting to work on the published version. "Show a man who is a natural idealist, a spoiled priest, giving in for various causes to the ideas of the haute bourgeoisie"—that is, of the old moneyed class—"and in his rise to the top of the social world losing his idealism, his talent and turning to drink and dissipation." In the very simplest terms, Dick Diver marries Nicole Warren and is destroyed by her money.

on Jordan Baker, on the Buchanans—he speaks as for ages to come.

All the other characters belong to their own brief era of confused and dissolving standards, but they are affected by the era in different fashions. Each of them represents some particular variety of moral failure; Lionel Trilling says that they are "treated as if they were ideographs," a true observation; but the treatment does not detract from their reality as persons. Tom Buchanan is wealth brutalized by selfishness and arrogance; he looks for a mistress in the valley of ashes and finds an ignorant woman, Myrtle Wilson, whose raw vitality is like his own. Daisy Buchanan is the butterfly soul of wealth and offers a continual promise "that she had done gay, exciting things just a while since and that there were gay, exciting things hovering in the next hour"; but it is a false promise, since at heart she is as self-centered as Tom and even colder. Jordan Baker apparently lives by the old standards, but she uses them only as a subterfuge. Aware of her own cowardice and dishonesty, she feels "safer on a plane where any divergence from a code would be thought impossible."

All these except Myrtle Wilson are East Egg people, that is, they are part of a community where wealth takes the form of solid possessions. Set against them are the West Egg people, whose wealth is fluid income that might cease to flow. The West Egg people, with Gatsby as their tragic hero, have worked furiously to rise in the world, but they will never reach East Egg for all the money they spend; at most they can sit at the water's edge and look across the bay at the green light that shines and promises at the end of the Buchanans' dock. The symbolism of place plays a great part in *Gatsby*, as does that of motorcars. The characters are visibly represented by the cars they drive: Nick has a conservative old Dodge, the Buchanans, too rich for ostentation, have an "easy-going blue coupé," and Gatsby's car is "a rich cream color, bright with nickel, swollen here and there in its monstrous length with triumphant hat-boxes and supper-boxes and tool-boxes, and terraced with a labyrinth of wind-shields that mirrored a dozen suns"—it is West Egg on wheels. When Daisy drives the monster through the valley of ashes, she runs down and kills Myrtle Wilson; then, by concealing her guilt, she causes the death of Gatsby.

The symbols are not synthetic or contrived, as are many of those in more recent novels; they are images that Fitzgerald instinctively found to represent his characters and their destiny. When he says, "Daisy took her face in her hands as if feeling its lovely shape," he is watching her act the charade of her self-love. When he says, "Tom would drift on forever seeking, a little wistfully, for the dramatic turbulence of some irrecoverable football game," he suggests the one appealing side of Tom's nature. The author is so familiar with the characters and their background, so absorbed in their fate, that the book has an admirable unity of texture; we can open it to any page and find another of the details that illuminate the story. We end by feeling that *Gatsby* has a double value: it is the best picture we possess of the age in which it was written, and it also achieves a sort of moral permanence. Fitzgerald's story of the suitor betrayed by the princess and murdered in his innocence is a fable of the 1920s that has survived as a legend for other times.

III HEMINGWAY
in Paris

1 ⚞ At the end of December 1921, when Ernest Hemingway was twenty-two years old and newly married, he came to Paris for a second visit. The first, in May 1918, had lasted only until he picked up a Red Cross ambulance, which he drove in convoy to the Italian front. There he had been gravely wounded early in July, and he had spent the following months in and out of military hospitals. After his return to Chicago he had written many stories and poems and had even started a novel, but he had so far published nothing over his own name except in high-school papers and in the weekly magazine of *The Toronto Star*. He now planned to finish out his apprenticeship as a writer, and this second visit—interrupted by four unhappy months in Toronto—was to last for nearly seven years. His apprenticeship, however, would end spectacularly in 1926, with the publication of *The Sun Also Rises*.

In days when many things have ended, it is a melancholy pleasure to go back over the records of that era when everything was starting, for Hemingway and others, and when almost anything seemed possible. He came to Paris with letters of introduction from Sherwood Anderson, whom he had known well in Chicago, and also with a roving commission from *The Toronto Star* to write color stories, for which he would be paid at space rates if the stories were printed. In those days such commissions were easy to obtain, since they did not obligate a newspaper to spend money, and usually they led to nothing but a few rejected or grudgingly printed manuscripts. Hemingway's stories were good enough to feature, and they quickly led to definite assignments, with travel expenses.

Suddenly elevated to the position of staff reporter and authorized to send cables—but not too many of them—Hemingway was dispatched to the Genoa Economic Conference in March 1922, to the Near East in September for the closing days of the Greco-Turkish War, and to Lausanne at the end of November for the peace conference that followed. He also worked for Hearst's International News Service on the last two of these assignments, earning while he learned. In Constantinople he listened to stories about the burning of Smyrna and studied the Greek retreat—so he afterward said—as if it were a laboratory experiment in warfare. At Lausanne he studied the mechanics of international relations, with the help of barside lectures from William Bolitho, already famous as a correspondent. In both places he studied the curious language known as cabelese, in which every word had to do the work of six or seven. At three dollars a word he would put a message something like this on the wires: KEMAL INSWARDS UNBURNED SMYRNA GUILTY GREEKS. The translation appearing in the Hearst papers would be: "Mustapha Kemal in an exclusive interview with the correspondent of the International News Service [KEMAL INSWARDS] denied vehemently that the Turkish forces had any part in the burning of Smyrna [UNBURNED SMYRNA]. The city, Kemal stated, was fired by incendiaries in the troops of the Greek rear guard before the first Turkish patrols entered the city [GUILTY GREEKS]."

Cabelese was an exercise in omitting everything that can be taken for granted. It contributed to Hemingway's literary method, just as the newspaper assignments contributed to his subject matter. Going back over the records, one is astonished to find how much he learned during that first year abroad. He said afterward, "A great writer seems to be born with knowledge. But he really is not; he has only been born with the ability to learn in a quicker ratio to the passage of time than other men and without conscious application, and with an intelligence to accept or reject what is already presented as knowledge." Hemingway had that gift to such an extent that one thinks of him as an instinctive student who never went to college. His motto through life was not that of Sherwood Anderson's groping adolescent, "I want to know why," but rather, "I want to know *how*"—how to write, first of all, but also how to fish, how to box, how to ski, how to act in the bull ring, how to remember his own sensations, how to nurse his talent, how to live while learning to write, and more broadly how to *live*, in the sense of mastering the rules that must be followed by anyone who wants to respect himself. Many of his stories can be read and have been read by thousands as, essentially, object lessons in practical ethics and professional decorum.

Since Hemingway could find no textbooks in many of his fields, or none that could be trusted, he went straight to the best teachers. Among those under whom he studied during his first Paris years were Gertrude Stein and Ezra Pound, who did not love each other, and a cross-eyed Negro jockey from Cincinnati named Jim Winkfield.

How much he learned from his two older literary friends is the subject of a long-standing argument, but I think he learned a great deal. He listened attentively, and he had too much confidence in himself to fear, as many young writers do, that he would end as somebody's disciple. He could afford to take from others because he gave much in return. What he gave to Miss Stein is partly revealed in his letters to her, now in the Yale Library: he got her work published in *The Transatlantic Review* when he was helping to edit it, and having learned that she had only a bound manuscript of *The Making of Americans*, he typed long sections of it for the printer. One thing he took partly from her was a colloquial—in appearance—American style, full of repeated words, prepositional phrases, and present participles, the style in which he wrote his early published stories. One thing he took from Pound—in return for trying vainly to teach him how to box—was the doctrine of the accurate image, which he applied in the "chapters" printed between the stories that went into *In Our Time*; but Hemingway also learned from him to bluepencil most of his adjectives and adverbs. What he learned from Jim Winkfield was simpler; it was the name of a winning horse.

To Sylvia with love [illegible]
Farewell to [illegible] Ernest Hemingway,

Hemingway with Sylvia Beach in front of Shakespeare and Company
(March 1928) after a bathroom skylight collapsed on his head.

I heard the story from the late Evan Shipman, poet, trotting-horse columnist, and one of Hemingway's lifelong friends. Winkfield, he told me, had won the Kentucky Derby in 1901, on His Eminence, and again the following year, on Alan-a-Dale. By 1922 black jockeys were not being employed on American tracks, and Winkfield was in France training horses for Pierre Wertheimer, who had a famous stable. There is no outside audience when colts are trained in France, and there are no professional clockers at their time trials; every stable has its own secrets. At Wertheimer's stable the secret was Epinard, a sensationally promising colt with an unfashionable sire. Winkfield, who was seeing a lot of Hemingway, told him that Epinard was going to run his first race at Deauville that summer. Having borrowed all the money he could, Hemingway laid it on Epinard's nose.

That wasn't his one lucky day at the track. In June of the same year—writing from Milan, where he said that most of the races were fixed—he reported to Gertrude Stein that he had picked seventeen winners out of twenty-one starts. Most of his winnings went into the bank, together with proceeds from a small trust fund inherited by his wife, born Hadley Richardson. He was a foresighted young man, and already he planned to stop working for newspapers. Miss Stein encouraged the decision. "If you keep on doing newspaper work," she told him, "you will never see things, you will only see words, and that will not do—that is, of course, if you intend to be a writer."

Hemingway had never intended to be anything else, but writing every day was a luxury he still couldn't afford. *The Star,* impressed by a series of articles he had lately submitted on the French occupation of the Ruhr, offered him a job in the home office at a top reporter's salary, for those days, of $125 a week. In September 1923 he left for Toronto with the intention of working two years and saving enough money to finish a novel. Soon he came into conflict with Harry C. Hindmarsh, then assistant managing editor of *The Star,* who tried to break his spirit with what seems to have been a series of nagging persecutions. Hemingway resigned explosively at the end of December, and the following month he was back in Paris with Hadley and their new baby, born in Toronto. He was resolved to get along as best he could while writing for himself.

2 ✍ The Paris of young American writers in the early and middle 1920s was both a city and a state of feeling induced, as I have already suggested, by the Great War and its aftermath. Like Hemingway, most of the writers had been in uniform and—with exceptions such as Fitzgerald and Faulkner—had served on the French or the Italian front. They had learned to admire French culture and had dreamed of a better world after the war. When they went back to the States, they found that the postwar world was worse for them than the world they had known before 1917. Prohibition, puritanism, philistinism, and salesmanship: these seemed to be the triumphant causes in America. Whoever had won the war, young American writers came to regard themselves as a defeated nation. So they went to Paris, not as if they were being driven into exile, but as if they were seeking a spiritual home.

Paris was freedom to dress as they pleased, talk and write as they pleased, drink as they pleased, and make love without worrying about the neighbors. Paris was a continual excitation of the senses. "There is a time in a man's life," Dos Passos says in his book of memoirs *The Best Times,* "when every evening is a prelude. Toward 5 o'clock the air begins to tingle. It's tonight if you drink enough, talk enough, walk far enough, that the train of magical events will begin." He happens to be writing about New York, but for most of us—and I suspect for Dos Passos too—Paris represented that moment in youth and that feeling of magical possibility.

Paris was also the capital of literature and art and music, with a central position that had been confirmed and in part created by the war. Until 1914 an American writer, if he lived abroad, would probably have lived in or near London, as did Henry James, Bret Harte, Ezra Pound (till after the Armistice), and T. S. Eliot. An American composer would have studied somewhere in Germany, and a painter, though he would probably have gone to Paris, might also have chosen Munich, which was becoming a second center of the arts. There was no second center for a dozen years after the war; almost every aspirant in every art spent more or less time in Paris. With Eliot as a lonely exception, almost everyone worshiped by the postwar generation could be found there, including Joyce, the half-blind Jove of the new age, and Hemingway's friend Miss Stein, its solid Minerva, as well as Picasso, Brancusi, Matisse, Pound (till he left for Rapallo), Valéry, Gide, and Stravinsky. It was as if the young American visitors had been transported to Olympus and had found themselves in the presence of the whole pantheon.

And living on Olympus was fantastically cheap by present standards, French or American. My own experience might serve as well as another's. In 1921 I was awarded an American Field Service fellowship of 12,000 francs, or about $1000 at the prevailing rate of exchange. With that sole capital, my wife and I went to France and lived there for a year, during which I earned a little extra money—not more than $500—by writing penny-a-word pieces for American magazines. The fellowship was renewed for the following year, and once more it was supplemented by literary earnings, which had not increased. On less than $1500 we lived comfortably in Giverny, then a painters' colony, fifty miles from Paris; we made weekly trips to see our friends in the city and catch up with events; we sat in cafés and rode in taxis, though we could not give American tips; and at the end of the second year, after paying our debts and buying our passage, we arrived in New York with exactly $5. By that time it seemed that everyone in Greenwich Village had heard the good news and was planning to live abroad.

The number of literary pilgrims grew larger every year, like the gross national product, and was largest at the end of the decade, just before the Wall Street crash. It was not until the spring of 1933, when this country went off the gold standard, that almost all the pilgrims came streaming home for want of money. America-in-Paris, among its other aspects, thus obeyed the simple laws of economics.

When the Hemingways came back from Toronto in 1924, young American writers, with contingents of painters and composers, were already beginning to crowd the second-class carriages of the boat trains from Cherbourg and Le Havre. First class was full of people with a slightly different destination. Geographically and socially, America-in-Paris was two separate communities. Perhaps it was three, if one considers the long-established American families that had little to do with either artists or tourists; but I am thinking now of the two noisier settlements composed respectively of the rich and the poor.

The Paris of rich Americans was on the right bank of the Seine and extended from the Place de l'Etoile eastward to the Louvre. It was the revelers' Paris, surviving from the Second Empire and once the dream city of German princelings (*Da geh' ich bei Maxim*), Russian grand dukes, Irish landlords, and Wallachian boyars. All these had disappeared after the war, partly giving place to strange new people, Chinese warlords and cotton millionaires from Egypt; but the best and biggest spenders of the time were Americans. Some landmarks of their Paris were the Arc de Triomphe and the *hôtels de grand luxe* in its neighborhood; then the nightclubs that clustered near the Place Blanche (in those days Zelli's was the most popular with Americans); then the dressmakers near the rue de la Paix; and finally the great hotels, especially the Ritz, and two American banks on the Place Vendôme.

For some years Scott Fitzgerald was to serve as ambassador of literature to that Paris of the rich (though he had several active colleagues, including the hospitable Gerald Murphys). One summer he had a literary luncheon each week with Hemingway and Dean Gauss of Princeton, but his function also involved making rounds of the nightclubs from midnight till dawn. The end of one such round is described at length in an abandoned manuscript from which Arthur Mizener quotes at length in *The Far Side of Paradise*. ". . . then six of us," Fitzgerald says, "oh, the best the noblest relics of the evening . . . were riding on top of thousands of carrots in a market wagon, the carrots smelling fragrant and sweet with earth in their beards—riding through the darkness to the Ritz Hotel and in and through the lobby—no, that couldn't have happened but we were in the lobby and the bought concierge had gone for breakfast and champagne." At the end of another night, Fitzgerald took a train for Brussels, though he didn't remember how or why, and woke in an utterly strange hotel.

Back in Paris, he spent a share of his time at the Ritz bar, which was a center for the males of his community. Until the crash it was always full of Princeton and Harvard men, with their sisters and their divorced wives drinking at a smaller sitdown bar across the room. They disappeared after the summer of 1930. When one of Fitzgerald's heroes—Charlie Wales of "Babylon Revisited"—goes back to the bar in the following autumn, the stillness there impresses him as being "strange and portentous. It was not an American bar any more—he felt polite in it, and not as if he owned it. It had gone back into France." Then Charlie takes a taxi to the Left Bank, where he had seldom ventured in the wild days before the crash, and thinks to himself that it has the look of a provincial town.

The Left Bank was the site of the other America-in-Paris, that of the mostly impecunious writers and artists. Geographically it was only a small portion of the French city, which is divided into twenty *arrondissements*. The American colony was largely confined to the Sixth, which extends from the river to the Boulevard du Montparnasse, though the colony spilled over into sections of the Fourteenth Arrondissement, south of the Boulevard. Its great public landmarks were three cafés at the corner of the Boulevard du Montparnasse and the Boulevard Raspail: the Dôme, the Rotonde, and the Select.

Life in Montparnasse has been commemorated in a long series of memoirs, at least eighteen by my incomplete count (which does not include unpublished manuscripts such as those by Nathan Asch and William Bird). Perhaps the best known of the memoirs are those by Gertrude Stein (*The Autobiography of Alice B. Toklas*), Sylvia Beach (*Shakespeare and Company*), Morley Callaghan (*That Summer in Paris*), Matthew Josephson (*Life among the Surrealists*), and Hemingway himself (*A Moveable Feast*). The liveliest and most candid is *Memoirs of Montparnasse,* by the Canadian John Glassco, a book written when he was twenty-two years old and expected to die on the operating table. The best title is that of a book by Robert McAlmon, hard to find in the original text, but reissued in a somewhat abbreviated version with interchapters by Kay Boyle: *Being Geniuses Together.* Hemingway's book renders the atmosphere that prevailed among the more devoted young writers, with due attention to their vendettas, but his mixture of bitterness and nostalgia expresses what he felt forty years after. For the spirit of the time as felt at the time, one might better read *The Sun Also Rises* in conjunction with some of E. E. Cummings' early poems:

> make me a child, stout hurdysturdygurdyman,
> waiter, make me a child. So this is Paris.

> 1 will sit in the corner and drink thinks and think drinks,
> in memory of the Grand and Old days:
> of Amy Sandburg
> of Algernon Carl Swinburned.
>
> Waiter a drink waiter two or three drinks
> what's become of Maeterlinck
> now that April's here?
> (ask the man who owns one
> ask Dad, He knows).

I can picture Cummings writing those lines at a café table with a drink in front of him—and no fear of having it snatched away by a Prohibition agent—but it would not be in the Dôme or the Rotonde or the Select, for he seldom or never appeared in them. There were other young writers who came to feel that avoiding them was a mark of social distinction. Nevertheless those three cafés in Montparnasse, and the Dôme in particular, were something more than a paperback edition of the Ritz bar; they were the heart and nervous system of the American literary colony.

When young writers came to Paris for the first time, they dropped their luggage at a hotel on the Left Bank and went straight to the Dôme, in hope of meeting friends who had preceded them. Either they met the friends or else they made new ones. When they left for Brittany or the Mediterranean, in July, they went to the Dôme before their departure. A word dropped to acquaintances there was a more effective means of announcing their movements than a paragraph in the Paris edition of *The New York Herald*. The Dôme created and disseminated gossip. Americans went there to see who was having breakfast with whom, or had quarreled with whom, or was invited to sit at whose table; it was their living newspaper.

Even before the war it had become an American café, just as the Rotonde across the Boulevard had attracted Russian revolutionists and international painters. There were stories of poker games that had lasted without intermission for several days, with fresh American players taking the places of those who dropped out. I saw no poker games in 1921 or later. The back room where they used to be played was then furnished, or upholstered, with four dispirited prostitutes who never seemed to have clients; they wrote a great many letters. The front room contained the bar and another busy counter licensed by the state to sell tobacco and postage stamps. But most of the varied transactions that went on in those rooms or at the sidewalk tables yielded no profit to the management, except from the incidental sale of drinks.

Transactions. . . . In one of its many aspects the Dôme served as an informal renting agency, the only one in the Quarter, and as a guide to cheap hotels. For some it was a loan office where they might, if lucky, obtain fifty francs to tide them over until the next check came from the States. For many it was the assembly point of parties that might end with onion soup at Les Halles, the central markets, while perhaps another party, that one composed of Right Bank Americans, roistered at the next table. Daybreak at Les Halles was one of the very few occasions when the two colonies mingled. The editors of little magazines went to the Dôme in search of contributors; it was easier than writing letters. Several American publishers went there to ask about young authors, for, in addition to its other functions, the Dôme was an over-the-table market that dealt in literary futures. I heard there in the early spring of 1923 that a young man named Hemingway, who sometimes came to the Dôme for his morning coffee, was writing a new kind of very short stories and showed them to people in manuscript, or sometimes read them aloud. Some thought they were marvelous, some held their noses. There was a chaffering about those early stories that preceded the later bidding and bargaining among critics.

Celebrities like Sinclair Lewis made a point of appearing at the Dôme to impress beginners. Tourists also appeared, as at the zoo, before taxiing off to the nightclubs near the Place Blanche. Fakes went there to prey on the tourists and sucks to gather round the artists in little absorptive groups: "Please God, let some of their talent rub off on me." The artists themselves and the self-respecting writers were to be frightened away long before the lack of dollars put an end to their happy exile. But every community needs a center, and the American settlement on the Left Bank was no exception. For ten years after the war, the Café Brasserie du Dôme de Montparnasse was truly "the place."

3   Hemingway was not often seen at the Dôme after his return from Toronto; he had begun to speak of it contemptuously. When he dreamed back on those years in *A Moveable Feast,* he was to say that "many people went to the cafés at the corner of the Boulevard Montparnasse and the Boulevard Raspail to be seen publicly and in a way such places anticipated the columnists as a daily substitute for immortality." He preferred the Closerie des Lilas, some blocks to the east, where he could write on cold mornings without being surrounded by make-believe artists. That year he was working hard, but not for newspapers, and was very poor since the income from Hadley's trust fund had dwindled away. Ernest reported that in 1924 he earned only 1100 francs by his writing, no more than $80. Most of that was for his contributions to Ford Madox Ford's magazine, *The Transatlantic Review,* of which he was the unpaid assistant editor, though he also had dirty poems printed in a German avant-garde magazine, *Der Querschnitt.* The family was living in a cheap little flat south of the Luxembourg Gardens, with windows that looked down at a sawmill in the courtyard. On his way back from the Closerie, Ernest might spend an hour in the Luxembourg Museum, where Cézanne, Manet, and Monet still hung on probation before being admitted to the Louvre. He was bent on describing a river—Big Two-Hearted River—the way that Cézanne would have painted it. At other times he walked in the Gardens and looked at pigeons flocking round the statues of famous authors. He reports that if there was no meat for dinner, he sometimes killed a pigeon with a slingshot and carried it home under his jacket.

Poor as he was that year, and published only in little magazines (except for *Three Stories & Ten Poems,* 1923, and *in our time,* 1924, two Paris booklets sent to the printer before his Canadian trip), Hemingway was already famous in the American literary colony. The colony included a number of young writers who had gained some reputation and would afterward be widely known. Besides those I have mentioned—Cummings, Dos Passos, Fitzgerald—there were among many others Archibald MacLeish, John Peale Bishop, Kay Boyle, Gilbert Seldes, Djuna Barnes, Donald Ogden

Stewart, Glenway Wescott, Janet Flanner, Matthew Josephson, Robert M. Coates, and Louis Bromfield. Hemingway knew all of these. He was the close friend of three or four (Dos Passos, Fitzgerald, Stewart, MacLeish) and the declared enemy of two or three others, but it was a still younger group that specially looked up to him. The group was composed of writers then in the process of being "discovered," which is to say that their first stories or poems were being printed in the little magazines that bloomed and faded like wildflowers; at least a brace of new talents was printed in every issue of every new magazine. Running over a list of names some years ago, I found that many of the group had gone into business or teaching, that others were dead—Evan Shipman, John Herrmann, Nathan Asch—and that still others, then including Morley Callaghan and Josephine Herbst, were writing well but in comparative obscurity while hoping to be rediscovered.

One couldn't say that Hemingway was a leader among them, because he stood apart from the group, but the others were proud to be seen with him. It was an event of the evening if he passed the Dôme, tall, broad, and handsome, usually wearing a patched jacket and sneakers and often walking on the balls of his feet like a boxer. Arms waved in greeting from the sidewalk tables and friends ran out to urge him to sit down with them. "The occasions were charming little scenes, as if spontaneous even though repeated," says Nathan Asch in one of his unpublished books. "In view of the whole terrace, Hemingway would be striding toward the Montparnasse railroad station, his mind seemingly busy with the mechanics of someone's arrival or departure, and he wouldn't quite recognize whoever greeted him. Then suddenly his beautiful smile appeared that made those watching him also smile; and with a will and an eagerness he put out his hands and warmly greeted his acquaintance, who, overcome by this reception, simply glowed; and who returned with Hem to the table as if with an overwhelming prize."

"No, I have no criticism to make of Hem's conduct," Asch said in a letter written not long before he died. "I do think it's a crazy situation, though, that the elimination was so brutal, that of all the writers in Paris then, Hem is holding the world by the handle and everybody else is either obscure or dead. But you can't blame it on Hem."

Others did blame it on Hem—for example, Robert McAlmon, a bitter but often generous man who regarded himself as an unacknowledged genius; he had paid for Hemingway's first trip to Spain and then had published *Three Stories & Ten Poems*. Hemingway had never liked him and took to insulting him in public. McAlmon, a homosexual, revenged himself by spreading baseless tales about Hemingway's relations with Fitzgerald; it was one of the feuds that kept tongues busy at the Dôme. After insults had been exchanged in another Montparnasse café, McAlmon said of him, "He's the original Limelight Kid, just you watch him for a few months. Wherever the limelight is, you'll find Ernest with his big lovable boyish grin, making hay." Ernest did have that gift for attracting public homage—"charisma" would be the later word for it—but he also had other gifts that distinguished him from the young writers at the sidewalk tables, now obscure or dead. He had more talent, he worked harder, and he had a peculiarly studious habit of mind that the sidewalk writers lacked. McAlmon, for instance, hardly ever read a book and was radically unteachable.

Hemingway "was gay, he was sentimental, but he was always at work," Lincoln Steffens says in his *Autobiography*. In 1924, when they were dining at a Chinese restaurant in Paris, Hemingway insisted to Mrs. Steffens that anyone could write. "You can," he told her, feinting as if to give her a left to the jaw, for he was always shadowboxing in those days. "It's hell. It takes it all out of you; it nearly kills you; but you can do it. Anybody can. Even you can, Stef." On another occasion he added, "I haven't done it yet, but I will." He seemed to think, Steffens reports, "that writing was a matter of honesty and labor, and maybe it is, utter honesty and hard labor."

Hemingway had met Steffens two years before, at the Lausanne Conference, and had shown him some of his dispatches from the Near East. It was a meeting which, in its consequences, had a decisive effect on Hemingway's apprenticeship. Immediately impressed by his work, Steffens asked to see more of it. Ernest told his wife to send it all on from Paris. Hadley was afraid it would be lost if she sent it by express, so she packed it in a suitcase and carried it herself. At the Gare de Lyon in Paris, she left the compartment for a moment to get a drink of water, and the suitcase was stolen. It contained everything he had saved till that time—an unfinished novel, eighteen stories, thirty poems; all the manuscripts, typescripts, carbon copies—and it was never recovered. There was a little salvage. *Poetry* had accepted six poems; the *Cosmopolitan* was rejecting a story, "My Old Man," which was then in the mail; and lying in a drawer was the manuscript of another story, "Up in Michigan," which Hemingway himself had rejected when Miss Stein told him it was *inaccrochable*, like a painting that couldn't be hung. For the rest, all the early work that he valued was irretrievably lost.

It was in some ways a fortunate disaster. With his work destroyed as if by fire, he could start from the beginning and build another structure on new lines. "I was trying to learn to write," he says on the second page of *Death in the Afternoon*, in a passage referring to those months, "commencing with the simplest things." That last phrase is almost unique in its mixture of simplicity and hardheadedness. I have known many apprentice writers, but not one other who was willing, at twenty-three, to put aside everything he thought he had learned and start again with the simplest things. "All you have to do is write one true sentence," he had told himself in one of the blue-covered notebooks he was keeping at the time. "Write the truest sentence that you know."

Before and after the Toronto venture, Hemingway studied writing in Paris as if he were studying geometry without a textbook and inventing theorems as he went along. He accepted as a postulate that the function of any literary work is to evoke some particular emotion from the reader; but how could that best be done? Most writers were content to describe an emotion as it was felt by themselves or their heroes, in hope that the reader would be moved by it, but this was a method that made him the mere auditor of someone else's fear or longing or rage. Hemingway wanted to make his readers feel the emotion directly—not as if they were being told about it, but as if they were taking part in it. The best way to produce this effect, he decided as a first theorem, was to set down exactly, in their proper sequence, the sights, sounds, touches, tastes, and smells that had evoked an emotion he remembered feeling. Then, without auctorial comments and without ever saying that he or his hero had been frightened, sad, or angry, he could make the reader feel the emotion for himself.

"I was trying to write then," he says in that same passage

of *Death in the Afternoon,* "and I found the greatest difficulty, aside from knowing truly what you really felt, rather than what you were supposed to feel, and had been taught to feel, was to put down what really happened in action; what the actual things were which produced the emotion that you experienced. In writing for a newspaper you told what happened and, with one trick and another, you communicated the emotion aided by the element of timeliness which gives a certain emotion to any account of something that has happened on that day; but the real thing, the sequence of motion and fact which made the emotion and which would be as valid in a year or in ten years or, with luck and if you stated it purely enough, always, was beyond me and I was working very hard to try to get it."

That often-quoted passage suggests a whole system of practical aesthetics—not the loftiest one, not one to which Hemingway would later confine himself, but a sound system within its self-imposed limitations and an excellent guide for young writers. Hemingway is suggesting, in substance, that a piece of writing might be regarded as a machine for producing a particular effect, and that its capacity for producing the effect should be permanent. "When you describe something that has happened that day," he would say elsewhere, "the timeliness makes people see it in their own imaginations. A month later that element of time is gone and your account would be flat and they would not see it in their minds nor remember it." Good writing, as Ezra Pound was already saying, is "news that STAYS news." It can stay news if it has achieved certain definite qualities, that is, if it is absolutely honest—a virtue that depends on "knowing truly what you really felt, rather than what you were supposed to feel, and had been taught to feel"—and if it presents "the real thing, the sequence of motion and fact which made the emotion." But a writer's luck, or unconscious, also plays a part in the process, and the real thing has to be stated "purely enough" if it is to remain valid.

"Purely enough," for Hemingway, meant without tricks of any sort, without conventionally emotive language, and with a bare minimum of adjectives and adverbs. It also meant that the permanent work had to be written like cabelese, with everything omitted that the reader could take for granted, and with each detail so carefully chosen that it did the work of six or seven. One of Hemingway's early studies was the art of omission. "If a writer of prose knows enough about what he is writing about," he says in another chapter of *Death in the Afternoon,* "he may omit things that he knows and the reader, if the writer is writing truly enough, will have a feeling of those things as strongly as though the writer had stated them. The dignity of movement of an ice-berg is due to only one-eighth of it being above water."

That sort of dignity is not simple to maintain, and Hemingway "was working very hard to try to get it." With his talent for methodology, for the *how,* he thought it could best be achieved, at the beginning, in very short pieces. The first ones he wrote after starting again with the simplest things were the vignettes, or "chapters," collected in one of his Paris booklets, *in our time* (and later printed in italics between the stories in the first of his books to be issued by a New York publisher, this time with the title capitalized: *In Our Time*). Much earlier six of the "chapters," all those he had finished at the moment, appeared in the April 1923 issue of *The Little Review.* One of these was the paragraph that afterward became "Chapter II," the one beginning "Minarets stuck up in the rain out of Adrianople across the mud flats." Perhaps it was the very first work in his new manner, and it exists in three separate versions, with a complicated history of changes that the late Charles A. Fenton studied at length in his *Apprenticeship of Ernest Hemingway.*

The earliest version is the first three paragraphs of a story that he cabled to *The Star* from Adrianople on October 20, 1922. It was not written in cabelese, as it would have been if he were sending it to International News Service, and it was a masterly piece of reporting. Lincoln Steffens, who read it at Lausanne in December, recollected much of it ten years later when writing the last chapters of his *Autobiography.* The paragraphs, however, were not in Hemingway's new manner. In their total length of 241 words there were no less than thirty adjectives, and some of these were compound words like "never-ending" and "muddy-flanked." There were also signposts to guide the reader toward having the proper emotions: that is, there were charged words and phrases like "ghastly," "in horror," and "to keep off the driving rain." These "tricks," as Hemingway called them, were permissible and even necessary in a newspaper story designed to produce its effect at a single hasty glance.

In the second version, the one that Hemingway published

in *The Little Review,* all the guideposts to emotion have disappeared and so have most of the adjectives. Some of the descriptive details have also been omitted, in order to bring the others into sharper focus. The process of sharpening and tightening the prose while suppressing even the implied comments of the author continued at intervals for several months. The results of it appear in the third and almost final version, as published in the Paris booklet *in our time.* The version reads:

> Minarets stuck up in the rain out of Adrianople across the mud flats. The carts were jammed for thirty miles along the Karagatch road. Water buffalo and cattle were hauling the carts through the mud. No end and no beginning. Just carts loaded with everything they owned. The old men and women, soaked through, walked along keeping the cattle moving. The Maritza was running yellow almost up to the bridge. Carts were jammed solid on the bridge with camels bobbing along through them. Greek cavalry herded along the procession. Women and kids were in the carts crouched with mattresses, mirrors, sewing machines, bundles. There was a woman having a kid with a young girl holding a blanket over her and crying. Scared sick looking at it. It rained all through the evacuation.

Here the "chapter," as it is called, has been shortened to 132 words, about half the length of the newspaper version. There are only ten descriptive adjectives instead of thirty, and every one of them is simple and definite. Four of the adjectives—"loaded," "soaked," "crouched," and "scared"—are past participles and have somewhat the effect of verbs in the passive voice: the right effect, since the refugees are the passive subjects of action. There are also nine present participles, three of which occur in the same sentence: ". . . *having* a kid with a young girl *holding* a blanket over her and *crying.*" They give a sense of action that continues under our eyes. This use, and sometimes abuse, of present participles was one of the habits that Hemingway had possibly acquired from Gertrude Stein, together with a fondness for prepositional phrases used in series (*in* the rain *out of* Adrianople *across* the mud flats) and a distrust of relative clauses. All the sentences are short, averaging only ten words. (Incidentally this is not a characteristic of Hemingway's later prose, in which there are sentences almost as long as Faulkner's.) Three sentences have been stripped of their verbs, and the others without exception are simple and declarative.

There were further changes, if slight ones, in 1925 when the Adrianople "chapter" was included in the much longer American *In Our Time,* and again in 1930 when the book was reissued by Scribners. Did the changes work, taken as a whole? To expand the question, what effects did Hemingway produce on his readers as a result of patient revisions in this and the other brief "chapters," eighteen in all (though two were later reprinted as stories), that he wrote during the months after he lost his manuscripts? I think the effects on sympathetic and attentive readers, at first a minority, were close to those he planned to produce. Other readers blamed Hemingway, insensitively, for being tough and insensitive. But the attentive ones were moved, though they seldom knew why, and they felt they were seeing events for themselves instead of just hearing about them. They felt that the exaggeratedly simple and awkward-looking style made everything seem authentic; and they also felt that the "chapters" had an impact not in proportion to their size, as if part of it depended on words that went unspoken. Written without tricks— except the great ones of understatement and omission—those very brief works proved to be news that stayed news. They have exerted a permanent influence even on writers who turned against Hemingway, and they brought about something like a revolution in American prose fiction.

(To make another incidental remark, they bear a resemblance to some of the "epiphanies" that Joyce recorded in manuscripts not published till after his death. Indeed, most of them *are* epiphanies in the Joycean sense that each is "a sudden spiritual manifestation, whether in the vulgarity of speech or of gesture or in a memorable phase of the mind itself." It was Hemingway's method, though, to present the vulgar background and to let the manifestation be inferred.)

He wrote no more "chapters" after his return from Toronto. Instead he went on to the second stage in his program, which consisted in writing stories. He began by applying the methods developed in his vignettes, but this time, besides presenting a scene, he included some of the events leading up to it, in strict chronological sequence. He also included dialogue, for which he had a naturally fine ear. But simple chronology, or narrative sequence, was the principal element that distinguished the stories from the "chapters," and Hemingway displayed an extraordinary talent for putting first things first, second things second, and for stopping short of what other writers would regard as the climax in order to let the reader go on for himself. That explains the power of suggestion of an early story like "Cat in the Rain," for instance: the climax is on the next page after the end.

In discussing the purely technical aspects of Hemingway's early work, I have omitted what he called the element of luck. He had that too, in the shape of an unusually rich subconscious and a stock of subject matter, both giving him an advantage over his teachers. Ezra Pound had only two closely related subjects at the time, art and the life of art. Gertrude Stein's principal subject was herself. Hemingway's subject was also himself, or his inner world, but that self had a passion for acquiring knowledge and for rushing forward to meet external challenges, so that his inner world already included a broad and highly colored segment of the outer world. He was a very complicated young man at twenty-six, with painful memories to exorcise, with grudges to pay off, and with something close to a genius for simplification. There were some readers—only a few at the time, for he had not been printed in American magazines (except *Poetry*)—who felt that his stories were completely new in American fiction.

In Our Time, which contains all the stories he had written since his manuscripts were stolen, appeared in New York at the beginning of October 1925. It was published by Boni and Liveright, then an enterprising young house that also published Anderson and Dreiser on long-term contracts and that now had taken an option on Hemingway's next three books. *In Our Time* had a sale in the first season of hardly more than five hundred copies. One of its early readers was Alfred Harcourt, an astute Yankee publisher who probably guessed at its failure as a business venture, but still wished that the book had been on his own list. Harcourt said in a letter to Louis Bromfield, who had called the book to his attention, "Hemingway's first novel might rock the country." The letter was sent to Paris in the late autumn of 1925, at a time when Hemingway had reached a third stage in his career. Having learned how to write stories as a second stage, he was then waiting to revise a hastily written draft of *The Sun Also Rises*.

4 ⚡ I don't mean to suggest that Hemingway spent all his time writing or preparing to write. He boxed regularly at a Paris gymnasium and sometimes earned a little money, ten francs a round, as a sparring partner for professionals. He played a good deal of tennis with, among others, Ezra Pound, William C. Bullitt the future ambassador to France, and Harold Loeb the former publisher of *Broom,* who had been a middleweight wrestler at Princeton. Rapidly Ernest had acquired a wide circle of friends, or rather a number of nonintersecting circles composed respectively of tennis friends, boxing friends, racetrack friends, newspaper friends, and older and younger writing friends. Some of the younger ones had been "discovered" in the issue of *The Transatlantic Review* (August 1924) that Hemingway had put together while Ford was trying to raise money in New York. But the magazine went under at the end of the year, and Hemingway had spent the winter skiing at the little Austrian town of Schruns, in the Vorarlberg. In the autumn of 1925, he was planning to spend a second winter at Schruns, where, so he reported, he was once offered the job of skiing instructor.

One is again surprised to find how much he learned in those early years and how quickly he reached a professional level in several fields of study. At one time he was a prizefight manager with, he told me, "a little stable of boxers" that included Larry Gaines, a black heavyweight from Toronto who later beat Max Schmeling in one of Schmeling's early bouts. That business career ended on a celebrated evening when Hemingway jumped into the ring with other spectators to save a young boxer from being killed in a fixed fight. Hemingway—so the story was repeated at the Dôme—grabbed a water bottle from one of the seconds and knocked out Francis Charles, the middleweight champion of France. After that he abandoned French boxing as a crooked sport and devoted more and more attention to the bullfights in Spain.

Told about that other sport by Gertrude Stein, he had seen his first bullfight in the late spring of 1923, on a trip to Seville with McAlmon, who paid the bills, and William Bird, a foreign correspondent whose avocation was hand-printing books in a little Paris shop. (One of the books, or booklets, was *in our time*.) A few weeks after that first trip, Ernest had taken Hadley to Pamplona for the *feria* of San Fermín, which always lasted from July 6 to July 12. "By God," he reported, "they have bullfights in that town." In 1924 he was back in Pamplona with, among others, Hadley, Dos Passos, Donald Ogden Stewart, and Ernest's Anglo-Irish military friend, Captain E. E. Dorman-Smith. He returned to Paris with photographs of the big pepper-and-salt bull that had carried him across the arena on its padded horns, besides cracking some of Don Stewart's ribs. He was also excited by trout fishing in the Irati River high in the mountains, where it came pouring out of a virgin beech forest.

He made another trip to the Irati just before the fiesta of 1925, this time with Hadley, Stewart, and Bill Smith, a friend of his Michigan days. They found that much of the beech forest had been cut down and that construction work on a dam had ruined the fishing. In some ways the fiesta itself was even less successful. The group in Pamplona included, besides the fishermen, Harold Loeb, Patrick Guthrie, who was an English remittance man, and his friend Lady Duff Twysden, who was said to be the heroine of Michael Arlen's immensely popular novel *The Green Hat*. Usually she did wear a floppy-brimmed green felt hat, but she was more widely known for her love affairs and her capacity for holding liquor. Ernest learned that Loeb had lately spent a week with her at Saint-Jean-de-Luz. Everybody drank a great deal at the fiesta and almost everybody quarreled. "Some fiesta," said Loeb, who later described it in his memoirs. Things went better at the bullring, where the principal attraction was Cayetano Ordóñez, also known as Niño de la Palma, who was then in his first season as a matador. After the fiesta, the Hemingways followed Ordóñez to Madrid. There he dedicated one of his bulls to Hadley, killed it to great applause, and presented her with its ear, which she wrapped in a handkerchief and carried back to the hotel.[1]

---

1. I heard a great deal about the fiesta at the time, from Harold Loeb and others, but it was years before I got straight in my mind who was there and exactly what happened. Loeb's book of memoirs, *The Way It Was* (1959), can be trusted for the facts, in spite of his justified sense of grievance. For what happened afterward, especially the writing of *The Sun Also Rises*, I am indebted to Carlos Baker's life of Hemingway, where the facts are double-checked.

The Hemingways went on to Valencia and it was there, on July 23, that Ernest started *The Sun Also Rises,* just eleven days after some of the events that were to be described (and considerably revised) in the novel. One of his early theorems was that the background of an experience should be presented truly, "the way it was," but that the story should be "made up," so as to become truer than what actually happened. Work on the novel continued uninterruptedly in Madrid, San Sebastian, Hendaye, and then Paris, where the first draft was finished on September 21, after less than two months of writing. "I knew nothing about writing a novel when I started it," Hemingway said many years later, "and so wrote too fast and each day to the point of complete exhaustion. So the first draft was very bad. I wrote it in six weeks and I had to rewrite it completely. But in the rewriting I learned much."

Before setting to work on the revision, he put the manuscript aside for nearly three months, to season. It was during this interval that he wrote *The Torrents of Spring,* a cruel parody of his friend Sherwood Anderson. Having produced a book-length manuscript in a little more than a week, he sent it on to Boni and Liveright as the next book under their contract. They could scarcely publish it, considering that Anderson, after Dreiser, was their leading author. If they rejected it, their option on Hemingway's future books would be canceled. He went back to the novel in December while he was at Schruns—but not skiing much, for that was the year of the avalanches—and worked hard on it at intervals, when he wasn't going for walks with Pauline Pfeiffer. At the end of the month he received a cablegram from Horace Liveright rejecting *The Torrents of Spring.* "So I'm loose," he said not unhappily. He had already received inquiries from other publishers. In February 1926 he made a hasty visit to New York, had an interview with Maxwell Perkins of Scribners, and signed a contract for both the parody (to be published first) and the novel. Work on the latter continued during March and included some ruthless cutting in the first or Paris section of the manuscript; here he was acting on advice from Fitzgerald. A final draft went to the typist April 1 and was published October 22. By that time Hemingway was living alone in Gerald Murphy's unheated studio. His first marriage had broken up and he was waiting for a divorce to marry Pauline.

The Sun Also Rises did not rock the country, but it received a number of hat-in-the-air reviews and it soon became a handbook of conduct for the new generation. That winter an observer in Greenwich Village noted that many of the younger writers had already begun to talk, walk, and shadowbox like Hemingway, when they weren't flourishing capes in front of an imaginary bull.

Though Hemingway said that he knew nothing about writing a novel when he started it, the book reveals his systematic or studentlike cast of mind and his habit of always starting with the simple before moving to the complex. In writing a first novel he applied the principles developed in his vignettes, along with the others developed in his stories. Once again, as he went on to another stage, his work incorporated a new element besides its greater length. Whereas each of his stories had dealt with one or two persons, or three at the most, his novel deals with the rather more complicated relations among a *group* of persons. That might lead to a general description of the novel—any novel—as a literary form: it is a long but unified narrative, designed to be read at more than one sitting, which presents a situation affecting a group of characters and leads to a change in their relations.

The situation in the background of *The Sun Also Rises* is the Great War, in which most of the characters have served and in which some of them have been physically or morally wounded. All the characters except Pedro Romero, the matador, have lost their original code of values. Feeling the loss, they are now trying to live by a simpler code, essentially that of soldiers on furlough, and it is this effort that unites them as a group. "I told you he was one of us," Lady Brett says of Count Mippipopolous after he has unashamedly stripped off his shirt and shown them where an arrow had passed completely through his body. The unashamedness, the wound, and the courage it suggests are all things they have in common. The war has deadened some of their feelings and has left them capable of enjoying only the simplest and strongest pleasures. It has also given them an attitude of resigned acceptance toward all sorts of disasters, including those caused by their own follies. Robert Cohn, however, has never been wounded and has never learned to be resigned; therefore he refuses to let Brett go, fights with his rivals including Romero, and is cast out of the group. Romero is their simple-minded saint. Brett is almost on the point of permanently corrupting him, but she obeys another article of the code and draws back. "You know, it makes one feel rather good deciding not to be a bitch," she says (and scores of junior Bretts have echoed). "It's sort of what we have instead of God."

The Sun Also Rises is not, as it is often called, Hemingway's best novel. After all it is his first, and there are signs in it of his struggle to master a new medium. In spite of his deletions from the manuscript, there are still details that do not seem essential, as notably in the street-by-street account of Jake Barnes's wanderings through Paris. There are also a few obvious guideposts for the reader, as when Jake says of Robert Cohn that "he was not so simple" after coming back from New York, "and he was not so nice." Although Cohn's fight with Romero is the physical climax of the action, it is reported at second hand—by Mike Campbell, who has heard the story from Brett, who was the only witness of the fight—instead of being directly presented. More serious than those technical flaws is the sort of timeliness that is always in danger of going stale. Brett was a pathetic brave figure for her time, but the pathos has been cheapened by thousands of imitation Bretts in life and fiction. Bill Gorton's remarks are not so bright now as they once seemed. "You're an expatriate," he tells Jake ironically. "You've lost touch with the soil. You get precious. Fake European standards have ruined you. . . . You hang around cafés." In those days, as I have been reminded by old newspaper clippings, editorial writers with nothing else to say used to deplore and deride the expatriates. Now that the editorials have been forgotten, a reader does not feel as he might have felt in 1926, that Gorton is making exactly the right rejoinder.

Not everything changes. After one has mentioned those wrinkles and scars revealed by age, how much of the novel seems as marvelously fresh as when it first appeared! Count Mippipopolous, his wound, and his champagne; the old couple from Montana on their first trip abroad; the busload of Basque peasants; the whole beautiful episode of the fishing trip in the mountains, in the harsh sunlight, with bright water tumbling over the dam; then by contrast the dark streets of Pamplona crowded with riau-riau dancers, who formed a circle round Brett as if she were a revered witch—as indeed she was, and as Jake in a way was the impotent Fisher King ruling over a sterile land—in all this there is nothing that has gone bad and not a word to be changed after so many years. It is all carved in stone, bigger and truer than life, and it is the work of a man who, having ended his busy term of apprenticeship, was already a master at twenty-six.

The work of the fifteen years that followed has been so much written about, and taught in so many college courses, that I feel no impulse to discuss it once again. After dealing with other writers, however, I shall come back to Hemingway in another chapter, one that deals with a much later stage in his career.

IV DOS PASSOS
The Learned Poggius

1   I like to remember Dos Passos as I saw him from time to time in the middle 1920s. Though still in his own twenties, just four years older than the century, he had published half a dozen books including *Three Soldiers* and *Manhattan Transfer,* both of which novels had been an outrage to the older generation. Younger people gathered round him at parties in the Village and strained to hear the understated but uproarious stories that he told about Russian commissars and waterfront dives in Marseilles; but soon he would drop out of the group, as if its homage made him uneasy, and stand in the background to watch and listen. He was above the average height and was usually dressed in a nondescript gray suit that might be worn at the seams. He had straight black hair, a wide forehead growing a little higher each year, and a wide mouth curving upward at the corners into apologetic grins. His most noticeable feature was a pair of spectacles with gollywog lenses, for he suffered from extreme shortsightedness until he was cured of it by a combination of middle-aged presbyopia and Dr. Bates's famous eye exercises. In

his twenties he had to peer at people and carried his head forward like that of a shy, inquisitive, easily frightened bird.

Sometimes he offered opinions in a tentative fashion: "Gosh, I d-don't know about that," he would say, or, "D-don't you think that perhaps—?" but the opinion that followed, though delivered in a low voice, would be his own and nobody else could change it. Sometimes, with a timid but mischievous smile, he stuttered out a devastating remark. "Intellectual workers of the world, unite!" he might say among a group of radical friends. "You have nothing to lose but your brains."

That particular remark, afterward widely repeated by others, was not actually spoken; it was scribbled as a message to another table at a Village speakeasy, where Dos Passos had come with Joseph Freeman and Michael Gold to discuss plans for bringing out a revolutionary magazine that they decided to call *The New Masses*. But were Joe and Mike and other radical journalists really his friends at the time, no matter how often he was seen with them? John Howard Lawson was a radical and a friend; they had served together in a Red Cross ambulance unit and soon they would be working together at the New Playwrights' Theater; but the others, it seems to me now, were merely allies in his crusade against a businessman's culture. The allies were usually Marxists of a sort, willing to be guided by the Communist Party, whereas Dos Passos was a libertarian with a touch of anarchism. He was also a writer essentially, more than a politician, and his closest friends were Cummings, Fitzgerald, Hemingway, Wilson, and other rising writers of the new generation. Even with these he was a little out of tempo. He was as interested as the friends in shaping a new language, but less interested in probing the depths of the mind, and vastly more interested in the social panorama. He looked back more than they did to the yellow or mauve 1890s, at least on one side of his work, while on another side, and at a time when other young writers were obstinately non-political, he looked forward to the 1930s, later to be called the Red Decade.

Meanwhile he had no sympathy with an element of showmanship that he detected in some of the friends. "I held them off as best I could," he was to say in his memoirs, speaking of Scott and Zelda Fitzgerald. ". . . the idea of being that kind of celebrity set my teeth on edge." Dos Passos didn't want to be any kind of celebrity or project a public image of any sort. He wanted to remain an observer, independent and almost anonymous, one to whom all sorts of people could speak their minds. As regards his private life, he wanted to keep it to himself. There was in fact one circumstance about the life that he was not ready to have discussed in public, though later he was to reveal it under a thin veil in his autobiographical novel *Chosen Country*, as well as candidly in his book of memoirs *The Best Times*. It was the cloud over his birth.

His father, John Randolph Dos Passos, was the son of a Portuguese immigrant who had married a Philadelphia Quaker. After serving as a drummer boy in the Civil War, the father had become a famous criminal lawyer, then a still more famous corporation lawyer. In 1891 he had guided the delicate maneuvers that led to the incorporation of the American Sugar Refining Company, the so-called Sugar Trust, and had received the largest legal fee on record up to that time. He was still radiant with this success and others when he fell in love with the novelist's mother, who was a penniless widow proud of her Virginia ancestry. The eminent lawyer had been living apart from his wife, an invalid. There were reasons why he could not ask for a divorce, but, after a long courtship, he persuaded the attractive widow to come with him to Europe. They were both in Chicago when their only child was born, in 1896. For the rest of her life the mother and the lawyer were together on most of his travels; it was a romantic union; but they could not live together in New York or Washington until the first wife died and they were finally married in 1910.

By that time Dos Passos was a boy in prep school. As a result of the family situation he had spent a lonely childhood in luxury hotels, always moving from city to city, always feeling himself the alien, always speaking the language with a foreign accent whether he was in France or Italy or Belgium—or in England, where he first went to school, or later among rich Americans at the Choate School in Connecticut—and never feeling at home except on trains or ocean steamers, where he could spend most of his time with a book held close to his gollywog glasses. Two of his favorite authors were Malory and Gibbon, both of whom he read from beginning to end. In *Le Morte d'Arthur* he preferred Book XX with its story of how, "as in the month of May, it befell a great anger and unhap that stinted not till the flower of chivalry of all the world was destroyed

Dos Passos radical (1931), his elbows on the galley proofs of *Nineteen Nineteen*.
THE GRANGER COLLECTION

Dos Passos conservative, in the 1950s.
THE BETTMANN ARCHIVE, INC.

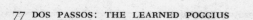

and slain." In *The Decline and Fall* he noted (and later transcribed for one of his novels) a passage about the last days of Pope Eugenius IV:

> . . . two of his servants, the learned Poggius and a friend, ascended the Capitoline Hille, reposed themselves among the ruins of columns and temples, and viewed from that commanding spot the wide and various prospect of desolation. The place and the object gave ample scope for moralizing on the vicissitudes of fortune, which spares neither man nor the proudest of his works, which buries empires and cities in a common grave. . . .

Sometimes Dos Passos called himself "the learned Poggius," witness, so he thought, to another decline and fall. He was shy, self-conscious, awkward in sports, and a brilliant student; in fact he graduated from Choate at fifteen, and his father had him spend a year abroad before going on to college. At Harvard he was again a lonely figure, standing outside the terribly snobbish social system of those days, not elected to Dickey or the Hasty Pudding, let alone to a final club; but after a time he found compensations. Becoming known for his contributions to *The Harvard Monthly*, he made his first close friends, most of whom belonged to a group afterward known as the Harvard Aesthetes. Although the group had some importance in literary history, principally because of Dos Passos and Cummings, it has never been properly described.

"The Aesthetes," I wrote of them briefly, many years ago, "had no interest whatever in social problems. They read Casanova's memoirs and *Les Liaisons Dangereuses*, both in the original French, and Petronius in Latin; they gathered at teatime in one another's rooms, or for punches in the offices of *The Harvard Monthly;* they drank seidels of dry gin topped with a maraschino cherry; they discussed the music of Pater, the rhythms of Aubrey Beardsley, and, growing louder, the voluptuousness of the Roman Church and the essential sanctity of prostitutes. They had crucifixes in their bedrooms and ticket stubs from last Saturday's burlesque at the Old Howard. They were trying to create in Cambridge, Massachusetts, an after-image of Oxford in the 1890s. They wrote, too," I continued; "dozens of them were promising poets, each with his invocations to Antinous, his mournful elegies to Venetian lagoons, and his sonnets that addressed a chorus girl as 'little painted poem of God.' " That last phrase is early Cummings, but Dos Passos had similar notions at the time, even though he put them into less metrical language.

The fact remains that he differed from the other Aesthetes in the scope of his rebellion. All rebels of a sort, the others protested as individuals; their hated enemies were puritanism and what they liked to call the tyranny of the mob, while Dos Passos dreamed of finding many allies in a revolution that would abolish the industrial system after putting an end to the war in Europe. He wrote to his classmate Arthur R. McComb two months after they left Harvard, "Really, Arthur, I am darned serious—'the forces of reason' must get together, must make a fuss—We want a new Enlightenment—new Byrons, new Shelleys, new Voltaires before whom 19th century stodginess—[on] the one hand—and 20th century reaction on the other shall vanish and be utterly worsted 'like souls from the enchanter fleeing.' " Shortly afterward Dos Passos went abroad to study architecture in Spain. From that country, obstinately neutral, but full of spies, refugees, and revolutionists, his letters to McComb became more violent. "Vive Adler," he wrote on January 4, 1917, after reading that Adler had assassinated the Austrian prime minister. The letter continued:

> I honestly see no reason on earth why a society for the assassination of statesmen shouldn't be formed that would promptly and neatly do to death all concerned in any declaration of war, "just" or "unjust."
>
> If Anarchists can murder people so successfully, I don't see why Pacifists can't.
>
> Chocolate and bombs forever.

A month later the elder Dos Passos died, and the bloodthirsty young pacifist hurried home. There he found that the father's estate was small for such a prominent man, that the will was likely to be contested, and that he would have to support himself thenceforth. Meanwhile he was trying to get into the army. Although he was opposed to the war more bitterly than ever, and exempt from the draft because of defective eyesight, he wanted to serve at the front "before the whole thing goes belly up," as more than one of his characters would later say. He wanted to write about the war from first-hand experience. Finally he was accepted by the Norton-Harjes Ambulance Corps, which had very few physical requirements. Before sailing for France he told McComb that his only hope was "in revolution—in wholesale assassination of all statesmen, capitalists, war-mongers, jingoists, inventors, scientists—in the destruction of all the machinery of the industrial world." So that his letters from the front might get past the censors, he adopted the code word "Nagel," actually the name of a young artist he knew. "Nagel—the name—" he said, "will stand for the chances of revolution and all the psychological fringe thereof." Another letter reported, "I've come to firmly believe that the only thing that can save America is Nagelism there."

After the American Army took over the Norton-Harjes ambulance units, Dos Passos enlisted in the Red Cross for service in Italy. There he got into trouble and was sent back to the States—chiefly for singing "Deutschland über Alles" during an air raid—and the experience gave depth to his feeling of rebellion. But what was the original source of the feeling? Partly it may have gone back to his lonely childhood, when he was forced to conceal his parentage and always felt himself to be the awkward outsider. He must have come to hate the social order that made him so unhappy. Also, it seems clear, he was rebelling against his eminent father. In the years after his mother died, he had drawn closer to the father—to whom he pays a warm tribute in his memoirs—but still he must have borne an obscure grudge against him, going back to the early years when this almost stranger had appeared at intervals to deprive him of the mother's undivided affection. Later it was natural to dream of destroying the corporations that the father had helped to create and of assassinating the bankers and politicians who had been the father's cronies.

Whatever the source of his revolutionary fervor, Nagelism persisted through the first fifteen years of his career as a writer. In all his early books it provided a hidden thesis: "Everything will be better when the revolution comes." He regarded each of the books as, in his own words, " 'arf a brick" heaved "into the temple of Moloch." The temple of Moloch was not much damaged, except for a broken window here and there, but, even by the middle 1920s, the books had won an international reputation for their author. In Paris he was admired by the American literary colony and had friends among the younger French writers. In Greenwich Village, where he reappeared between expeditions to Russia, Persia, Mexico, and wherever, he was taken to be an elusive and even a mysterious figure. Very few of his companions knew where he was living in any given week. He never seemed to have a nest, but only to be perched on a branch, as if he were a migrating bird. At parties he left his soft brown Harvard hat near the door "so as to be ready to bolt," he says, "at a moment's notice." I am quoting from *The Best Times*, where he also tells us:

> At the slightest excuse, and particularly upon the occasion of the publication of a book, I bolted for foreign parts. . . . Young women I met at cocktail parties liked to tell me I was running away from myself.
>
> That was partly true. Maybe I was running away from them. I never got around to explaining that I was running toward something too. It was the whole wide world. I still had an insatiable appetite for architecture and painting, particularly the work of the so-called scientists of the early Italian renaissance. . . . I wanted to see everything they had ever painted. I wanted to see country and landscape and plants and animals and people: men, women and children in city, town and hamlet. I had to hurry. There would never be time to satisfy such multifarious curiosity.

The same note of eagerness and multifarious curiosity is sounded in the first pages of his most ambitious work, a trilogy of novels first published separately in the years from 1930 to 1936. When the novels reappeared in 1937 as one huge volume called *U. S. A.*, he added three pages by way of a prologue that offers a portrait of the author as he was in his twenties.

> The young man walks by himself [Dos Passos says], fast but not fast enough, far but not far enough (faces slide out of sight, talk trails into tattered scraps, footsteps tap fainter in alleys); he must catch the last subway, the streetcar, the bus, run up the gangplanks of all the steamboats, register at all the hotels, work in the cities, answer the wantads, learn the trades, take up the jobs, live in all the boardinghouses, sleep in all the beds. One bed is not enough, one job is not enough, one life

is not enough. At night, head swimming with wants, he walks by himself alone.

No job, no woman, no house, no city.

That young man once published a book called, without much exaggeration, *In All Countries*. As early as 1927, however, his itinerary had changed. He had become deeply involved in the struggle to save the lives of Sacco and Vanzetti, and the execution of "those anarchist bastards," as Judge Thayer had called them, made Dos Passos feel more deeply than ever that his own country had lost compassion under the rule of faceless monopolies. Might he dream of becoming a contemporary Gibbon? Might he write a series of novels that would chronicle the moral decay of the whole nation since the Spanish-American War? To carry out such a project he would need more knowledge about many sections of the United States, and the search for that knowledge was to guide most of his activities for the following eight or nine years. He made a trip to Russia in 1928, but he wasn't tempted to go back. For the rest, instead of bolting up the gangplanks of steamers bound for it didn't matter what foreign ports, he caught trains for the Middle West, the Carolina cotton mills, the Kentucky coal fields, or the San Francisco waterfront, wherever people were suffering and class wars were bursting out. Especially during the early years of the Depression, he attended mass meetings and congressional hearings, he walked on picket lines before reporting strikes for the labor press, once he worked in Hollywood, and always he listened and observed.

The trilogy of novels recording what he learned from his travels is an impressive work that embodies a paradox. Dos Passos was primarily interested in presenting his *material*, that is, in offering a panorama of American life at all levels over a period of thirty years. But no previous novelist had found a method of painting such a panorama. Tolstoy? one asks. His *War and Peace* had achieved a breadth beyond the dreams of other novelists, but even Tolstoy had devoted most of his attention to four great families of the Russian nobility. Dos Passos wanted to present typical persons from many levels of society, giving sharp attention to each—even using their special idioms—while suggesting the movement of society as a whole. To do so he was forced to invent devices of his own. These included "Newsreels," as he called them, consisting of phrases from newspapers and snatches of popular songs that would suggest the voice of an era; then short biographies of various American worthies, the leaders of their time (but subject to the same impersonal forces as lesser people); then the "Camera Eye," which gave his own reaction to the scenes described—as in those early-renaissance religious paintings, Dos Passos explained, where we find a self-portrait of the artist in one corner. There were to be hundreds of characters, but the substance of the novel would be the life stories of twelve more or less typical men and women, each from a different section of the country and each disastrously involved in great events. The new technical devices, if successful, would all contribute to a general effect. At this point the learned Poggius, the intensely curious observer of history, was setting out to make himself a master technician.

The paradox is that the technique, much more than the observed material it was designed to present, has had an effect on literary history in more than one country. Dos Passos' picture of America succumbing to decay as competitive capitalism gave way to monopoly capitalism is powerful, but in the end subjective; one is not obliged to accept his notion of a catastrophic decline and fall. One has to acknowledge, however, that his technical inventions soon reappeared in the mainstream of fiction. *The Grapes of Wrath, The Naked and the Dead,* and scores of other American novels concerned with a collective event or with the fortunes of a group, large or small—a squad, a ship's company, a village, a labor union on strike— have owed a debt to Dos Passos for solving some of their problems in advance. So have novels by famous Europeans, as Jean-Paul Sartre explained in *The Atlantic Monthly:*

> . . . it was after reading a book by Dos Passos that I thought for the first time of weaving a novel out of various, simultaneous lives, with characters who pass by without knowing one another and who all contribute to the atmosphere of a historical period.
> . . . Dos Passos, in order to make us feel more keenly the intrusion of group thinking in the most secret thoughts of his characters, invented a social voice, commonplace and sententious, which chatters incessantly round about them, without our ever knowing whether it is a chorus of conformist mediocrity or

a monologue which the characters themselves keep locked in their hearts.

. . . Dos Passos has revealed the falseness of unity of action. He has shown that one might describe a collective event by juxtaposing twenty individual and unrelated stories. These revelations permitted us to conceive and to write novels which are to the classic works of Flaubert and Zola what non-Euclidean geometry is to the old geometry of Euclid.

Sartre is wrong about one matter: the characters in *U. S. A.* do not "pass by without knowing one another." Each of the twelve principal characters meets at least two of the others and, as the trilogy draws to its close, most of the survivors assemble at a cocktail party that marks the catastrophic end of the New Era. Dos Passos was more of an architect in fiction than Sartre realized, but still that article in *The Atlantic* suggests the effect on other writers of his technical discoveries. There is, however, another paradox, this time involving the material or message of *U. S. A.* and its reception when the trilogy first appeared in separate volumes. *The 42nd Parallel* in 1930 and *Nineteen Nineteen* two years later were both regarded as "revolutionary novels," a phrase that carried weight at the time; they were praised by radicals, if with reservations, and violently damned by conservatives. Dos Passos in 1932 had joined with fifty-one other intellectuals in signing a manifesto supporting the Communist candidate for President, William Z. Foster, and the Communists welcomed him as one of their own; "Comrade," they called him, using their title of honor. They did more than welcome him, for in those days the Communists were looking for a famous writer who might strengthen their position in the cultural world by serving as the American Maxim Gorky. That was almost a political post, and they offered it in succession to a number of writers, including Edmund Wilson and Theodore Dreiser, both of whom declined the nomination. Now at last Dos Passos appeared to be the man they were seeking, and he was celebrated in one left-wing book (*The Great Tradition*, 1933, by Granville Hicks) as the towering novelist who had avoided the blindness and the compromises of James, Howells, and Mark Twain. Meanwhile Dos Passos himself was becoming less and less revolutionary. He had dropped out of Communist-front organizations after a protest meeting in Madison

Square Garden at which the Communists disgracefully howled down the Socialists. In the last volume of his trilogy, *The Big Money* (1936), the radicals turn out to be almost as devious as the conservatives and all the characters come to unhappy ends, no matter what their political opinions.

A year later Dos Passos underwent a traumatic experience. In the early spring of 1937 he went to Spain with Hemingway, still his close friend; they planned to work together on a film, *The Spanish Earth*, that would tell the story of the Spanish Civil War. When they reached Valencia, Dos Passos heard that another friend of long standing, José Robles Pazos, an official in the Loyalist Ministry of War, had been arrested under suspicion of treason. In Madrid Dos Passos went from one ministry to another trying to establish his friend's innocence; then suddenly he learned that Robles had already been shot—at whose instigation it has never been learned. Government figures blamed the Anarchists, but Dos Passos became convinced, perhaps rightly, that the Russians in Spain had ordered the execution because Robles knew too much and might be undependable politically. It was a shock to the novelist's former beliefs and one from which he never recovered. From that moment he was willing to impute all evil to the Communists and, by extension, to anyone he suspected of furthering their designs.

Hemingway stayed in Spain for some months to work on *The Spanish Earth* and to send home dispatches that reflected an intimate knowledge of what the Loyalist commanders were saying. Soon he was to write a melodrama, *The Fifth Column*, in which the American hero is a secret agent apparently under Communist discipline. Dos Passos hurried back to the States and published an article, "Farewell to Europe!" in which he said that America offered the last hope for individual freedom and thanked God that the Atlantic was a good wide ocean. The two novelists were never again close friends.

2   I was tempted to end this chapter with Dos Passos' return from Spain at the age of forty-one. The rest of the story is interesting politically and biographically rather than from the standpoint of a

literary historian. Dos Passos lived until 1970 and continued to work with the ideal in mind of becoming a contemporary Gibbon. He published more books than in his early years—historical essays and reports on the war and the nation as well as novels—but nothing he wrote after *U. S. A.* had the same widespread and lasting effect. The most ambitious of his later works is *District of Columbia,* a political trilogy in which the first novel *(Adventures of a Young Man,* 1939) is devoted to American communism, the second *(Number One,* 1943) to Huey Long's brand of fascism, and the third *(The Grand Design,* 1949) to the New Deal in wartime. The most appealing of the works, though badly organized, is *Chosen Country* (1951), which is partly a fictionalized life of the author and partly a tribute to his first wife, Katherine Smith, who had died in a motor accident four years before the book appeared. The nearest to being a popular success was *Midcentury* (1961), a long novel mostly concerned with the misdeeds of labor leaders. All these are solid works after their fashion, but they lack the inventiveness and daring of his earlier fiction, and most of all they lack a young man's eagerness to see with his own eyes "country and landscape and plants and animals and people: men, women and children in city, town and hamlet." The learned Poggius now saw what he expected and intended to see. While remembering a brighter past, he looked down as from the Capitoline Hill at a various prospect of desolation.

His Capitoline was now on the political right, toward which Dos Passos had moved not faster but farther than others who once shared his radical opinions. Twenty years after signing a manifesto for Willam Z. Foster, he signed another for Senator Taft, then the most conservative of the Republican presidential candidates. Instead of reporting strikes and trials for *The New Masses,* he joined the staff of William Buckley's stoutly conservative weekly, *The National Review.* His name appeared on the same letterheads as those of prominent cold-warriors and drop-the-big-bombers. The change, however dramatic, was in some ways less fundamental than it appeared to be. Dos Passos from the beginning had been an individualist who distrusted bureaucracies of every sort. The bigger they were, the more he distrusted them, whether they represented big capital, as in his early novels, or big labor and the welfare state. "Organization is death," he had once repeated to himself in French, Latin, Greek, and Italian; that was in 1918, when he was washing barracks windows as a private in the American Army (which had finally accepted him as a volunteer). Organized communism was death, he later came to believe, and still later the New Deal was death because he thought that its "grand design" was to remake America into a communized state.

In other ways, however, the change in opinions revealed a deeper change in values. Some of the recognizable figures that had been derided in his early novels, for instance the head of the Norton-Harjes Ambulance Corps, reappear in *Chosen Country* as heroes of conscience, while some of his formerly admired friends, Hemingway in particular, are presented there as grotesques. Jack Lawson becomes the villain of another late novel, one that Dos Passos might have thought twice before publishing: *Most Likely to Succeed* (1954). Speaking more broadly, one might say that the novelist, after rebelling against his father, was making himself over in the father's image—with the proviso that the corporation lawyer was less conservative politically toward the end of his life than the novelist later became. Dos Passos looked back more and more toward the America in which his father had risen high. Happily married for a second time, he settled down in the Northern Neck of Virginia, on part of his father's big farm.

He continued to peer about him, said Granville Hicks, "with the grim, puzzled honesty that has been his distinctive virtue, almost his trademark." Nobody thought that Dos Passos was trying to profit by his new beliefs. On the contrary, they involved a financial sacrifice, since they deprived him of his former audience and plunged him into a period of partial neglect. They seemed extreme to the editors of *Life,* not a radical magazine, who stopped printing his reports on the state of the world. The contemporary historian was losing touch with contemporary feelings. In all those years Dos Passos made few compromises, and one admired him for that, but also one felt that his integrity was displayed more in his personal life and opinions than it was in the structure and style of his fiction. Some of his later work appeared to be written with more haste than his early novels, with less rigor and with fewer demands on his imagination.

Simple physiology, a factor that critics neglect, might explain some of the change. A man with hardening arteries can no longer write with a young man's vigor and multifarious curiosity.

But patience and depth may compensate for the loss of those qualities, at least in part, and prolonged attention may take the place of passionate attention. It did not do so for Dos Passos. His loss of literary stature might tempt one into making a false generalization about fiction and politics. Dos Passos was a radical and wrote works of great inventiveness and power; then he became conservative and produced such bald, embittered tracts as *Most Likely to Succeed* and *The Great Days;* so therefore— But that is entirely too simple. The history of fiction seems to show that great novelists can hold almost any sort of position, radical or conservative, aristocratic or egalitarian; they can be monarchists like Balzac or angry reformers like Dickens, or they can shift positions like Dostoevsky without necessarily harming their work—but on one absolute condition, that they should believe in their characters more firmly than they hold to their opinions. Dos Passos in his later work often failed to meet that condition, and there too he broke another rule that seems to have been followed by great novelists. They can regard their characters with love or hate or anything between, but cannot regard them with tired aversion. They can treat events as tragic, comic, farcical, pathetic, or almost anything but consistently repulsive.

Aversion and repulsion are dominant moods in, for example, *The Great Days* (1958). There among the minor characters, the first to appear sets a tone for all the others; she is a waitress in the airport at Miami who "limps around behind the saggy counter with a rag in her hand. Her frizzy hair has grown out since it was bleached so that the dark ends show against her head. Bags under her eyes. Crowsfeet. Saggy granulated skin. Fagged. Up too late last night. Middleaged. Forlorn." Almost everyone else in the story is either young and brutally stupid or else, like the waitress, middle aged, dispirited, and corrupt. The only appealing characters are two of those remembered out of the past.

The Great Days was a low point for Dos Passos. In other books he published during the later years there are admirable passages, though it must be added that almost all of them are retrospective. In *The Best Times* (1966), to use his memoirs as an example, there is a long, candid, affectionate portrait of his father, one that explains much about the author. There are two or three fine chapters in *Chosen Country,* especially those dealing with the adventures of the autobiographical hero in Europe after the Great War, in Greenwich Village, and during the Sacco-Vanzetti case (here moved for purposes of fiction to Indiana City). The story ends with the hero's first marriage while the case is still in progress, and the book of memoirs, which becomes disjointed toward the end, breaks off at about the same point. It is as if the learned Poggius were saying that the best times were all in the past, or as if, in the various prospect of desolation, he could not bear to contemplate his literary decline and fall.

V CUMMINGS
One Man Alone

"Gertrude Stein who had been much impressed by The Enormous Room said that Cummings did not copy, he was the natural heir of the New England tradition with its aridity and its sterility, but also with its individuality."

—The Autobiography of Alice B. Toklas, p. 208.

1   It was a curious background for a rebel poet. Edward Estlin Cummings was born (1894) and brought up on a quiet street north of the Harvard Yard, one where distinguished professors lived. William James and Josiah Royce were neighbors, and Charles Eliot Norton had a wooded estate nearby that bordered on Somerville and its Irish tenements. Cambridge in the early 1900s . . . good manners, tea parties, Browning, young women with their minds adequately dressed in English tweeds. I think it was T. S. Eliot who said that life there was so intensely cultured it had ceased to be

civilized. The younger poet's family was part of that life. Edward Cummings, the father (Harvard '85), had been an instructor in sociology, but then had become a clergyman, preaching in Boston as the assistant, the colleague, and finally the successor of Edward Everett Hale at the South Congregational Society, Unitarian. Sometimes on Sundays little Estlin, as the family called him, passed the plate. The father, famous for rectitude, was also president of the Massachusetts Civic League and was later executive head of the World Peace Foundation.

The son attended a public high school, Cambridge Latin, where he tells us that the admired principal was a Negro.[1] Sending Estlin there was apparently one of his father's democratic ideas, and another—when the son went on to Harvard, class of '15—was to have him live at home for the first three years. That encouraged his bookish habits and also cut him off from college life, including the club system with its societies, waiting clubs, and final clubs—always something ahead to make students act with propriety for fear of being blackballed. Cummings joined nothing but the Musical Society and the board of a literary magazine that had published some of his early poems. There were two such magazines at Harvard in those days, *The Monthly* and *The Advocate,* and they looked down on each other—or, to be accurate, they nodded to each other coldly from the facing doors of their respective sanctums on the dusty third floor of the Harvard Union. The Monthlies thought that the board of *The Advocate,* which then appeared fortnightly, was composed of journalists, clubmen, athletes, and disciples of Teddy Roosevelt, a former editor, with not a man of letters among them. The Advocates suspected that the Monthlies were aesthetes (as indeed most of them came to be called), scruffy poets, socialists, pacifists, or worse. It was for *The Monthly* that Cummings chose to write.

In his last undergraduate year he took a room at college and became a gossiped-about figure in the group that surrounded *The Monthly.* It was the only time in his life that he formed part of a group, but even then he stood apart from most of the others and preferred to keep his relations one to one. He was intensely shy and private in the Cambridge fashion. Still, among the ones he saw

---

1. Cummings' biographer, Charles Norman, says that the black principal, a woman, was at a grade school the boy attended.

often were Dos Passos, Robert Hillyer the conservative poet (though with some distrust on both sides), S. Foster Damon ("who opened my eyes and ears," Cummings was to write, ". . . to all ultra, at that moment, modern music and poetry and painting"), and two very rich young men, James Sibley Watson and Scofield Thayer, who greatly admired his poems and drawings. Cummings decided to stay at Harvard for a year of postgraduate work. At commencement he was awarded a degree *magna cum laude,* with honors in Literature, Greek and English. He was also chosen to give the Disquisition and shocked his classmates and their parents—those who listened—by speaking on "The New Art," with examples from Amy Lowell and Gertrude Stein.

At the time he was in full revolt against almost everything—except personal integrity—that Cambridge and his father stood for. Cleanliness, godliness, decorum, public spirit, then chastity went by the board. Cummings developed a taste for low life, something that teemed in Boston. One night the Boston police were embarrassed to find his father's car, with its clergyman's license plates, parked outside a joint near Scollay Square. Cummings and Dos Passos, both virgins at the time, were not "upstairs"; they were drinking in the parlor while holding a polite conversation with the madam.

> *When you rang at Dick Mid's Place*
> *the madam was a bulb stuck in the door.*

In the autumn after his postgraduate year, Cummings went to New York, where he spent three months at the only office job he was ever to hold. The experiment having failed by reason of pure boredom, he went to work seriously on his drawing and painting (the drawing was often inspired; the paintings were impressionistic and weak in color). He took no part in the debate over preparedness for war, one which shook the country in the winter of 1916–17 and which, as a minor effect, disrupted the board of *The Harvard Monthly.* Four of the editors were pacifists, the other four were superpatriots, all eight were impractical, and they couldn't agree on what to print. In April 1917, when Congress declared war, *The Monthly* disappeared from Harvard, but not from memory. An editorial that carefully didn't mention the war explained that publication was being suspended because of "existing circumstances."

Cummings in 1938, the year of his first *Collected Poems*.

93 CUMMINGS: ONE MAN ALONE

Cummings by that time was on his way to France as a volunteer in the Norton-Harjes Ambulance Corps.

On the old *Touraine* of the French Line, a tub that wallowed its way through the submarine zone, he met William Slater Brown, another New Englander. Brown, lately a student at Columbia, was a pacifist proud of knowing the anarchist Emma Goldman. Cummings was mildly patriotic, but he didn't allow opinions, at the time, to interfere with his friendships. Through a mistake at headquarters, the two young men were not immediately assigned to an ambulance unit and had a month to spend in Paris. They roamed the streets in all the glow of youth, went to the Russian Ballet, and learned to speak passable French, apparently with the help of Paris ladies ("little ladies more / than dead exactly dance / in my head"). Finally they went to the front in Section 21, whose commanding officer, Lieutenant Anderson, distrusted them because they wore dirty coveralls and were too friendly with the French mechanics. An artillery company quartered in their village had mutinied that spring, and Brown talked about war weariness in letters to friends (as well as in one to Emma Goldman). A French censor reported his remarks to Lieutenant Anderson, who said that Brown was a dangerous character and that Cummings should be arrested too. Cummings might have been cleared—of what charge? there was none—but a sense of personal honor kept him from assuring the military examiners that he detested all Germans. Together the friends were shipped off to La Ferté, to a detention barracks that Cummings was later to celebrate as "the Enormous Room."

The three months he spent there were another watershed, after the rebellion of his last two years at college. Confined with men of all nations, mostly illiterate, even inarticulate, all used to living outside the law, Cummings found that he liked some of them—especially those he called the Delectable Mountains—vastly more than he liked his college classmates. They gave him a new sense of human values: individuals could be admired for their generosity and courage, but social authority was always and everywhere stupid. By example they encouraged him to exalt feeling over knowledge, and they also gave him a new aesthetic. He was soon to say, on page 249 of *The Enormous Room*, "that there is and can be no such thing as authentic art until the *bons trucs* (whereby we are taught to see and imitate on canvas and in stone and by words this so-called world) are entirely and thoroughly and perfectly annihilated by that vast and painful process of Unthinking which may result in a minute bit of purely personal feeling. Which minute bit is Art."

The honors student in Literature, Greek and English was busy unthinking his five years at Harvard and was getting ready to write poems that would each, he hoped, embody a moment of intensely alive and personal feeling. Meanwhile Dr. Edward Cummings, having learned of his son's disappearance, made vigorous efforts first to find where he was, a difficult task in itself, and then to obtain his release. As pastor of the South Church, he was not without friends in Washington. When the French received official inquiries, they gave the son another farcical hearing and finally set him free. Brown, with his letters as evidence, was condemned to the military prison at Précigny, from which nobody had come out living since the first days of the war. There he fell victim to scurvy, but Dr. Cummings was busy with his problem, too, and he was released before the disease had crippled him.

After the Armistice, Brown and Cummings rented a Greenwich Village apartment that became a model of squalor. Cummings liked to roam through the Lower East Side and the Syrian quarter near the southern tip of Manhattan. He was painting "all the time," Brown says, but was also writing scores, even hundreds of poems in many new manners. Meanwhile the death of *The Harvard Monthly* had an unexpected sequel. Scofield Thayer and Sibley Watson had bought a moribund political fortnightly, *The Dial,* which they set about transforming into the most distiguished magazine of the arts that had appeared in this country. In some ways and in some contributors it carried on the tradition of *The Monthly,* this time with a national audience. The first issue, for January 1920, featured the poems and drawings of E. E. Cummings. I remember how they provoked indignant remarks from more conservative poets and, in particular, how Bobby Hillyer fumed.

In the autumn of that year Cummings wrote *The Enormous Room* at his father's house near Silver Lake, New Hampshire. He wrote it at the father's suggestion and partly to keep Dr. Cummings from suing the French government for a million dollars; also he wrote it very fast, in a style close to the spoken idiom he had fashioned for himself over the years. Dr. Cummings had the manuscript copied by his secretary, then went over it with a blue pencil, crossing out the bad words and making other minor changes (for example, a character whom the son called Jesus Christ was renamed Judas). It was hard to find a publisher, but the new firm of Boni and Liveright was more venturesome than others, and Dr. Cummings persuaded them to accept the book. When it appeared in 1922, it was read with enthusiasm by younger writers, and the free-ranging, partly colloquial, partly involved style had a lasting effect on American prose. *The Enormous Room* was not a commercial success. Horace Liveright, who thought he had been fooled, came to dislike the book so much that he wouldn't allow the unsold copies of the first edition to be remaindered; he sold them for wastepaper.[2]

2 ✍ In the years from 1923 to 1926 Cummings published four books of poetry: *Tulips and Chimneys, &* (he wore his titles cut short), *XLI Poems,* and *Is 5.* Many or most of the poems in all four were written either at college or during the burst of activity and experiment that followed his release from the detention barracks at La Ferté, but the first and the last book stand somewhat apart from the other two. In *Tulips and Chimneys* there are some of his recent experiments, but there are also earlier long pieces full of oriental or medieval color, and these seem utterly traditional in their effort to be exotic. Only one of them has life in it, "All in green went my love riding," a lyrical ballad that is a gifted exercise in Preraphaelitism. The fourth book, *Is 5,* contains many satirical pieces written in what seems to have been a new manner for Cummings. "Poem, or Beauty Hurts Mr. Vinal," "she being Brand-new," "workingman with hand so hairy-sturdy," "my sweet old etcetera": these and others deal mostly with contemporary subjects, using catch phrases and advertising slogans that are strictly of the time (as note "pretty littleliverpill-hearted-Nujolneeding-There's-A-Reason americans" in the diatribe against Harold Vinal, a harmless lyric poet from Maine); yet their wit and their headlong rhythms give them an inner life that makes

---

2. Later he must have regretted the gesture, when he found that there was a revived demand for the book. *The Enormous Room* was reprinted three or four times during the 1920s.

them nearly indestructible. Among all the books of poetry that Cummings published, *Is 5* is still the liveliest.

None of the first four books was a popular success. The audience for poetry was even smaller at the time than in earlier and later periods, and most of it shared Mr. Vinal's tastes for conventional beauty. With Cummings the critics were severe: they condemned his fleshly realism, his experiments with typography, and his custom of using a small "i" for the first-personal pronoun. "e. e. cummings" they called him, with a visible curl of the lip. But the more his work was condemned by critics, the more it was admired by many of the younger writers and the more he was adopted as one of their spokesmen, along with Dos Passos and Hemingway. Fitzgerald had been the first spokesman, but rebels lost faith in him when he appeared too often in *The Saturday Evening Post*. Cummings too was making a keep-alive compromise, by writing prose pieces for *Vanity Fair,* but most of these were signed with a pseudonym. As for his private life, he kept it private, and that added to his prestige.

He wasn't often seen at parties in the middle 1920s, though hostesses tried to capture him and though he had overcome his shyness to the point of liking to have an audience. "I've watched him operating among strangers," another poet said rather envyingly. "He starts talking to one person in a low confidential voice and the person starts laughing. Then another person drifts up, glass in hand, and bends forward to hear what is being said. Cummings talks lower, faster, and funnier, without cracking a smile, and a third person appears. Pretty soon the whole room is grouped around Cummings, everybody laughing, everybody with eyes on him so as not to miss a word." "Jesus, he was a handsome man," as he had written of Buffalo Bill. He had large, well-shaped features, carved rather than molded, eyes set wide apart, often with a glint of mischief in them, and in those days a good deal of fine khaki-colored hair. "Doesn't he look like a faun!" I heard a young woman say. "Or like a bad boy," another said, also admiringly. In later years, when he had lost most of the hair and the rest was clipped off, he looked more like a bare-skulled Buddhist monk.

He was the most brilliant monologuist I have known. What he poured forth was a mixture of cynical remarks, puns, hyperboles, outrageous metaphors, inconsequence, and tough-guy talk spoken from the corner of his wide, expressive mouth: pure Cummings, as if he were rehearsing something that would afterward appear in print. Sometimes it did: "His Royal Highness said 'peek-a-boo' and thirty tame fleas left the prettily embroidered howdah. . . . Thumbprints of an angel named Frederick found on a lightning-rod, Boston, Mass." Perhaps the style of those harangues is better suggested by his *i: six nonlectures* as these were delivered at Harvard in the early 1950s. The second nonlecture, for instance, starts by praising the world in which he grew to manhood: "a reckless world, filled with the curiosity of life herself; a vivid and violent world welcoming every challenge; a world worth hating and adoring and fighting and forgiving: in brief, a world which was a world." Then, after ridiculing the later ideal of "quote security unquote," he tells a story that has to be repeated in his own words.

Back in the days of dog-eat-dog [he says] . . . there lived a playboy; whose father could easily have owned the original superskyscraper-de-luxe; a self-styled Cathedral of Commerce, endowed with every impetus to relaxation; not excluding ultraelevators which (on the laudable assumption that even machinery occasionally makes mistakes) were regularly tested. Testing an ultraelevator means that its car was brought clean up, deprived of safety devices, and dropped. As the car hurtled downward, a column of air confined by the elevator shaft became more and more compressed; until (assuming that nothing untoward happened) it broke the car's fall completely—or so I was told by somebody who should know. At any rate, young Mr. X was in the habit not only of attending these salubrious ceremonies, but of entering each about-to-be-dropped car, and of dropping with it as far as the laws of a preEinsteinian universe permitted. Eventually, of course, somebody who shouldn't know telephoned a newspaper; which sent a reporter; who (after scarcely believing his senses) asked the transcender of Adam point-blank why he fell so often. Our playful protagonist shrugged his well-tailored shoulders—"for fun" he said simply; adding (in a strictly confidential undertone) "and it's wonderful for a hangover."

Here, I feel, we have the male American stance of my adolescence; or (if you prefer) the adolescent American male stance

of what some wit once nicknamed a "lost generation"; whereof
—let me hastily append—the present speaker considers himself no worthy specimen. My point, however, isn't that many
of us were even slightly heroic; and is that few of us declined
a gamble. I don't think we enjoyed courting disaster. I do feel
we liked being born.

In Cummings' published work, that passage is one of the
very few in which he used the pronoun "we" as referring to any
group larger than the one composed of the poet and his love. Usually
other groups were "they," alien and hostile. But "we," meaning his
generation, were reckless persons who liked to accept a challenge,
and "we" sometimes gambled with death simply "for fun" and to
reaffirm our joy in being alive. That is surely a theme or feeling that
pervaded the 1920s; an adolescent feeling, if you will—Cummings
makes that concession to critics—but one to which he looked back in
the 1950s with a continuing sense of we-ness.

The 1920s had other favorite themes and one is amazed, in
rereading his early work, to find out how often Cummings expressed
them. Of course he was a lyric poet in the bad-boy tradition, broadly
speaking, of Catullus and Villon and Verlaine. Of course he kept
returning to the standard lyrical subjects of love, death, April, and
the special quality of a moment. But traditional as he was on one
side of his work, and determinedly unique on another, he was also
a man of his generation. Much oftener than one might expect, he
said what other young writers were saying at the time, or would soon
be saying, and he usually said it with more ingenuity and morning
freshness.

I won't revert to themes directly connected with his adventures in wartime: the feeling that death was omnipresent and life all
the more to be enjoyed; the other feeling, for American ambulance
drivers, that they were spectators of the greatest show on earth; and
the notion that everyone in authority was stupid and that only
common soldiers deserved sympathy. All this one finds in his early
poems, together with other war-connected themes. More than other
postwar writers, Cummings made fun of the big words, especially
when spoken by politicians. Better and more amusingly than others
he expressed his mistrust of almost everyone over thirty: "o the sweet
& aged people who rule this world(and me and you if we're not very

careful) . . . OH the bothering dear unnecessary hairless old." But Cummings also wrote poems on other themes that were popular with a whole generation of rebel writers, and here I might give a few examples.

There is first of all the revolt against Victorian standards, especially those prescribing chaste language and chaste behavior. Cummings made himself a leader in the revolt by describing, explicitly and often, the act of sex. Thus, in his second book of poems, &, there are nine rather labored sonnets recording visits to various prostitutes, including "Cecile . . . Alice . . . Loretta, cut the comedy, kid . . . Fran Mag Glad Dorothy."

There is the expatriate theme of praise for "superb and subtle" Paris, with its churches at twilight, its cafés, its streets that "turn young with rain," and its little ladies.

There is the tourist without Baedeker wandering beside his mistress among Roman ruins. "Ponder, darling, these busted statues," he tells her; but then he exhorts her to turn aside from the unimportant past and "instigate constructive horizontal business."

There is the spectator's report on New York as another such Greatest Show as the war had been. Dos Passos embodied the report in a long novel, *Manhattan Transfer,* but Cummings was more succinct:

> *by god i want above fourteenth*
>
> *fifth's deep purring biceps, the mystic screech*
> *of Broadway, the trivial stink of rich*
>
> *frail firm asinine life*

There is the supercilious delight in advertising slogans and the habit of using them in poems. Cummings used them only for satire—"what's become of Maeterlinck / now that April's here / (ask the man who owns one / ask Dad, He knows)"—but later Hart Crane and others began to exploit them seriously.

There is the contempt for citizens who lead ordinary lives, "impersons" who accept the slogans at face value.

There is the utter scorn for conventional poets still feeding on the past:

if we are to believe these gently O sweetly
melancholy trillers amid the thrillers
these crepuscular violinists among my and your
skyscrapers—Helen & Cleopatra were Just Too Lovely,
The Snail's On The Thorn enter Morn and God's
In His andsoforth.

There is the respect for rebels of all sorts, even for Communists in those early days. Thus, in his report of a Paris demonstration broken up by the police, Cummings says that "the communists have fine Eyes . . . none look alike," whereas the police, "tidiyum, are very tidiyum reassuringly similar."

There is compassion for outcasts, not excluding the drunk lying in his pool of vomit as people carefully step around him, and there is the feeling that poets are outcasts too, for all their pride. "why are these pipples taking their hets off?" Cummings asks in an idiom borrowed from Krazy Kat of his favorite comic strip. He answers:

the king & queen
alighting from their limousine
inhabit the Hôtel Meurice(whereas
i live in a garret and eat aspirine)

There is finally the deep strain of anti-intellectualism that I have already mentioned. Among its manifestations is a prejudice against scientists and "pruient philosophers" who poke and prod the earth, combined with praise for a child's direct vision that sees the earth as "mud-luscious" and "puddle-wonderful."

There is, in fact, almost every theme that was to be widely treated by new writers in the 1920s, except for Hemingway's theme of giving and accepting death, and Fitzgerald's theme of the betrayed suitor for the very soul of money. Cummings spoke of money not often and then with the disdain of a barefoot friar. Besides the themes he treated, his poems embody various attitudes that lay behind them: the passion for reckless experiment in life and art, the feeling that a writer's duty was to be unique, and the simple determination to enjoy each moment and make the most of having been born. In spite of his aloofness, it is no wonder at all that the rebel writers had come to regard him as an indispensable spokesman for their cause.

The question in the middle 1920s was what Cummings would do next.

3 ᨺ His next work, to their surprise, was for the theater and it was not so much a play as a brilliant vaudeville. *Him* (1927) was abused by the drama critics, but it was deliriously enjoyed by the younger people in the audience. Once again Cummings had spoken for them, and *Him* is in fact so much "of the twenties"—in the attitudes it reveals toward women, politics, Negroes (here admired for their sexual freedom), and the life of art—that it has seldom or never been revived. During the original production by the Province-town Players, the very small auditorium was crowded every night, but the production was expensive, the Players were losing money they didn't have, and the piece had to be withdrawn after a few weeks. Cummings went back to painting and writing verse.

A new book of poems, *VV* (which he also called *"ViVa"*), appeared in 1931 and was a mild disappointment to his readers. Mostly the book deals with the same themes as his earlier work, but it is less exuberant than *Is 5*—much less of a hurrah than the title promises—and it speaks less directly for the poet's generation. There is a growing bitterness in the satires directed against politicians, generals, and run-of-the-mine people. The bitterest of all has proved to be the most enduring: it is the ballad of blond Olaf, the con-scientious objector who is prodded with bayonets, then beaten to death while repeating "I will not kiss your f.ing flag." As a general thing, however, the development revealed in the book is a matter much less of tone than of technique.

Although Cummings' technique is a confusing subject, one argued back and forth since his poems first appeared in *The Dial,* much of it depends on the elaboration of a few devices that are fairly simple in themselves. Too much of it so depends, a reader may end by feeling. The two principal devices employed in *VV* had ap-peared at times in his earlier work, but here he carries them both to extremes. One is the calligram—or picture writing, to use a more general term—and the other is the word scramble, which might also be called the cryptogram. Cummings' use of the two devices has been discussed more than once, and I do not propose to resume the discussion here. It is enough to say that when he combines calligram with cryptogram, as he sometimes does in *VV*, the result in three or four cases is something beyond my ability to decipher. Even worse, a deciphered statement may be one that Cummings has made elsewhere, in plainer words, and thus it leaves a reader with the impression that his time and the poet's have both been wasted. *VV* is the most ingenious of Cummings' books, but—aside from the ballad of blond Olaf, a tribute to the poet's mother, and a few other moving poems—it is by far the least successful.

On the technical side, however, *VV* gives more than a hint of two additional devices that the poet was to cultivate more intensively in his later books. One of these is his use of negative terms—especially those formed by the prefixes "un-," "im-," and "not-" and the suffix "-less"—to imply special shades of meaning. In Poem XLII, for instance, he speaks of an "upward deep most invincible unthing," which I should take to be a spiritual essence. Poem LXVII tells of watching "unhands describe what mimicry," and here I don't know exactly what he means, although "unhands" would be a sinister word in Cummings' idiom. In later books one finds a host of such expressions: "an undream of anaesthetized impersons," "a notalive undead too-nearishness," "unfools unfree / undeaths who live," "till unwish returns on its unself," and the adjective "whereless," one that might pass into general usage. The poet says of politicians who want to save the world, "scream, all ye screamers, till your if is up / and vanish under prodigies of un." If such prodigies do not unexist, it is because Cummings has performed them.

The other device is the game he was beginning to play with parts of speech. It is a game with elastic rules or none at all: roughly, any part of speech can be transformed into any other. Verbs, adjectives, pronouns, even some adverbs and conjunctions, are used instead of nouns. Nouns become verbs ("but if a look should *april* me"), or they become adverbs by adding "-ly," or adjectives in the superlative by adding "-est" (thus, instead of writing "most like a girl," Cummings has "girlest"). Adjectives, adverbs, and conjunctions, too, become participles by adding "-ing" ("onlying," "softlying,"

"whying"); participles become adverbs by adding "-ly" ("kneelingly").
Some of those practices are foreshadowed in *VV*, where one finds,
for instance, "footprints on the sands of was"—of time, obviously,
though "was" in later books becomes "the past." Also in *VV* one finds
"the smallening World" and "laughtering blocks"—the latter a hide-
ous phrase—as well as "togethering" and "foreverfully," both more
effective. In the later books—which include *50 Poems* (1940), *1 x 1*
(1944), *XAIPE* ("Rejoice!" 1950), and *95 Poems* (1958)—such
coined words and transposed parts of speech come close to being a
new language. An example in *50 Poems* is Poem 29, of which the
first stanza reads:

> *anyone lived in a pretty how town*
> *(with an up so floating many bells down)*
> *spring summer autumn winter*
> *he sang his didn't he danced his did.*

A translation—omitting the second line, which means whatever it means—might be, "The poet lived year by year in an ordinary
town, where he sang his negations and danced his affirmations."
Need one say that Cummings' new language has a marvelous way
of lending strangeness to sometimes rather commonplace statements? It also serves as a means of avoiding various words that he
detested. Later in the same poem, when he says that "noone loved
him more by more," it is obvious that "noone" is the poet's wife.
After his second divorce, Cummings was happily married for nearly
thirty years, a fact attested by some of his finest poems, but the
word "wife" appears in none of them.

Any words involved in his game with parts of speech acquired a plus or a minus value. Thus, "was" as a noun is minus;
"is" and "am" and "become" are plus. "Who" is plus, but "which" is
minus, especially when it refers to impersons, and so is the adjective
"whichful." "It," another neuter, seems to be the negative of "he" or
"him" and leads to "itmaking," a term of utter condemnation.
"Where" and "when" are both minus as nouns; "wherelings" and
"whenlings" are pitiable people, "sons of unless and children of
almost"—one might say the Jukes and Kallikaks of Cummings' world.
The honorifics are "here" and "now." "beautiful most is now," he
says, and elsewhere, in a fine tribute to his father,

> *this motionless forgetful where*
> *turned at his glance to shining here.*

All such words have become abstractions, and the meanings they imply are ethical and metaphysical. Usually ethics and ontology are fatal subjects for modern poets, but Cummings was feeling impelled to venture into them. The anti-intellectual was about to become, in limited ways, an ideologist. There had been changes in his life and they had led to a number of ideas that were partly new for him and were completely opposed at the time to those held by "mostpeople," as he called the American public. When one looks back at his career, it would seem that he had to invent his new language as the only fresh and serviceable means of expressing the ideas in poetry.

4 ⟨ Changes in his life. . . . His father had been killed in a motor accident (at a grade crossing in a blinding snowstorm), his second marriage had broken up, and in 1931 he had made a trip to Russia. This last was a shattering experience, much on the order of Dos Passos' visit to Loyalist Spain in 1937. Cummings wrote a prose book about the trip (*Eimi*, 1934), which is hard to read because of its pointillist style, but in which the conclusions are forthright. Russia, he reported, was a country racked by fear and suspicion. Living under the shadow of Stalin, Communists were the bigoted defenders of a system that destroys individuals. Soon the same conclusions were being stated in his poems:

> *every kumrad is a bit*
> *of quite unmitigated hate*
> *(travelling in a futile groove*
> *god knows why)*
> *and so do i*
> *(because they are afraid to love*

Cummings was not afraid to love, but he hated, too, and his hatred (or call it his feeling of revulsion) circled out from Stalin and his "kumrads" to wider and wider social groups. First to be encompassed were politicians who abetted communism by making appeals to the same public yearning for a better life. Cummings had always detested politicians, but now he raged against them:

> a politician is an arse upon
> which everyone has sat except a man

Reformers and crusaders, especially those who supported the New Deal, came next into the circle of aversion:

> then up rose pride and up rose pelf
> and ghibelline and guelph
> and ladios and laddios
> (on radios and raddios)
> did save man from himself

Growing still wider, the circle was drawn about salesmen of every type: "a salesman is an it that stinks . . . whether it's in lonjewray or shrouds"—a salesman in shrouds being anyone in favor of entering World War II on Stalin's side. Labor unions were still another abomination:

> when serpents bargain for the right to squirm
> and the sun strikes to gain a living wage—
> when thorns regard their roses with alarm
> and rainbows are insured against old age

—then, Cummings says, "we'll believe in that incredible unanimal mankind." At this point the circle of those rejected has become so wide that it includes almost everyone living except "you and me," that is, the poet, his love, and perhaps a handful of friends.

Not since the trip to Russia had Cummings been a spokesman for his literary generation. Most of its other members—with almost all the younger writers—had been moving in an opposite direction from his. During the 1930s a dream that haunted many was that of joining forces with all the dispossessed and of moving forward shoulder to shoulder into a brighter future. Even Hemingway shared the dream for a time. *To Have and Have Not*, published during the Spanish Civil War, has a hero who lives by his own law, but his dying words are "No matter how a man alone ain't got no bloody fucking chance." "It had taken him a long time to get it out," Hemingway adds in his own voice, "and it had taken him all his life to learn it." Steinbeck, a younger man, was more affirmative in *The Grapes of Wrath* (1939): he tells how the mistreated Okies in California acquired a sense of collective purpose, until each of them— as Preacher Casy prophesies before his death—was on the point of becoming only a little piece of "one big soul." Cummings had no patience with this religion of humanity, or with humanity itself. He was to write during World War II:

> *pity this busy monster,manunkind,*
> *not. . . .*
>
> > *listen:there's a hell*
> *of a good universe next door;let's go*

Long before that other war, his statements of opinion had begun to seem inopportune and embarrassing. *Eimi,* for instance, appeared at a moment when much of the book-reading public was entranced by the Russian Five Year Plan, and it proved to be a commercial disaster. Its publisher rejected Cummings' next book of poems. After extensive travels in manuscript, and with a change in title, this was finally printed at his own expense as *No Thanks* (1935). It was dedicated, with no thanks, to fourteen publishers: Farrar and Rinehart, Simon and Schuster, Coward-McCann, Limited Editions, Harcourt Brace, Random House, Equinox Press, Smith and Haas, Viking, Knopf, Dutton, Harpers, Scribners, and Covici Friede. Cummings' first *Collected Poems* (1938) had less trouble in finding a home, and the books that followed had none at all, but I can't remember that they were widely discussed. In the left-wing press, hardly anyone excoriated Cummings or pleaded with him sorrowfully, as some did with Dos Passos; the books were mostly passed over in silence, as if they were social blunders. Perhaps it was the feeling of simply not being heard that made the poet's voice too shrill in some of the later diatribes.

Most of the poems, however, didn't suffer in themselves from his changed opinions, as the later novels of Dos Passos undoubtedly suffered. Dos Passos had different problems, having cast himself in the role of contemporary Gibbon. One of his self-imposed tasks was to report events in such a way as to reveal underlying forces. If he had been wrong about those forces during his early career, mightn't he be equally wrong after his loss of faith in the workers' revolution? That question must have nagged at him—though he didn't mention it to others—and it would help to explain the discouraged tone of his later fiction. Cummings took no interest in historical forces. He was essentially a lyric poet, and in the best of his later work he continued to deal with the traditional lyric themes of love and death, of springtime and the ineffable quality of moments. There was less exuberance than in the early poems, less inventiveness in spite of the game he played with parts of speech, but there was at times more depth, combined with the effort I mentioned to express a coherent attitude, almost a metaphysic.

This last was something that Dr. Edward Cummings would have understood, and indeed it represented, in some measure, a return to the father. Such returns can be traced in the lives of many writers: Dos Passos is one of them, but there are scores of examples from which to choose. How often rebellion against the father—perhaps under the sign of the mother—is revealed in early works, and how often the father's image looms behind the later career! A younger poet, Wendell Berry, has written about such a change in his own life. Of his father he says:

> Now he speaks in me
> as when I knew him first,
> as his father spoke
> in him . . .
>   and I have grown
> to be brother to all
> my fathers, memory
> speaking to knowledge,
> finally, in my bones.[3]

If Cummings too admired his father more and more, it was obviously not for the social doctrine one assumes that the father preached to his congregation at the South Church, Unitarian. It was for personal qualities: love, kindness, utter independence, and faith based on an inner rightness of feeling:

> Scorning the pomp of must and shall
> my father moved through dooms of feel;

---

3. From "The Gathering" (*The Nation*, January 31, 1972, p. 151).

> *his anger was as right as rain*
> *his pity was as green as grain*

The New England tradition to which the poet returned was not that of the Unitarians or of the Calvinists, much less of the Come-outers, but that preached by Emerson in the years after he left the pulpit and before he became an Abolitionist. It was the tradition of the autonomous individual standing before God (or the Oversoul), living by universal laws in harmony with nature, obeying an inner voice, and letting society take care of itself. Emerson . . . there is no record that Cummings ever read his essays, yet his ideas had once pervaded the Cambridge air, and Cummings' later poems are Emersonian in more respects than one.

Thus, Emerson in the flush of his thought was an individualist to such an extent that he could not conceive of history as a process involving social systems and masses of people. "An institution," he wrote, "is the lengthened shadow of one man . . . and all history resolves itself into the biography of a few stout and honest persons." He regarded events of the past as mere decorations of the contemporary mind. "This life of ours," he said, "is stuck round with Egypt, Greece, Gaul, England, War, Colonization, Church, Court and Commerce, as with so many flowers and wild ornaments grave and gay. I will not make more account of them." For Cummings too, history was supremely unimportant:

> *all history's a winter sport or three:*
> *but were it five,i'd still insist that all*
> *history is too small for even me;*
> *for me and you,exceedingly too small.*

Here "me and you" are of course the poet and his love, the only group to which Cummings proclaimed his loyalty. He could do so because "me and you" were really not a group; they were "wonderful one times one." For him almost every group of more than two was either mythical or malevolent, or both. "swoop(shrill collective myth)into thy grave," he exclaimed in that same poem. In other poems we read that the state is an "enormous piece of nonsense" and that its citizens (or "sit-isn'ts") are a huge "collective pseudobeast / (sans either pain or joy)." Emerson wrote, and Cummings would have agreed, that "Society everywhere is in conspiracy against the manhood of every one of its members." As a rule, however, Emerson expressed less hostility to groups than Cummings did; he simply disregarded them in his scheme of things (while acknowledging the existence of "races," as he called the English and the French; of course what he meant was nations). He was interested in the moral character of each nation, but not at all in its politics. I am sure he would have assented when Cummings said:

> a state submicroscopic is—
> compared with pitying terrible
> some alive individual

Cummings also wrote that "there are possibly 2½ or improbably 3 individuals every several fat thousand years," and here the echo seems unmistakable. Emerson had said in "The American Scholar," "Men in history, men in the word of to-day, are bugs, are spawn, and are called 'the mass' and 'the herd.' In a century, in a millennium, one or two men; that is to say, one or two approximations to the right state of every man." I can imagine that Emerson would have nodded happily—as Whitman would have nodded too—when Cummings suggested that any man truly alive contains the universe within himself:

> (his briefest breathing lives some planet's year,
> his longest life's a heartbeat of some sun;
> his least unmotion roams the youngest star)

Emerson was more of a mystic, in the technical sense of the word, than most critics have realized, and some of his essays refer explicitly to an "ecstatical state" in which the soul is reunited with the Oversoul.[4] Such a state is to be understood in a famous passage near the beginning of *Nature*: "Standing on the bare ground—my head bathed in the blithe air and uplifted into infinite space—all mean egoism vanishes. I become a transparent eyeball; I am nothing; I see all; the currents of the Universal Being circulate through me; I am part and parcel of God." Time and space being abolished at such moments, the soul is bathed in a higher Reason to be distin-

---

4. He is most explicit in "The Method of Nature," an address delivered at Colby College in 1841. The address, not often read today, is almost a handbook of "the perennial philosophy."

guished from mere Understanding. The distinction in Cummings' later poems is between "know" or "because," both contemptuous nouns in his language, and "feel," which is something to be honored ("my father moved through dooms of feel"). As for the states of ecstasy, they are possibly foreshadowed in the early poems by Cummings' effort to render the special quality of moments. In later poems that sense of the moment, the now, is so intensified that it comes close to being a mystical vision. "ten centuries of original soon"—that is, of history—are "plunged in eternal now." "dimensionless new alls of joy" flood over the poet as he perceives the "illimitably spiralling candy of tiniest forever." "now the ears of my ears awake," another poem ends, "and now the eyes of my eyes are opened." In passages like these Cummings appears to be writing as the latest—though I suspect not the last—of the New England Transcendentalists.

The parallel can be carried too far. Where Emerson was essentially a Neoplatonist, Cummings was a scoffer in his youth, then more and more a Christian. He does not think of Christ as the most perfect man, in Emerson's way of speaking, but rather prays to him as a divine intercessor. In theological terms his God is less immanent than Emerson's and more transcendent. He says in a poem addressed to God—here I translate into prose—"How should any tasting, touching, hearing, seeing, breathing, merely human being—lifted from the no of all nothing—doubt unimaginable You?" As regards a future life, one of the subjects on which Emerson remained ambiguous, Cummings lets us infer that he believes in the resurrection of the flesh. "our now must come to then," he tells his love in a late sonnet—

> our then shall be some darkness during which
> fingers are without hands;and i have no
> you:and all trees are(any more than each
> leafless)its silent in forevering snow
>
> —but never fear(my own,my beautiful
> my blossoming)for also then's until

Other poems of the time make it clear that "until," for Cummings, was the moment when lovers shall rise from the grave.

5 ⚹ Cummings lived into the late summer of 1962 and continued working to the last day. His career, if not his opinions, had been remarkably self-consistent. Except for his painting, carried on through the years, and except for a few lively incursions into prose—of which *The Enormous Room* is the most durable—he had never worked at any trade except that of writing verse. *"Peintre et poète,"* he had told a French policeman who asked his profession before arresting him; I think that was in 1923. Poet and painter—and nothing else—he remained to the end.

He wrote twelve books of poetry, including one that appeared after his death (73 *poems*, 1963), but not including collected or selected works. The books contain 770 poems in all, an impressive output for a lyric poet and one recalling that of another New Englander, Emily Dickinson. Most of the poems are as short as hers, with perhaps one-fourth of them variations on the traditional fourteen-liner. After the early romantic pieces in *Tulips and Chimneys,* Cummings never ventured again into longer forms. Not all the poems are on the same level, and some of the more ingenious ones remind me that there is a drawer in our house full of kitchen gadgets made of stamped tin and wire, all vastly ingenious—U.S. patent applied for—but many of them unworkable and most of them seldom used. Cummings' inventions, too, are sometimes gimcrack and wasted, but the best of them have enriched the common language. The best of his lyrics, early and late, and not a few of the sonnets—more, it seems to me, on each rereading—have a sweep and music and underlying simplicity that make them hard to forget. And where does he stand among the poets of our time? He suffers from comparison with those who built on a larger scale—Eliot, Aiken, Crane, Auden among others—but still he is unsurpassed in his special field, one of the masters.

One may feel that in his later years, when he was groping his way back toward Emerson, Cummings wrote rather more new poems than he had new things to say. He might have been more severe with his work, and with his acolytes, but he had earned the privilege, after all, of being a little self-indulgent. He did not abuse the privilege. Except for those six nonlectures at Harvard, his only concession to the public, and to the need for earning money, was reading his poems aloud to mostly undergraduate audiences in all parts of the country. It required physical courage, for by that time he was partly crippled by arthritis, wore a brace on his back that jutted out two inches from his shoulderblades, and had to read while sitting in a straight-backed kitchen chair. After reading for half an hour, he had to rest for ten minutes; then he came back to finish the program. Nevertheless he held and charmed the audience, which was usually acquainted with his work and well prepared to listen.

He was speaking in the McCarthy years to what had come to be known as the silent generation. Sometimes he scolded the youngsters, as at Harvard, for being obsessed with security. "What is that?" he asked them. "Something negative, undead, suspicious and suspecting; an avarice and an avoidance; a self-surrendering meanness of withdrawal; a numerable complacency and an innumerable cowardice. . . . How monstrous and how feeble seems some unworld which would rather have its too than eat its cake!" The youngsters, cautious as they were at the time, liked to dream about the romantic freedom of the 1920s. They specially enjoyed his early poems, with their recklessness and brio, but they did not object to the conservative Christian anarchism of the later poems. Once again Cummings, the man stubbornly alone, found himself accepted by others as a spokesman.

VI WILDER
Time Abolished

1 ✍   Let us go back once again to the middle 1920s, which were famous years for American writing. A group of powerful novelists who had started as idol smashers were at last being accepted by the public. They would become idols themselves, but first they were producing their mature and most characteristic work as if in a burst of creative energy. *An American Tragedy, Arrowsmith, Dark Laughter, Barren Ground,* and *The Professor's House* all appeared in 1925. So did *Manhattan Transfer* and *The Great Gatsby,* but these were works by younger men who pictured what seemed to be a different world. Soon the picture would be enlarged by other members of the World War I generation. Hemingway's first book of stories was published in 1925, as I have noted, and his first novel in 1926. That same year Faulkner came forward with *Soldier's Pay,* and Hart Crane with *White Buildings,* a first collection of poems that carried a first introduction, by Allen Tate. It was the year when Cummings published *Is 5,* not a first book of verse, but his wittiest, and when Edmund Wilson wrote a series of critical dialogues,

Discordant Encounters. In 1926 a new galaxy of writers was taking shape, with its novelists, poets, playwrights, and critics.

That was also the year when Thornton Wilder published *The Cabala*. I was lucky enough to be sent an advance copy—a young book for a young reviewer—and it became a personal discovery for me as for many others. From the opening sentence—"The train that first carried me into Rome was late, overcrowded, and cold"—it announced a new writer who was not a novice, who knew how to set a scene and how to make simple words stand cleanly on a page. "It was Virgil's country," he said at the end of the first paragraph, "and there was a wind that seemed to rise from the fields and descend upon us in a long Virgilian sigh." That had the authority of rightness; nobody could improve it by changing words or the order of words, and it also hinted that the story, although set in the present, would have something to do with the past. A circle was closed when the shade of Virgil appeared in the last chapter and spoke to the young traveler on his way back to America. The book had form, and hardly anyone doubted from the first that Wilder would be an important member of the new galaxy.

But did he really belong to it in any sense except that of being the same age as the others and hence of having lived, in some respects, the same sort of life? . . . He was born in 1897, a year after Dos Passos and Fitzgerald, two years before Hemingway and Hart Crane, and like those others he was born in the Middle West. He was the second of five children, two boys and three girls. His father, Amos P. Wilder, was a Down East Yankee and a devout Congregationalist who had taken a doctorate in economics at Yale and then had bought a newspaper in Madison, Wisconsin. As a publisher Dr. Wilder also played a part in Republican politics, and during the Taft administration he was sent to China, where he served as consul general at Hong Kong and Shanghai. He tried to instill a sense of duty into all his children and to pick a career for each of them: for example, Amos, the older son, was designed to be a theologian, and he carried out the father's plan; later he became a professor at Harvard Divinity School.

About Thornton's future there was more doubt. He read wildly, wrote plays for his sisters to act in cheesecloth robes, and used the margins of his schoolbooks for taking literary notes. "Poor Thornton, poor Thornton," his father used to say, "he'll be a burden all his life." It was decided to make him a teacher, on the theory that he would fail in any other profession. Among the schools he attended were Thacher, in Ojai, California; a missionary school at Chefoo, on the China coast; and the Berkeley, California, high school, from which he was graduated after the family returned to the States. He was sent East to Oberlin College for two years because his father thought that Yale was too worldly for an underclassman. In 1918 he enlisted in the Coast Artillery, rising, he said, "by sheer military ability to the rank of corporal." He then went back to Yale, where he wrote for the *Lit* and read his one-act plays to classmates who crowded his room. In 1920–21 he was studying archaeology at the American Academy in Rome. Then his father summoned him home with a cablegram: "HAVE JOB FOR YOU TEACHING NEXT YEAR LAWRENCEVILLE LEARN FRENCH." Wilder knew French already, having always been quick with languages, but he set about learning to teach it.

He was launched in the profession that had been picked out for him, and he enjoyed it—at Lawrenceville, the preparatory school near Princeton where he taught for six years, as later at the University of Chicago and briefly at Harvard. He was a born teacher, and in that respect he shows more resemblance to writers of a later generation than to those of his own. Sometimes he remains a teacher even when he is writing plays and novels. At Lawrenceville, where he was a housemaster as well as an instructor, his only time for literary work was "after the lights of the House were out and the sheaf of absurd French exercises corrected and indignantly marked with red crayon." Then, writing in a bound ledger with a fountain pen, he might set down the first draft of a three-minute play for three actors—he wrote more than forty of these, and the best of them were later collected in a volume called *The Angel That Troubled the Waters* (1928)—or he might work on a more ambitious project growing out of his year in Europe and called in its first state *Notes of a Roman Student*.

He became a novelist as if by request. Friends from the Yale *Lit* wrote and asked him, "Why haven't you published a book when you were the most brilliant in your class and all your friends have published?" His answer was to copy out from his *Notes* about a hundred pages of manuscript, which afterward became the first three chapters of *The Cabala*. He finished the book during a summer at the MacDowell Colony in Peterborough, New Hampshire; almost

Wilder takes his turn at playing the Stage Manager in the Broadway
production of *Our Town* (1938), when Frank Craven, the starred
actor, was on a brief vacation. BROWN BROTHERS

always his writing has been done away from home, during three or four months spent in some new corner of the globe. Then, having read galley proofs of *The Cabala* not too carefully—the first edition was full of misspellings—he wrote the first sentence of a new novel: "On Friday noon, July the twentieth, 1714, the finest bridge in all Peru broke and precipitated five travelers into the gulf below."

From its publication in November 1927, *The Bridge of San Luis Rey* was a success with the public. There were six new printings in the one month of December. In May it received the Pulitzer Prize. During the year after its publication it had a sale of two hundred thousand copies (the publisher claimed three hundred thousand) without benefit of book clubs or cheap editions. It was popular in England too, and was soon translated into most of the European languages. Its success—still a little hard to understand, for the best qualities of *The Bridge* are not those usually regarded as being popular—was one of the accidents or miracles that sometimes happen in the lives of young writers and that happened a little more frequently in the 1920s, though seldom on this grand scale. One day the author was a housemaster in a boys' boarding school with a passion for writing in his spare time, to please himself. The next morning he could read with a little incredulity that he had "already attained to the front rank of living novelists" and that his book was quite simply "a work of genius." The critic was William Lyon Phelps of Yale, who had always been given to superlatives, but in England Arnold Bennett agreed with him. "The writing," Bennett said, "has not been surpassed in the present epoch. It dazzled me by its accomplishment."

Wilder resigned his post at Lawrenceville and spent much of the next two years traveling in Europe. His third novel, *The Woman of Andros* (1930), was started in England—where parts of it, he says, were thought out during church services—and was continued on the Riviera, at New Haven, where he was planning a house in the suburbs—"the house that *The Bridge* built"—and at Oxford, Paris, and Munich. For a pastoral novel about Greece in the last century before the Christian era, it appeared at an unpropitious moment—a year after Black Thursday, in a month marked by bank failures, apple sellers at street corners, and stockbrokers jumping out of high-story windows. It was mildly praised, as a general rule, but *The New Republic* printed a famous review by Michael Gold that abused Wilder as the "Prophet of the Genteel Christ," as "this Emily Post of culture," and challenged him to write about the sufferings of his fellow Americans. Wilder accepted the challenge, in part, by writing *Heaven's My Destination* (1934), a novel in which the hero comes from the Middle West, is a traveling salesman in the Depression years, and makes laughable efforts to be a saint. This time most of the reviewers were indifferent or puzzled. It was an early sign of the coolness that has long existed between Wilder and the critics; one might speak of them as nodding distantly or respectfully when they pass him in the street, but almost never stopping to talk. His work has been crowned or clobbered with all sorts of official honors— with almost everything but the Nobel Prize—but for thirty years or more it has received less critical attention than the work of any other major American writer.

2   His life until 1930 had resembled, in most respects, the lives of other Americans born at the turn of the century who were making their way as novelists. It was distinguished from those other lives chiefly by the fact that two of his boyhood years had been spent in China—an experience that had more of a negative than a positive effect on his work—and by his professional interest in teaching. Everything else seems on the surface to be part of a familiar picture: the early delight in reading, the literary reputation gained in college, the wartime service in the army (although it was his older brother, the future theologian, who went abroad with the ambulance corps), the year in Europe as a spectator of greatness and decay, the critical recognition of a first book and the popular success of a second, followed by more wanderings abroad; all the novelists of his generation have been great travelers. On the Riviera in 1928–29, he was one of the brilliant young men who often met at Gerald and Sara Murphy's: some of the others were Hemingway, MacLeish, Cole Porter, Dos Passos, and Fitzgerald, whose next novel, *Tender Is the Night,* would be dedicated to the Murphys. *Tender* was praised even less than Hemingway's books of the early 1930s, while Faulkner, then writing his best work, was condemned or passed over

in silence. Thus, even the attacks on Wilder in the early Depression years were part of a pattern in many lives.

Yet under the surface there was an essential difference between his life and those of the others, a difference not so much in events as in the quality of experience, and it helps to explain a quality in his work. As immensely varied as that work has been, in fiction, drama, and criticism, with each new book presenting a different period and place—from the Ice Age to the Atomic Age and from Peru to the isles of Greece, passing through Omaha and Grover's Corners, New Hampshire—still it has been animated from the beginning by the same spirit, and by one that is almost unique in our time and country. Perhaps, by contrasting Wilder with the other novelists of his generation, we can find at least an approximate statement of what the spirit is.

Most of the others had a geographical starting point, a sort of rock to which their early books were attached like mussels. One thinks of Faulkner's county in Mississippi, of Hemingway's Michigan woods, of Wolfe's Asheville (or Altamont), and of Summit Avenue in St. Paul, the locus of many stories by Scott Fitzgerald. With this generation, a strong sense of place re-entered American literature for almost the first time since Hawthorne and Thoreau. But the place that most of them cherished was the country of their childhood where they had felt at home. They were always thinking back on it, or saying good-by to it (as Glenway Wescott in *Good-bye, Wisconsin*), and often they complained, as Wolfe did in the title of his last novel, that *You Can't Go Home Again.*——In all his travels Wilder never had that sense of being exiled or expatriated, because there was no one place that he regarded as home. Perhaps that was the chief result of his boyhood years in China; they did not make him a citizen of the world, but they took him away forever from Madison, Wisconsin. He ceased to be a Midwesterner, and he did not become a Californian in spite of his schooling. Later he was a little more of a New Englander, but chiefly he is an American, whose home is wherever he opens a ledger, uncaps a fountain pen, and begins writing about people anywhere.

The others had a home place, but no longer had a family. That doesn't mean they had quarreled with their parents; the days of tears and final separations had ended for writers with the Great War. Now the young men simply went their way, but it was so different from the parents' way, there was such a gulf between generations (as again there would be in the late 1960s), that sons couldn't talk sincerely with their fathers and be understood. They had rejected the standards by which the fathers lived.——There was no such rejection in Wilder's early career. He never belonged to a conspiracy of youth, leagued in a moral rebellion against middle age. He had worshiped in his father's church and followed the profession his father picked out for him. In a way he represented continuity and tradition, so far as they existed in American society.

The others lived in a new world, but not one they had fashioned for themselves. They were disillusioned by the postwar reaction, cynical about politics, hostile to the institutions of society, and pessimistic about the future, while having a good time in the present and feeling a little guilty about it, or hung over. Some of them were becoming connoisseurs of decay. Fitzgerald called them "all the sad young men."——Wilder describes himself as "fundamentally a happy person." He likes to find the goodness or greatness in people and books. He is optimistic by instinct, in the fashion of an older America.

The others were new or at least tried to be new; they made experimental forays in all directions. Each of them wanted to write what might have been the first novel since the beginning of time, from a fresh vision of life, in a new language. Some of the minor writers, now forgotten, would have liked to abolish all literature before Joyce or Baudelaire or whoever might be their idol of the month. I have heard a toast drunk to Caliph Omar for burning the library at Alexandria.——Wilder is devoted to books, the older the better, and he says that his writing life has been "a series of infatuations for admired writers." He likes to acknowledge that most of his plots are borrowed and to specify their sources, as in a note that precedes *The Woman of Andros*: "The first part of this novel is based upon the *Andria,* a comedy of Terence, who in turn based his work upon two Greek plays, now lost to us, by Menander." But Wilder transforms the borrowed material, with a richness of invention that would be rare in any age, and becomes original through trying not to be.

Each of the others had an ideal of art that was allied to symbolism, or to naturalism, or to impressionism, or was a mixture of all three. In any case the ideal was an outgrowth of the romantic movement, and some of the writers tried to make their lives romantic too, most often Byronic or Baudelairean.——Wilder holds to the classical ideal of measure and decorum. Most of his infatuations have been for classical authors, including Sophocles, Catullus, Virgil, Mme. de Sévigné, and La Bruyère, as well as the severely classical Noh drama of Japan, although he has also taken lessons from Proust and Joyce. Among his models he makes little distinction of time or place, for he remembers what he was told by an admired professor at Oberlin: "Every great work was written this morning." Perhaps his tastes are more Roman than Greek, and more English Augustan than Roman. Yale in his day was a center of eighteenth-century studies, and there has always been something of that century in his habit of mind; possibly he is the one contemporary author who would subscribe to most of the axioms that Pope advanced in his *Essay on Criticism:*

Like Kings we lose the conquests gain'd before
By vain ambition still to make them more;
Each might his sev'ral province well command,
Would all but stoop to what they understand.

Those RULES of old discover'd, not devis'd,
Are Nature still, but Nature methodiz'd.

Regard not then if Wit be old or new,
But blame the false, and value still the true.

Men must be taught as if you taught them not,
And things unknown propos'd as things forgot.

Pope's ideal, and Wilder's, is to restate in new, but not shockingly new, language "What oft was said, but ne'er so well express'd." I doubt whether any other writer of his generation would exclaim, as Wilder did to a reporter from *Time,* that "Literature is the orchestration of platitudes."

3

But there is a more fundamental difference between his work and that of his contemporaries. The others write novels about a social group—sometimes a small group, as in *Tender Is the Night,* sometimes a very large one, as in *U. S. A.*—or they write about an individual in revolt against the group, as in *A Farewell to Arms*. The central relation with which they deal is between the many and the one. Very often—to borrow a pair of terms from David Riesman —their theme is the defeat of an inner-directed hero by an other-directed society. They feel that the society and its standards must be carefully portrayed, and these writers are all, to some extent, novelists of manners. ——Wilder is a novelist of morals.

Manners and morals are terms that overlap, sometimes confusingly, but here I am using the two words in senses that are easier to distinguish. Manners would be the standards of conduct that prevail in a group, large or small, and hence they would change from group to group and year to year. Morals would be defined as the standards that determine the relations of individuals with other individuals, one with one—a child with each of its parents, a husband with his wife, a rich man with a poor man (not *the* rich with *the* poor)—and also the relations of any man with himself, his destiny, and his God. They are answers found by individuals to the old problems of faith, hope, charity or love, art, duty, submission to one's fate . . . and hence they are relatively universal; they can be illustrated from the lives of any individuals, in any place, at any time since the beginning of time.

The characters in Wilder's novels and plays are looking for such answers; his work is not often concerned with the behavior of groups. An outstanding exception might be *Our Town* (1938), in which the Stage Manager speaks with the voice of the community. But the community hasn't much to say about itself and will not admit to having local color; it might be any town, a fact that explains the success of the play in towns all over the country, and other countries. The events portrayed are coming of age, falling in love, getting married, and dying; in other words they are not truly events— except for the characters, who are not truly characters—but rather they serve as examples of a universal pattern in human lives; and they are not greatly affected, in the play, by the special manners of this one community. *The Cabala* also starts by dealing with a group, but very soon the young American narrator shifts his attention to its separate members, explaining that he is "the biographer of the individuals and not the historian of the group." The statement applies to the author himself, and in a simpler form: Wilder is not a historian. In Rome he had studied archaeology and had learned to look backward and forward through a long vista of years; that sort of vision is a special quality of all his work. But what he sees at the end of a vista is what the archaeologist often sees, that is, fragments of a finished pattern of life in many ways similar to our own. It is not what the historian tries to see: a living community in a process of continual and irreversible change.

The other novelists of his generation are all in some way historians. Their basic perception was of the changes in their own time, from peace to war, from stability to instability, from a fixed code of behavior to the feeling that "It's all right if you can get away with it." For them the Great War was a true event, in the sense that afterward nothing was the same. All of them were "haunted fatally by the sense of time," as Wolfe says of his autobiographical hero. His second novel was *Of Time and the River*. Hemingway's first book was *In Our Time* and he let it be understood, ". . . as in no other time." Faulkner saw his time in the South as one of violent decay. When Dos Passos tried to put thirty years of American life into one big novel, he invented a device called the Newsreel, intended to convey the local color of each particular year. Fitzgerald put the same sort of material into the body of his stories; he wrote as if with an eye on the calendar. *The Great Gatsby* belongs definitely to the year 1923, when the Fitzgeralds were living in Great Neck, Long Island, and *Tender Is the Night* could have ended only in 1930; no other year on the Riviera had quite the same atmosphere of things going to pieces. Both books are historical novels about his own time, so accurately observed, so honestly felt, that the books are permanent. ——Wilder would never attempt to draw such a picture of his time. He is the great unsocial and antihistorical novelist, the master of the anachronism.

Like Dos Passos he gives us a newsreel, or rather two of them, to introduce the first two acts of *The Skin of Our Teeth* (1942). The contrast here is complete. Where Dos Passos recalls such episodes as the capture of the bobbed-hair bandit, the Florida real-estate boom, and the suppression of a revolt in Canton (to the refrain of "I'm Dancing with Tears in My Eyes"), Wilder presents another order of phenomena. Before the first act, when the lights go out, the name of the theater flashes on the screen and we hear the Announcer's voice:

The management takes pleasure in bringing to you—the news of the world! (*Slide 2. The sun appearing above the horizon.*) Freeport, Long Island. The sun rose this morning at 6:32 a.m. This gratifying event was first reported by (*Slide 3*) Mrs. Dorothy Stetson of Freeport, Long Island, who promptly telephoned the Mayor. The Society for Affirming (*Slide 4*) the End of the World at once went into a special session and postponed the arrival of that event for *twenty-four hours* (*Slide 5*). All honor to Mrs. Stetson for her public spirit.

New York City. (*Slide 6, of the front doors of the theater.*) The Plymouth Theater. During the daily cleaning of this theater a number of lost objects were collected, as usual (*Slide 7*), by Mesdames Simpson, Pateslewski, and Moriarity. Among these objects found today was (*Slide 8*) a wedding ring, inscribed: To Eva from Adam. Genesis 2:18. The ring will be restored to the owner or owners, if their credentials are satisfactory.

Wilder's news of the world is first what happens every day, and then what happened at the beginning. In all his work—except for that hint of the Creation—I can think of only one event that marks a change in human affairs: it is the birth of Christ, as announced on the first and the last page of *The Woman of Andros*. Perhaps another event is foreshadowed in a much later novel, *The Eighth Day* (1967): it is the birth of new messiahs, something that might resemble a Second Coming. That other Christian event, the Fall, is nowhere mentioned and seems to play no part in Wilder's theology. Everything else in his plays and novels—even the collapse of a famous bridge—is merely an example or illustration of man's universal destiny. Nothing is unique, the author seems to be saying; the Ice Age will return, as will the Deluge, as will Armageddon. After each disaster man will start over again—helped by his books, if he has saved them—and will struggle upward until halted by a new disaster. "Rome existed before Rome," the shade of Virgil says at the end of *The Cabala*, "and when Rome will be a waste there will be Romes after her." "There are no Golden Ages and no Dark Ages," we read in *The Eighth Day*. "There is the oceanlike monotony of the generations of men under the alternations of fair and foul weather." The same book says, "It is only in appearance that time is a river. It is rather a vast landscape and it is the eye of the beholder that moves."

4 ✍ At this point I think we might glimpse a design that unites what Wilder has written from beginning to end. He has published not quite a dozen books, each strikingly different from all the others in place, in time, in social setting, and even more in method, yet all the books illustrate the same feeling of universally shared experience and eternal return. *Everything that happened might happen anywhere and will happen again.* That principle explains why he is able to adopt different perspectives in different books, as though he were looking sometimes through one end of a telescope, sometimes through the other. In *The Ides of March* (1948) a distant object is magnified and Rome in 45 B.C. is described as if it were New York two thousand years later. In *Our Town* he reverses the telescope and shows us Grover's Corners as if it had been preserved for two thousand years under a lava flow and then unearthed like Herculaneum. He has many other fashions of distorting time. *The Long Christmas Dinner* (1931) is a one-act play in which the dinner lasts for ninety years, with members of the family appearing from a bright door and going out through a dark door, to indicate birth and death. *The Skin of Our Teeth* epitomizes the story of mankind in three acts and four characters: Adam, Eve, Lilith, and Cain. They are living in Excelsior, New Jersey, when the glacial cap comes grinding down on them. In Atlantic City, just before the Deluge, they launch an ark full of animals two by two from the Million Dollar Pier.

Because Wilder denies the importance of time, his successive books have proved to be either timely or untimely in a spectacular fashion—and in both cases by accident. *The Bridge* exactly fitted the mood of the moment, and nobody knows exactly why. *The Woman of Andros* was published thirty years too late or too soon. *The Skin of Our Teeth* had a more complicated history. Produced on Broadway in 1942, it was a success largely because of Tallulah Bankhead's so-jolly part of Lilith, or Lily Sabina. Hardly anyone said that the play expressed the mood of the moment, or of any other moment.

But when it was staged in Central Europe after World War II, it was not only a success but a historic one, for any cast of actors that played in it. The Germans and the Austrians seem to have felt that it was a topical drama written especially for them, to soften their defeat and give them strength to live.

The Skin of Our Teeth is derived in part from Finnegans Wake, as The Woman of Andros is based in part on Terence's Andria, and as the plot of The Bridge was suggested by one of Mérimée's shorter plays. We read in a note on The Matchmaker (1954), "This play is based upon a comedy by Johann Nestroy, Einen Jux Will Er Sich Machen (Vienna, 1842), which was in turn based upon an English original, A Day Well Spent, by John Oxenford." There are many other acknowledged derivations in Wilder's work, from authors of many times and countries, and together they reveal another aspect of his disregard for history. He feels that a true author is independent of time and country, and he also feels, apparently, that there is no history of literature, but only a pattern consisting of books that continue to live because they contain permanent truths. Any new author is at liberty to restate those truths and to borrow plots or methods from older authors, so long as he transforms the borrowed material into something of his own. Not only was every great book written this morning, but it can be read tonight as on the first day. That principle, in two of Wilder's plays, becomes a metaphor that is a masterpiece of foreshortening. In a one-acter called Pullman Car Hiawatha and again in the third act of The Skin of Our Teeth, the great philosophers are presented as hours of the night. One of the characters explains: "Just like the hours and stars go by over our heads at night, in the same way the ideas and thoughts of the great men are in the air around us all the time and they're working on us, even when we don't know it." Spinoza is nine o'clock, Plato is ten, Aristotle is eleven, and Moses is midnight. Three thousand years of thought are reduced to four hours, which pass in less than two minutes on the stage.

This foreshortening of time becomes an opportunity for the novelist as well as for the playwright. When history is regarded as a recurrent pattern rather than as a process, it becomes possible to move a character from almost any point in time or space to almost any other. In The Bridge Mme. de Sévigné reappears in Peru as the Marquesa de Montemayor. Keats is presented in The Cabala, with his genius, his illness, his family problems; and he dies again in 1920 among a group of strange characters who might be resurrected from the *Memoirs* of the Duc de Saint-Simon, or who also might be classical gods and goddesses in modern dress. Persons can be moved backward in time as well as forward. Edward Sheldon, the crippled and blinded dramatist who lived for thirty years in retirement, dispensing wisdom to his friends, appears in *The Ides of March* as Lucius Manilius Turrinus, and one suspects that Cicero, in the same novel, is a preincarnation of Alexander Woollcott. As for the hero of the novel, he is not a historical character but a model or paradigm of the man of decision, as such a man might exist in any age. Wilder has called him Julius Caesar, much as Paul Valéry called his man of intellect Leonardo da Vinci, and much as Emerson gave the title of "Plato" to his essay on man as philosopher.

So Emerson's name comes up again, as it did in the case of E. E. Cummings (though it wouldn't make sense to mention the name in connection with any other writer of the Lost Generation). Emerson was of course the prophet who gave no importance to groups or institutions and refused to think of history as a process. When he discussed Montaigne or Shakespeare, it was not against the background of their times, but rather as "representative men" whom he might meet at any dinner of the Saturday Club. Wilder, in the brilliant series of lectures that he gave at Harvard in 1950–51, started with Emerson, Thoreau, and other classical American writers, notably Melville and Whitman. What he tried to deduce from their works was the character of the representative American, but what he actually presented was, I suspect, partly a reflection of his own character. Here are some of his statements:

> From the point of view of the European an American is nomad in relation to place, disattached in relation to time, lonely in relation to society, and insubmissive to circumstances, destiny, or God.

> Americans could count and enjoyed counting. They lived under a sense of boundlessness. . . . To this day, in American thinking, a crowd of ten thousand is not a homogeneous mass of that number, but is one and one and one . . . up to ten thousand.

Since the American can find no confirmation of identity from the environment in which he lives, since he lives exposed to the awareness of vast distances and innumerable existences, since he derives from a belief in the future the courage that animates him, is he not bent on isolating and "fixing" a value on every existing thing in its relation to a totality, to the All, to the Everywhere, to the Always?

Those are perceptive statements, but I should question whether they apply to most Americans today, or to many American writers since the First World War. Their primary application is to all the big and little Emersonians, beginning with Thoreau (who is Wilder's favorite) and Whitman. In our own day they apply to Wilder himself more than to any other writer—more than to Cummings, even, whose later work revives the Emersonian tradition, but chiefly on its romantic, mystical, anarchistic side. Wilder is neoclassical, as I said. He goes back to Pope and Addison in his attitude toward the art of letters, but in other habits of thought he clearly goes back to the Transcendentalists. His work has more than a little of the moral distinction they tried to achieve, and like their work it deals with the relation of one to one, or of anyone to the All, the Everywhere, and the Always. Like theirs it looks toward the future with confidence, though not with the bland confidence that some of the Emersonians displayed. "Every human being who has existed can be felt by us as existing now," Wilder says in another of his Norton lectures, as if to explain his foreshortening of history. "All time is present for a single time. . . . Many problems which now seem insoluble will be solved when the world realizes that we are all bound together as the population of the only inhabited star."

VII FAULKNER
The Yoknapatawpha Story

Most of what follows was written in 1945, at a time when Faulkner's books were little read and often disparaged. He had a few enthusiastic defenders, but no one, so it seemed to me then, had more than distantly suggested the scope and force and interdependence of his work as a whole. I was writing to overcome a general misconception, and that explains why the emphasis, at various points, was different from what it would be today. Yet I find it hard to change what I said, except in the comparatively simple matter of bringing facts up to date. The original text was longer than my introduction to *The Portable Faulkner* (1946) and was written with some valued hints from Faulkner himself. It still maps out the straightest road into his imaginary country. I should like to follow that early text except for a few revisions, while saving my comments for the end.

1 ✍ When the war was over—the other war—William Faulkner went back to Oxford, Mississippi. He had served in 1918 as a cadet in the Royal Canadian Air Force. Now he was home again and not at home, or at least not able to accept the postwar world. He was writing poems, most of them worthless, and dozens of immature but violent and effective stories, while at the same time he was brooding over his own situation and the decline of the South. Slowly the brooding thoughts arranged themselves into the whole interconnected pattern that would form the substance of his novels.

The pattern was based on what he saw in Oxford or remembered from his childhood, on scraps of family tradition (the Falkners, as they spelled the name, had played their part in the history of the state), on kitchen dialogues between the black cook and her amiable husband, on Saturday-afternoon gossip in Courthouse Square, on stories told by men in overalls squatting on their heels while they passed around a fruit jar full of white corn liquor; on all the sources familiar to a small-town Mississippi boy—but the whole of it was elaborated, transformed, given convulsive life by his emotions; until by simple intensity of feeling the figures in it became a little more than human, became heroic or diabolical, became symbols of the old South, of war and reconstruction, of commerce and machinery destroying the standards of the past. There in Oxford, Faulkner performed a labor of imagination that has not been equaled in our time, and a double labor: first, to invent a Mississippi county that was like a mythical kingdom, but was complete and living in all its details; second, to make his story of Yoknapatawpha County stand as a parable or legend of all the Deep South.

For this double task, Faulkner was better equipped by talent and background than he was by schooling. He was born in New Albany, Mississippi, September 25, 1897; he was the oldest of four brothers. Soon the Falkners moved to Ripley, in the adjoining county, then fifty miles southwestward to Oxford, where the novelist attended the public school, but without being graduated from high school. For a year or two after the war, he was a student at the University of Mississippi, where veterans could then matriculate without a high-school diploma, but he neglected his classroom work and left early in the second year. He had less of a formal education than any other good writer of his age group, except Hart Crane—less even than Hemingway, who never went to college, but who learned to speak several languages and studied writing in Paris with Ezra Pound and Gertrude Stein. Faulkner taught himself, largely, as he says, by "undirected and uncorrelated reading." [1]

Among the authors either mentioned or echoed in his early stories and poems are Keats, Balzac, Flaubert, Swinburne, Verlaine, Mallarmé, Wilde, Housman, Joyce, Eliot, Conrad Aiken, Sherwood Anderson, and E. E. Cummings, with fainter suggestions of Hemingway (looking at trout in a river), Dos Passos (in the spelling of compound words), and Scott Fitzgerald. The poems he wrote in those days were wholly derivative, but his prose from the beginning was a form of poetry, and in spite of the echoes it was wholly his own. He traveled less than any of his writing contemporaries. There was a lonely time in New York as salesclerk in a bookstore; there were six months in New Orleans, where he lived near Sherwood Anderson and met the literary crowd—he even satirized them in a bad early novel, *Mosquitoes*—then another six months in Italy and Paris, where he did not make friends on the Left Bank. Except for writing assignments in Hollywood and summers on the Gulf Coast, the rest of his life has been spent in the town where he grew up, less than forty miles from his birthplace.

Although Oxford, Mississippi, is the seat of a university, it is even less of a literary center than was Salem, Massachusetts, during Hawthorne's early years as a writer; and Faulkner himself has shown an even greater dislike than Hawthorne for literary society. His novels are the books of a man who broods about literature, but doesn't often discuss it with his friends; there is no ease about them, no feeling that they come from a background of taste refined by

---

1. The reading, though, was extensive. There was no public library in Oxford when Faulkner was a boy, but there were books in the house—a well-thumbed set of Dickens, for example. Also there was an older friend and neighbor, Phil Stone, who came back from Yale in 1914 apparently with trunkloads of books that were otherwise unavailable in Oxford. They included most of the authors, French, English, and American, who were read and prized by members of the literary generation.

Faulkner in his last year, at "Rowanoak" in Oxford, Mississippi,
in front of the log stable where he kept his riding horse.

MARTIN J. DAIN, MAGNUM

argument and of opinions held in common. They make me think of a passage from Henry James's little book on Hawthorne:

> The best things come, as a general thing, from the talents that are members of a group; every man works better when he has companions working in the same line, and yielding to the stimulus of suggestion, comparison, emulation. Great things of course have been done by solitary workers; but they have usually been done with double the pains they would have cost if they had been produced in more genial circumstances. The solitary worker loses the profit of example and discussion; he is apt to make awkward experiments; he is in the nature of the case more or less of an empiric. The empiric may, as I say, be treated by the world as an expert; but the drawbacks and discomforts of empiricism remain to him, and are in fact increased by the suspicion that is mingled with his gratitude, of a want in the public taste of a sense of the proportion of things.

Like Hawthorne, Faulkner is a solitary worker by choice, and he has done great things not only with double the pains to himself that they might have cost if produced in more genial circumstances, but sometimes also with double the pains to the reader. Two or three of his books as a whole and many of them in part are awkward experiments. All of them are full of overblown words like "imponderable," "immortal," "immutable," and "immemorial" that he would have used with more discretion, or not at all, if he had followed Hemingway's example and served an apprenticeship to an older writer. He is a most uncertain judge of his own work, and he has no reason to believe that the world's judgment of it is any more to be trusted; indeed, there is no American author who would be justified in feeling more suspicion of "a want in the public taste of a sense of the proportion of things." His early novels, when not condemned, were overpraised for the wrong reasons; his later and in many ways better novels have been ridiculed or simply neglected; and in 1945 all his seventeen books were effectively out of print, with some of them unobtainable in the second-hand bookshops.[2]

---

2. I have let this paragraph stand, with the one that follows, as an accurate picture of Faulkner's reputation in 1945.

Even his warm admirers, of whom there are many—no author has a higher standing among his fellow novelists—have shown a rather vague idea of what he is trying to do; and Faulkner himself has never explained. He holds a curious attitude toward the public that appears to be lofty indifference (as in the one preface he wrote, for the Modern Library edition of *Sanctuary*), but really comes closer to being a mixture of skittery distrust and pure unconsciousness that the public exists. He doesn't furnish information or correct misstatements about himself (most of the biographical sketches that deal with him are full of preposterous errors). He doesn't care which way his name is spelled in the records, with or without the "u"— "Either way suits me," he says. Once he has finished a book, he is apparently not concerned with the question of how it will be presented, to what sort of audience, and sometimes he doesn't bother to keep a private copy of it. He said in a letter, "I think I have written a lot and sent it off to print before I actually realized strangers might read it." Others might say that Faulkner, at least in those early days, was not so much composing stories for the public as telling them to himself—like a lonely child in his imaginary world, but also like a writer of genius.

2 ✍ Faulkner's mythical kingdom is a county in northern Mississippi, on the border between the sand hills covered with scrubby pine and the black earth of the river bottoms. Except for the storekeepers, mechanics, and professional men who live in Jefferson, the county seat, all the inhabitants are farmers or woodsmen. Except for a little lumber, their only commercial product is baled cotton for the Memphis market. A few of them live in big plantation houses, the relics of another age, and more of them in substantial wooden farmhouses; but still more of them are tenants, no better housed than slaves on good plantations before the Civil War. Yoknapatawpha County—"William Faulkner, sole owner and proprietor," as he inscribed on one of the maps he drew—has a population of 15,611 persons scattered over 2400 square miles. It sometimes seems to me that every house or hovel has been described in one of Faulkner's novels, and that all the people of the imaginary county, black and

white, townsmen, farmers, and housewives, have played their parts in one connected story.

He has so far [1945] written nine books wholly concerned with Yoknapatawpha County and its people, who also appear in parts of three others and in thirty or more uncollected stories. *Sartoris* was the first book to be published, in the spring of 1929; it is a romantic and partly unconvincing novel, but with many fine scenes in it, such as the hero's visit to a family of independent pine-hill farmers; and it states most of the themes that the author would later develop at length. *The Sound and the Fury,* published six months later, recounts the going-to-pieces of the Compson family, and it was the first of Faulkner's novels to be widely discussed. The books that followed, in the Yoknapatawpha series, are *As I Lay Dying* (1930), about the death and burial of Addie Bundren; *Sanctuary* (1931), for a long time the most popular of his novels; *Light in August* (1932), in some ways the best; *Absalom, Absalom!* (1936), about Colonel Sutpen and his ambition to found a family; *The Unvanquished* (1938), a cycle of stories about the Sartoris dynasty; *The Wild Palms* (1939), half of which deals with a convict from back in the pine hills; *The Hamlet* (1940), a first novel about the Snopes clan, with others to follow; and *Go Down, Moses* (1942), in which Faulkner's principal theme is the relation between whites and Negroes. There are also many Yoknapatawpha stories in *These 13* (1931) and *Doctor Martino* (1934), besides other stories privately printed (like *Miss Zilphia Gant,* 1932) or published in magazines and still to be collected or used as episodes in novels.[3]

---

3. That was the tally in 1945. With one exception, all the books that Faulkner published after that year are concerned with Yoknapatawpha County. The exception is *A Fable* (1954), about a reincarnated Christ in the First World War. The Yoknapatawpha books, eight in number, are *Intruder in the Dust* (1948), about a lynching that is averted by a seventy-year-old spinster and a pair of boys; *Knight's Gambit* (1949), recounting the adventures in detection of Gavin Stevens; *Collected Stories of William Faulkner* (1950), containing all the stories in *These 13* and *Doctor Martino* as well as several not previously collected; *Requiem for a Nun* (1951), a three-act drama, with narrative prologues to each act, about the later life of Temple Drake; *Big Woods* (1955), a cycle of hunting stories, some of them revised from chapters of *Go Down, Moses; The Town* (1957), second volume in the Snopes trilogy; *The Mansion* (1959), concluding the trilogy; and *The Reivers,* published a month before Faulkner's death on July 6, 1962. In all, sixteen of his books belong to the Yoknapatawpha cycle, as well as half of another book (*The Wild Palms*) and it is hard to count how many stories.

Just as Balzac, who may have inspired the series, divided his *Comédie Humaine* into "Scenes of Parisian Life," "Scenes of Provincial Life," "Scenes of Private Life," so Faulkner might divide his work into a number of cycles: one about the planters and their descendants, one about the townspeople of Jefferson, one about the poor whites, one about the Indians, and one about the Negroes. Or again, if he adopted a division by families, there would be the Compson-Sartoris saga, the continuing Snopes saga, the McCaslin saga, dealing with the white and black descendants of Carothers McCaslin, and the Ratliff-Bundren saga, devoted to the backwoods farmers of Frenchman's Bend. All the cycles or sagas are closely interconnected; it is as if each new book was a chord or segment of a total situation always existing in the author's mind. Sometimes a short story is the sequel to an earlier novel. For example, we read in *Sartoris* that Byron Snopes stole a packet of letters from Narcissa Benbow; and in "There Was a Queen," a story published five years later, we learn how Narcissa got the letters back again. Sometimes a novel contains the sequel to a story, and sometimes an episode reappears in several connections. Thus, in the first chapter of *Sanctuary,* we hear about the Old Frenchman place, a ruined mansion near which the people of the neighborhood had been "digging with secret and sporadic optimism for gold which the builder was reputed to have buried somewhere about the place when Grant came through the country on his Vicksburg campaign." Later this digging for gold served as the subject of a story printed in *The Saturday Evening Post:* "Lizards in Jamshyd's Courtyard." Still later the story was completely rewritten and became the last chapter of *The Hamlet.*[4]

As one book leads into another, the author sometimes falls into inconsistencies of detail. There is a sewing-machine agent named V. K. Suratt who appears in *Sartoris* and some of the stories written at about the same time. When we reach *The Hamlet,* his name has changed to Ratliff, although his character remains the same (and his age, too, for all the twenty years that separate the backgrounds of the two novels). Henry Armstid is a likable figure in *As I Lay Dying* and *Light in August;* in *The Hamlet* he is mean and half-

---

4. The Old Frenchman place was built in the 1830s by Louis Grenier, as Faulkner tells us in the prologue to the first act of *Requiem for a Nun* (1951).

demented. His wife, whose character remains consistent, is called Lula in one book and Martha in another; in the third she is nameless. There is an Indian chief named Doom who appears in several stories; he starts as the father of Issetibeha (in "Red Leaves") and ends as his nephew (in "A Justice"). The mansion called Sutpen's Hundred was built of brick at the beginning of *Absalom, Absalom!*, but at the end of the novel it is all wood and inflammable except for the chimneys. But these errors are inconsequential, considering the scope of Faulkner's series, and I should judge that most of them are afterthoughts rather than oversights.

All his books in the Yoknapatawpha cycle are part of the same living pattern. It is the pattern, not the printed volumes in which part of it is recorded, that is Faulkner's real achievement. Its existence helps to explain one feature of his work: that each novel, each long or short story, seems to reveal more than it states explicitly and to have a subject bigger than itself. All the separate works are like blocks of marble from the same quarry: they show the veins and faults of the mother rock. Or else—to use a rather strained figure—they are like wooden planks that were cut, not from a log, but from a still-living tree. The planks are planed and chiseled into their final shapes, but the tree itself heals over the wound and continues to grow.

Faulkner is incapable of telling the same story twice without adding new details. In compiling *The Portable Faulkner* I wanted to use part of *The Sound and the Fury*, the novel about the fall of the Compson family. I thought that the last part of the book would be most effective as a separate episode, but still it depended too much on what had gone before. Faulkner offered to write a very brief introduction that would explain the relations of the characters. What he finally sent me was the much longer passage printed at the end of the *Portable*: a genealogy of the Compson family from their first arrival in America. Whereas the novel is confined (except for memories) to a period of eighteen years ending on Easter Sunday, 1928, the genealogy goes back to the battle of Culloden in 1745, and forward to the year 1943, when Jason, last of the Compson males, has sold the family mansion and Sister Caddy has last been heard of as the mistress of a German general. The novel that Faulkner wrote about the Compsons had long before been given what appeared to be its final shape, but the pattern or body of legend behind the novel—and behind his other books—was still developing.

Although the pattern is presented in terms of a single Mississippi county, it can be extended to the Deep South as a whole; and Faulkner always seems conscious of its wider application. He might have been thinking of his own novels when he described the ledgers in the commissary of the McCaslin plantation, in *Go Down, Moses.* They recorded, he says, "that slow trickle of molasses and meal and meat, of shoes and straw hats and overalls, of plowlines and collars and heelbolts and clevises, which returned each fall as cotton"—in a sense they were local and limited; but they were also "the continuation of that record which two hundred years had not been enough to complete and another hundred would not be enough to discharge; that chronicle which was a whole land in miniature, which multiplied and compounded was the entire South."

3   "Tell about the South," says Quentin Compson's roommate at Harvard, a Canadian named Shreve McCannon who is curious about the unknown region beyond the Ohio. "What's it like there?" he asks. "What do they do there? Why do they live there? Why do they live at all?" And Quentin, whose background is a little like that of Faulkner himself and who sometimes seems to speak for him— Quentin answers, "You can't understand it. You would have to be born there." Nevertheless, he tells a long and violent story that reveals something essential in the history of the Deep South, which is not so much a region as it is, in Quentin's mind, an incomplete and frustrated nation trying to relive its legendary past.

The story he tells—I am trying to summarize the plot of *Absalom, Absalom!*—is that of a mountain boy named Thomas Sutpen whose family drifted into the Virginia lowlands, where his father found odd jobs on a plantation. One day the father sent him with a message to the big house, but he was turned away at the door by a black man in livery. Puzzled and humiliated, the mountain boy was seized upon by the lifelong ambition to which he would afterward refer as "the design." He too would own a plantation with slaves and a liveried butler; he would build a mansion as big as any of those in the Tidewater; and he would have a son to inherit his wealth.

A dozen years later Sutpen appeared in the frontier town of Jefferson, where by some presumably dishonest means he managed to obtain a hundred square miles of land from the Chickasaws. With the help of twenty wild Negroes from the jungle and a French architect, he set about building the largest house in northern Mississippi, using timbers from the forest and bricks that his Negroes molded and baked on the spot; it was as if the mansion, Sutpen's Hundred, had been literally torn from the soil. Only one man in Jefferson—he was Quentin's grandfather, General Compson—ever learned how and where Sutpen had acquired his slaves. He had shipped to Haiti from Virginia, worked as an overseer on a sugar plantation, and married the rich planter's daughter, who had borne him a son. Then, finding that his wife had Negro blood, he had simply put her away, with her child and her fortune, while keeping the twenty slaves as a sort of indemnity. He explained to General Compson, in the stilted speech he had taught himself as appropriate to his new role of Southern gentleman, that she could not be "adjunctive to the forwarding of the design."

"Jesus, the South is fine, isn't it," Shreve McCannon says. "It's better than the theater, isn't it. It's better than Ben Hur, isn't it. No wonder you have to come away now and then, isn't it."

In Jefferson he married again, Quentin continues. This time Sutpen's wife belonged to a pious family of the neighborhood and she bore him two children, Henry and Judith. He became the biggest cotton planter in Yoknapatawpha County, and it seemed that his "design" had already been fulfilled. At this moment, however, Henry came home from the University of Mississippi with an older and worldlier new friend, Charles Bon, who was in reality Sutpen's son by his first marriage. Charles became engaged to Judith. Sutpen learned his identity and, without making a sign of recognition, ordered him from the house. Henry, who refused to believe that Charles was his half-brother, renounced his birthright and followed him to New Orleans. In 1861 all the male Sutpens went off to war, and all survived four years of fighting. Then, in the spring of 1865, Charles suddenly decided to marry Judith, even though he was certain by now that she was his half-sister. Henry rode beside him all the way back to Sutpen's Hundred, but tried to stop him at the gate, killed him when he insisted on going ahead with his plan, told Judith what he had done, and disappeared.

"The South," Shreve McCannon says as he listens to the story. "The South. Jesus. No wonder you folks all outlive yourselves by years and years." And Quentin says, remembering his own sister with whom (or with a false notion of whom) he was in love—just as Charles Bon, and Henry too, were in love with Judith—"I am older at twenty than a lot of people who have died."

But Quentin's story of the Deep South does not end with the war. Colonel Sutpen came home, he says, to find his wife dead, his son a fugitive, his slaves dispersed (they had run away before they were freed by the Union Army), and most of his land about to be seized for debt. Still determined to carry out "the design," he did not pause for breath before undertaking to restore his house and plantation as nearly as possible to what they had been. The effort failed; Sutpen lost most of his land and was reduced to keeping a crossroads store. Now in his sixties, he tried again to beget a son; but his wife's younger sister, Miss Rosa Coldfield, was outraged by his proposal ("Let's try it," he seems to have said, though his words are not directly repeated—"and if it's a boy we'll get married"); and later poor Milly Jones, whom he seduced, gave birth to a girl. At that Sutpen abandoned hope and provoked Milly's grandfather into killing him. Judith survived her father for a time, as did the half-caste son of Charles Bon by a New Orleans octoroon. After the death of these two by yellow fever, the great house was haunted rather than inhabited by an ancient mulatto woman, Sutpen's daughter by one of his slaves. The fugitive Henry Sutpen came home to die; the townspeople heard of his illness and sent an ambulance after him; but old Clytie thought they were arresting him for murder and set fire to Sutpen's Hundred. The only survivor of the conflagration was Jim Bond, a half-witted, saddle-colored creature who was Charles Bon's grandson.

"Now I want you to tell me just one thing more," the Canadian roommate says after hearing the story. "Why do you hate the South?"—"I dont hate it," Quentin says quickly, at once. "I dont hate it," he repeats, apparently speaking for the author as well as himself. *I dont hate it,* he thinks, panting in the cold air, the iron New England dark; *I dont. I dont hate it! I dont hate it!*

The reader cannot help wondering why this somber and, at moments, plainly incredible story has so seized upon Quentin's mind that he trembles with excitement when telling it, and why

Shreve McCannon felt that it revealed the essence of the Deep South. It seems to belong in the realm of Gothic romance, with Sutpen's Hundred taking the place of a haunted castle on the Rhine, with Colonel Sutpen as Faust and Charles Bon as Manfred. Then slowly, if you read it again, it dawns on you that most of the characters and incidents have a double meaning; that besides their place in the story they serve as symbols or metaphors with a general application. Sutpen's great design, the land he stole from the Indians, the French architect who built his mansion with the help of wild Negroes from the jungle, the woman of mixed blood whom he married and disowned, the unacknowledged son who ruined him, the poor white whom he robbed and who killed him in anger, and the final destruction of the mansion like the downfall of a social order . . . all these might belong to a tragic fable of Southern history. With a little cleverness, the whole novel might be explained as a connected and logical allegory, but this, I think, would be going far beyond the author's intention. First of all he was writing a story, and one that affected him deeply, but he was also brooding over a social situation. More or less unconsciously, the incidents in the story came to represent the forces and elements in the social situation, since the mind naturally works in terms of symbols and parallels. In Faulkner's case, this form of parallelism is not confined to *Absalom, Absalom!* It can be found in the whole fictional framework that he has been elaborating in novel after novel, until his work has become a myth or legend of the South.

I call it a legend because it is obviously no more intended as a historical account of the country south of the Ohio than *The Scarlet Letter* was intended as a history of Massachusetts or *Paradise Lost* as a factual account of the Fall. Briefly stated, the legend might run something like this: The Deep South was ruled by planters some of whom were aristocrats like the Sartoris clan, while others were new men like Colonel Sutpen. Both types were determined to establish a lasting social order on the land they had seized from the Indians (that is, to leave sons behind them). They had the virtue of living single-mindedly by a fixed code; but there was also an inherent guilt in their "design," their way of life; it was slavery that put a curse on the land and brought about the Civil War. [I must add, in deference to Cleanth Brooks, that although Sutpen had more than his share of the guilt, he never pretended to follow the code of conduct that in some measure atoned for it. Temperamentally he was less of a Southerner than a Northern robber baron out of his time and place; or he might even stand for the blindly ambitious man of all ages. To the other planters, he was always an alien. Quentin Compson, their descendant, regarded him as "trash, originless"—so Faulkner told me in a letter—but Quentin also grieved the fact that a man like Sutpen "could not only have dreamed so high but have had the force and strength to have failed so grandly." Thus, it was not at all in his character, but rather in his fate, that Sutpen became emblematic of the South.]

After the war was lost, partly as a result of the Southerners' mad heroism (for who else but men as brave as Jackson and Stuart could have frightened the Yankees into standing together and fighting back?), the planters tried to restore their "design" by other methods. But they no longer had the strength to achieve more than a partial success, even after they had freed their land from the carpetbaggers who followed the Northern armies. As time passed, moreover, the men of the old order found that they had Southern enemies too; they had to fight against a new exploiting class descended from the landless whites of slavery days. In this struggle between the clan of Sartoris and the unscrupulous tribe of Snopes, the Sartorises were defeated in advance by a traditional code that kept them from using the weapons of the enemy. As a price of victory, however, the Snopeses had to serve the mechanized civilization of the North, which was morally impotent in itself, but which, with the aid of its Southern retainers, ended by corrupting the Southern nation. In a later time, the problems of the South are still unsolved, the racial conflict is becoming more acute, and Faulkner's characters in their despairing moments foresee or forebode some catastrophe of which Jim Bond and his like will be the only survivors.

4   This legend of Faulkner's, if I have stated it correctly, is clearly not the plantation legend that has been embodied in hundreds of romantic novels. Faulkner presents the virtues of the old order as being moral rather than material. There is no baronial pomp in his novels; no profusion of silk and silver, mahogany and moonlight and

champagne. The big house on Mr. Hubert Beauchamp's plantation (in "Was") had a rotted floorboard in the back gallery that Mr. Hubert never got round to having fixed. Visitors used to find him sitting in the springhouse with his boots off and his feet in the water while he sipped his morning toddy. Visitors to Sutpen's Hundred were offered champagne: it was the best, doubtless, yet it was "crudely dispensed out of the burlesqued pantomime elegance of Negro butlers who (and likewise the drinkers who gulped it down like neat whisky between flowery and unsubtle toasts) would have treated lemonade the same way." All the planters lived comfortably, with plenty of servants, but Faulkner never lets us forget that they were living on what had recently been the frontier. What he admires about them is not their wealth or their manners or their fine horses, but rather the unquestioning acceptance—by the best planters —of a moral code that taught them "courage and honor and pride, and pity and love of justice and of liberty." Living with single hearts they were, says Quentin Compson's father,

> . . . people too as we are, and victims too as we are, but victims of a different circumstance, simpler and therefore, integer for integer, larger, more heroic and the figures therefore more heroic too, not dwarfed and involved but distinct, uncomplex, who had the gift of living once or dying once instead of being diffused and scattered creatures drawn blindly limb from limb from a grab bag and assembled, author and victim too of a thousand homicides and a thousand copulations and divorcements.

The old order was a moral order: briefly that was its strength and the secret lost by its heirs. But also—and here is another respect in which it differs from the Southern story more commonly presented—it bore the moral burden of a guilt so great that the Civil War and even Reconstruction were in some sense a merited punishment. There is madness, but there is metaphorical meaning too, in Miss Rosa Coldfield's belief that Sutpen was a demon and that his sins were the real reason "why God let us lose the War: that only through the blood of our men and the tears of our women could He stay this demon and efface his name and lineage from the earth." Colonel Sutpen himself has a feeling not exactly of guilt, since he has never questioned the rightness of his design, but rather of amazement that so many misfortunes have fallen on him. Sitting in General Compson's office, he goes back over his career, trying to see where he had made his "mistake," for that is what he calls it. Sometimes the author seems to be implying that the sin for which Sutpen and his class are being punished is that of cohabiting with Negroes. But before the end of *Absalom, Absalom!* we learn that miscegenation is only part of it. When Charles Bon's curious actions are explained, we find that he was taking revenge on his father for having refused to recognize him by so much as a glance. Thus, heartlessness was the "mistake" that ruined Sutpen, not the taking of a partly Negro wife and Negro concubines.

The point becomes even clearer in the long fourth part of that tremendous story "The Bear." When the protagonist, Isaac Mc-Caslin, is twenty-one he insists on relinquishing the big plantation that is his by inheritance; he thinks that the land is cursed. It is cursed in his eyes by the deeds of his grandfather: "that evil and un-regenerate old man who could summon, because she was his property, a human being because she was old enough and female, to his widower's house and get a child on her and then dismiss her because she was of an inferior race, and then bequeath a thousand dollars to the infant because he would be dead then and wouldn't have to pay it." At this point Faulkner seems to be speaking through Ike Mc-Caslin. The lesson is that the land was cursed—and the Civil War was part of the curse—because its owners had treated human beings as instruments; in a word, it was cursed by slavery.

All through his boyhood, Faulkner must have dreamed of fighting in the Civil War. It was a Sartoris war and not a Snopes war, like the later one in which he had enlisted for service in a foreign army. And yet his sympathies did not wholly lie with the slave-holding clan of Sartoris, even though it was his own clan. The men he most admired and must have pictured himself as resembling were the Southern soldiers—after all, they were the vast majority—who owned no slaves themselves and suffered from the institution of slavery. The men he would praise in his novels were those "who had fought for four years and lost . . . not because they were opposed to freedom as freedom, but for the old reasons for which man (not the generals and politicians but man) has always fought and died in wars: to preserve a status quo or establish a better future one to endure for his children." One might define the author's position as that of an antislavery Southern nationalist.

Faulkner's novels of contemporary Southern life [those written before 1945] continue the legend into a period that he regards as one of moral confusion and social decay. He is continually seeking in them for violent images to convey his sense of outrage. *Sanctuary* is the most violent of all his novels; it has been the most popular and is by no means the least important (in spite of Faulkner's comment that it was "a cheap idea . . . deliberately conceived to make money"). The story of Popeye and Temple Drake has more meaning than appears on a first hasty reading—the only reading that early critics were willing to grant it. Popeye himself is one of several characters in Faulkner's novels who represent the mechanical civilization that has invaded and conquered the South. He is always described in mechanical terms: his eyes "looked like rubber knobs"; his face "just went awry, like the face of a wax doll set too near a hot fire and forgotten"; his tight suit and stiff hat were "all angles, like a modernistic lampshade"; and in general he had "that vicious depthless quality of stamped tin." Popeye was the son of a professional strikebreaker, from whom he had inherited syphilis; he was the grandson of a pyromaniac, and he had spent most of his childhood in an institution. He was the man "who made money and had nothing he could do with it, spend it for, since he knew that alcohol would kill him like poison, who had no friends and had never known a woman" —in other words, he was a compendium of all the hateful qualities that Faulkner assigns to finance capitalism. *Sanctuary* is not a connected allegory, as George Marion O'Donnell condemned it for being—he was the first critic to approach it seriously—but neither is it a mere accumulation of pointless horrors. It is an example of the Freudian method turned backward, being full of sexual nightmares that are in reality social symbols. It is somehow connected in the author's mind with what he regards as the rape and corruption of the South.

In his novels dealing with the present Faulkner makes it clear that the descendants of the old ruling caste have the wish but not the courage or the strength to prevent this new disaster. They are defeated by Popeye (like Horace Benbow), or they run away from him (like Gowan Stevens, who had been to college at Virginia and learned how to drink like a gentleman, but not to fight for his principles), or they are robbed and replaced in their positions of influence by the Snopeses (like old Bayard Sartoris, the president of the bank), or they drug themselves with eloquence and alcohol (like Quentin Compson's father), or they retire into the illusion of being inviolable Southern ladies (like Mrs. Compson, who says, "It can't be simply to flout and hurt me. Whoever God is, He would not permit that. I'm a lady."), or they dwell so much on the past that they are incapable of facing the present (like Reverend Hightower of *Light in August*), or they run from danger to danger (like young Bayard Sartoris) frantically seeking their own destruction. Faulkner's novels are full of well-meaning and even admirable persons, not only the grandsons of the cotton aristocracy, but also pine-hill farmers and storekeepers and sewing-machine agents and Negro cooks and share-croppers; but they are almost all of them defeated by circumstances and they carry with them a sense of their own doom.

They also carry, whether heroes or villains, a curious sense of submission to their fate. "There is not one of Faulkner's characters," says André Gide in his dialogue on "The New American Novelists," "who properly speaking has a soul"; and I think he means that not one of them exercises the faculty of conscious choice between good and evil. They are haunted, obsessed, driven forward by some inner necessity. Like Miss Rosa Coldfield in *Absalom, Absalom!* they exist in "that dream state in which you run without moving from a terror in which you cannot believe, toward a safety in which you have no faith." Or, like the slaves freed by General Sherman's army, in *The Unvanquished*, they blindly follow the road toward any river, believing that it will be their Jordan:

> They were singing, walking along the road singing, not even looking to either side. The dust didn't even settle for two days, because all that night they still passed; we sat up listening to them and the next morning every few yards along the road would be the old ones who couldn't keep up any more, sitting or lying down and even crawling along, calling to the others to help them; and the others—the young ones—not stopping, not even looking at them. "Going to Jordan," they told me. "Going to cross Jordan."

Most of Faulkner's characters, black and white, are a little like that. They dig for gold frenziedly after they have lost their hope of finding it (like Henry Armstid in *The Hamlet* and Lucas Beauchamp in *Go Down, Moses*); or they battle against and survive a Mississippi flood for the one privilege of returning to the state prison farm (like the tall convict in "Old Man"); or, a whole family together, they carry a body through flood and fire and corruption to bury it in the cemetery at Jefferson (like the Bundrens in *As I Lay Dying*); or they tramp the roads week after week in search of men who had promised but never intended to marry them (like Lena Grove, the pregnant woman of *Light in August*); or, pursued by a mob, they turn at the end to meet and accept death (like Joe Christmas in the same novel). Even when they seem to be guided by a conscious purpose, like Colonel Sutpen, it is not something they have chosen by an act of will, but something that has taken possession of them: Sutpen's great design was "not what he wanted to do but what he just had to do, had to do it whether he wanted to or not, because if he did not do it he knew that he could never live with himself for the rest of his life." In the same way, Faulkner himself writes, not what he wants to, but what he just has to write whether he wants to or not.

5   It had better be admitted that most of his novels have some obvious weakness in structure. Some of them combine two or more themes having little relation to each other, as *Light in August* does, while others, like *The Hamlet*, tend to resolve themselves into a series of episodes resembling beads on a string. In *The Sound and the Fury*, which is superb as a whole, we can't be sure that the four sections of the novel are presented in the most effective order; at any rate, we can't fully understand the first section until we have read the three that follow. *Absalom, Absalom!* though at first it strikes us as being pitched in too high a key, is structurally the soundest of all the novels in the Yoknapatawpha series—and it gains power in retrospect; but even here the author's attention seems to shift from the principal theme of Colonel Sutpen's design to the secondary theme of incest and miscegenation.

Faulkner seems best to me, and most nearly himself, either in long stories like "The Bear," in *Go Down, Moses,* and "Old

Man," which was published as half of *The Wild Palms,* and "Spotted Horses," which was first printed separately, then greatly expanded and fitted into the loose framework of *The Hamlet,* or else in the Yoknapatawpha saga as a whole. That is, he has been most effective in dealing with the total situation always present in his mind as a pattern of the South, or else in shorter units which, though often subject to inspired revision, have still been shaped by a single conception. It is by his best that we should judge him, as every other author; and Faulkner at his best—even sometimes at his worst—has a power, a richness of life, an intensity to be found in no other American writer of our time. He has—once again I am quoting from Henry James's essay on Hawthorne—"the element of simple genius, the quality of imagination."

Moreover, he has a brooding love for the land where he was born and reared and where, unlike other writers of his generation, he has chosen to spend his life. It is ". . . this land, this South, for which God has done so much, with woods for game and streams for fish and deep rich soil for seed and lush springs to sprout it and long summers to mature it and serene falls to harvest it and short mild winters for men and animals." So far as Faulkner's country includes the Delta, it is also (in the words of old Ike McCaslin)

> . . . this land which man has deswamped and denuded and
> deriverod in two generations so that white men can own planta-
> tions and commute every night to Memphis and black men own
> plantations and ride in jimcrow cars to Chicago and live in
> millionaires' mansions on Lake Shore Drive, where white men
> rent farms and live like niggers and niggers crop on shares and
> live like animals, where cotton is planted and grows man-tall
> in the very cracks of the sidewalks, and usury and mortgage and
> bankruptcy and measureless wealth, Chinese and African and
> Aryan and Jew, all breed and spawn together.

Here are the two sides of Faulkner's feeling for the South: on the one side, an admiring and possessive love; on the other, a compulsive fear lest what he loves should be destroyed by the ignorance of its native serfs and the greed of traders and absentee landlords.

No other American writer takes such delight in the weather. He speaks in various novels of "the hot still pinewiney silence of the August afternoon"; of "the moonless September dust, the trees along the road not rising soaring as trees should but squatting like huge fowl"; of "the tranquil sunset of October mazy with windless wood-smoke"; of the "slow drizzle of November rain just above the ice point"; of "those windless Mississippi December days which are a sort of Indian summer's Indian summer"; of January and February when there is "no movement anywhere save the low constant smoke . . . and no sound save the chopping of axes and the lonely whistle of the daily trains." Spring in Faulkner's country is a hurried season, "all coming at once, pell mell and disordered, fruit and bloom and leaf, pied meadow and blossoming wood and the long fields shearing dark out of winter's slumber, to the shearing plow." Summer is dust-choked and blazing, and it lasts far into what should be autumn. "That's the one trouble with this country," he says in *As I Lay Dying.* "Everything, weather, all, hangs on too long. Like our rivers, our land: opaque, slow, violent; shaping and creating the life of man in its implacable and brooding image."

And Faulkner loves these people created in the image of the land. After a second reading of the novels, you continue to be impressed by his villains, Popeye and Jason and Flem Snopes; but this time you find more space in your memory for other figures standing a little in the background yet presented by the author with quiet affection: old ladies like Miss Jenny Du Pre, with their sharp-tongued benevolence; shrewd but affable traders like Ratliff, the sewing-machine agent, and Will Varner, with his cotton gin and general store; long-suffering farm wives like Mrs. Henry Armstid (whether her name is Lula or Martha); and backwoods patriarchs like Pappy MacCullum, with his six middle-aged but unmarried sons named after the generals of Lee's army. You remember the big plantation houses that collapse in flames as if a whole civilization were dying, but you also remember men in patched and faded but quite clean overalls sitting on the gallery—here in the North we should call it the porch—of a crossroads store that is covered with posters advertising soft drinks and patent medicines; and you remember the stories they tell while chewing tobacco until the suption is out of it (everything in their world is reduced to anecdote, and every anecdote is based on character). You remember Quentin Compson not in his despairing moments, but riding with his father behind the dogs as they quarter a sedge-grown hillside after quail; and not listening to his father's story, but still knowing every word of it because, as he thought to himself, "You had learned, absorbed it already without the medium of speech somehow from having been born and living beside it, with it, as children will and do; so that what your father was saying did not tell you anything so much as it struck, word by word, the resonant strings of remembering."

Faulkner's novels have the quality of being lived, absorbed, remembered rather than merely observed. And they have what is rare in the novels of our time, a warmth of family affection, brother for brother and sister, the father for his children—a love so warm and proud that it tries to shut out the rest of the world. Compared with that affection, married love is presented as something calculating, and illicit love as a consuming fire. And because the blood relationship is central in his novels, Faulkner finds it hard to create sympathetic characters between the ages of twenty and forty. He is better with children, Negro and white, and incomparably good with older people who preserve the standards that have come down to them "out of the old time, the old days."

In the group of novels beginning with *The Wild Palms* (1939), which attracted so little attention at the time of publication that they seemed to go unread, there is a quality not exactly new to Faulkner—it had appeared already in passages of *Sartoris* and *Sanctuary*—but now much stronger and no longer overshadowed by violence and horror. It is a sort of homely and sobersided frontier humor that is seldom achieved in contemporary writing (except sometimes by Erskine Caldwell, also a Southerner). The horse-trading episodes in *The Hamlet,* and especially the long story of the spotted ponies from Texas, might have been inspired by the Davy Crockett almanacs. "Old Man," the story of the convict who surmounted the greatest of the Mississippi floods, might almost be a continuation of *Huckleberry Finn.* It is as if some older friend of Huck's had taken the raft and drifted on from Aunt Sally Phelps's farm into wilder adventures, described in a wilder style, among Chinese and Cajuns and bayous crawling with alligators. In a curious way, Faulkner combines two of the principal traditions in American letters: the tradition of psychological horror, often close to symbolism, that begins with Charles Brockden Brown, our first professional novelist, and extends through Poe, Melville, Henry James (in his later stories), Stephen Crane, and Hemingway; and the other tradition of frontier humor and realism, beginning with Augustus Longstreet's *Georgia Scenes* and having Mark Twain as its best example.

But the American author he most resembles is Hawthorne, for all their polar differences. They stand to each other as July to December, as heat to cold, as swamp to mountain, as the luxuriant to the meager but perfect, as planter to Puritan; and yet Hawthorne had much the same attitude toward New England that Faulkner has to the South, together with a strong sense of regional particularity. The Civil War made Hawthorne feel that "the North and the South were two distinct nations in opinions and habits, and had better not try to live under the same institutions." In the spring of 1861 he wrote to his Bowdoin classmate Horatio Bridge, "We were never one people and never really had a country." "New England," he said a little later, "is quite as large a lump of earth as my heart can really take in." But it was more than a lump of earth for him; it was a lump of history and a permanent state of consciousness. Like Faulkner in the South, he applied himself to creating its moral fables and elaborating its legends, which existed, as it were, in his solitary heart. Pacing the hillside behind his house in Concord, he listened for a voice; one might say that he lay in wait for it, passively but expectantly, like a hunter behind a rock; then, when it had spoken, he transcribed its words—more cautiously than Faulkner, it is true; with more form and less fire, but with the same essential fidelity. "I have an instinct that I had better keep quiet," he said in a letter to his publisher. "Perhaps I shall have a new spirit of vigor if I wait quietly for it; perhaps not." Faulkner is another author who has to wait for the spirit and the voice. He is not so much a novelist, in the usual sense of being a writer who sets out to observe actions and characters, then fits them into the framework of a story, as he is an epic or bardic poet in prose, a creator of myths that he weaves together into a legend of the South.

AN AFTERWORD

Except for minor revisions that I couldn't help making, that is what I wrote about Faulkner in 1945, on the basis of the seventeen books he had then published. There would be nine additional books in the subsequent years, and eight of them would contribute to the Yoknapatawpha cycle. In the same years there would be a

Mississippi flood of critical studies dealing with various aspects of Faulkner's novels (most often with their symbolic elements). The question is how this chapter might change in emphasis if I were writing it today, in the light of his critical reputation and on the basis of his life's work.

A few of the statements I made in 1945, or quoted with approval from others, would have to be revised on the ground that they do not apply to the later novels. I note, for example, André Gide's comment, "There is not one of Faulkner's characters who properly speaking has a soul"—to which my echo was, "I think he means that not one of them exercises the faculty of conscious choice between good and evil." Though broadly true in 1945, the statement would eventually be riddled with exceptions. Temple Drake, to mention only one of these, had been a morally supine creature from the beginning to the end of *Sanctuary*. Twenty years later, when she reappears in *Requiem for a Nun* (1951), she drives herself into making an agonized confession, and she makes it "to save my soul," which she has discovered for the first time.

Another statement contradicted by Faulkner's later career is that he "finds it difficult to create sympathetic characters between the ages of twenty and forty." Again that is true of the early novels, but the later ones contain many characters between those ages who are meant to elicit not only sympathy but admiration. Nancy Mannigoe, who first appeared in "That Evening Sun"—"a nigger dopefiend whore," as Temple calls her—has become the saint or nun for whom Faulkner sounds a requiem. The villains forgo a little of their villainy, and one of them, Mink Snopes, is the real hero of *The Mansion* (1959). There are even happy endings of the conventional type. Lucas Beauchamp is saved from being lynched (*Intruder in the Dust*, 1948). Temple Drake, having found a soul, goes back to her husband and her surviving child. Gavin Stevens (in *Knight's Gambit*, 1949) stops talking long enough to marry a widow to whom he had first proposed when she was a girl of sixteen.

In Faulkner's later novels, the Yoknapatawpha story is traced backward to the founding and naming of Jefferson, as well as being carried forward almost to the time of his death. Those novels might be regarded as sequels to the earlier books, yet they almost seem to be written by a different man. The sense of doom and outrage that brooded over the early ones has been replaced by pity for human beings, even the worst of them ("The poor sons of bitches," Gavin Stevens says, "they do the best they can") and by the obstinate faith, expressed in the Nobel Prize address, "that man will not only endure; he will prevail"—all this combined with more than a touch of old-fashioned sentiment. In Faulkner's case, as in those of many other writers, there had been a return to the fathers. I respect the later author, with most of his demons exorcised, but the younger possessed and unregenerate Faulkner is the man whose works amaze us, as they never ceased to puzzle and amaze himself.

Even in a chapter confined to those works, I should, if I were writing it today, adopt a somewhat different emphasis. In 1945 I was arguing against the scandalous neglect of his novels. Not only were they little read at the time, but it seemed to me, as I kept saying, that hardly any critic had looked for a general design in which one novel was linked to another. So it was the design that I chiefly emphasized: the imaginative effort to understand the present in terms of the past that led Faulkner to elaborate a legend of Southern history. In so doing I shifted my attention from book to book without pausing long enough on any one of them—even *The Sound and the Fury* or *Absalom, Absalom!*—and without examining each of them as a separate achievement. Fortunately that emphasis has been corrected and overcorrected by a host of later critics.

Perhaps I dwelt too much on what is in the foreground, that is, on the story of a single county in northern Mississippi presented as, in Faulkner's words, "that chronicle which was a whole land in miniature, which multiplied and compounded was the entire South." Faulkner in his early novels is indubitably a Southern nationalist and an heir of the Confederacy—for all his sense of guilt about the Negroes—but he is something else besides, a fact that I failed to make sufficiently clear. What he regarded as his ultimate subject is not the South or its destiny, however much they occupied his mind, but rather the human situation as revealed in Southern terms—to quote from one of his letters, "the same frantic steeplechase toward nothing everywhere." He approached that steeplechase in terms of Southern material because, as he also said, "I just happen to know it, and dont have time in one life to learn another one and write at the same time." There was of course another reason, for it was the South that aroused his apprehensions, that deeply engaged his loyalties ("*I dont. I dont hate it!*"), and that set his imagination to work. He dreamed, however, that his Yoknapatawpha story might stand for the human drama everywhere and always. Thus, he said in a famous interview with Jean Stein (reprinted in *Writers at Work*, 1958), "I like to think of the world I created as being a kind of keystone in the universe; that, small as the keystone is, if it were ever taken away the universe itself would collapse."

VIII WOLFE
Homo Scribens

In the summer of 1931 Thomas Wolfe was living in the Syrian quarter of Brooklyn, alone as always. He was trying hard to write a second novel while spending some of his nights with an attractive young woman in Manhattan. At last she wrote him one of those serious letters which, for lovers both living on the subway circuit, foreshadow either marriage or the end of an affair. Wolfe wasn't looking forward to either alternative, but he didn't rush over to see the young woman, as she doubtless hoped he would do. Instead he wrote another serious letter that began

> Dear ————:
>
> I just found your special delivery upstairs and my first impulse on reading it was to call you up right away. But your letter seemed so fine and clear to me that I thought I would try to answer you in the same way, before talking to you, and I wonder that I did not try it before—this is my usual means of expression—paper and pencil—and I believe I can be much more direct and less confused in this way than in conversation.

The letter went on for more than twenty pages of Wolfe's urgent scrawl. It was admirably frank and considerate, and it said at great length what could have been said less clearly, but more effectively for his purpose, in a few stammered words and an embrace. Wolfe was never at home in those other languages that most persons employ in most of their intimate relations: the language of gestures, the language of hints and indirections. He was completely articulate only when he had a pencil in his long fingers, but then he was more at home than anyone else who has lived on this continent.

He thought as if with the pencil that raced over sheet after sheet. Sometimes he wrote a letter to discover how he felt, and it might even be the writing that gave birth to his feelings. There are letters in which he started calmly, grew angry as he wrote, then furious, but overcame his fury in expressing it and was reconciled before the scrawled signature. Some of his most revealing letters were never mailed, but they had served a purpose: they satisfied his passion for digesting every experience into written words.

What he wrote he saved, as other persons save money or heirlooms or press clippings and photographs. This particular letter, not one of the unmailed ones, has a history that casts light on more than one aspect of Wolfe's character. After the affair was broken off, he demanded that the letter be returned—perhaps because he was afraid that the young woman would use it against him, for he had periods of unreasoning suspicion; but he must have wanted it for another reason too. Doubtless he thought that it might eventually be used in a section of the many-volumed novel—"the book," as he called it—in which he tried to include everything he had felt or thought or observed, the whole world of Thomas Wolfe.

Long after his death in 1938, Elizabeth Nowell, his literary agent and loyal friend, found the letter among his papers in the Houghton Library at Harvard. She printed it with seven hundred others, mailed and unmailed, in a collection that helps to advance his own design. The Selected Letters of Thomas Wolfe (1957) includes everything of importance except the letters to his mother, which had already been printed, and the more intimate letters to the late Aline Bernstein, which Mrs. Bernstein had some notion—never carried out—of publishing separately. The result is a very large volume, as seems appropriate to Wolfe, and one that bears no resemblance to the usual interesting collection of letters that reflect a time, a place, or an order of society.

Not much of the world is reflected here. There is little discussion of public affairs, there is almost no gossip, personal or literary, and there are no sidelights on famous characters; in fact, Wolfe's correspondence can hardly be said to depict any characters except the author and his editor Maxwell Perkins. There is not much of the "you" except when he is writing to his family; many or most of the other letters might have been addressed To Whom It May Concern. Essentially they are letters from Thomas Wolfe about Thomas Wolfe; their action is reflexive. They are a man expressing himself, explaining himself, and painting a self-portrait. They are the story of a man writing a novel about a man writing a novel.

But the story is no less absorbing for having been told elsewhere. A boy from the North Carolina mountains with an insatiable appetite for experience is reared not in poverty, but in emotional promiscuity and squalor. He goes to the state university, goes to Harvard, goes to New York, and there pours his resentments into a book. At twenty-nine he finds himself a famous author without ceasing to be a small-town boy at heart. He has fiercer joys and sorrows than other people, but achieves a sort of maturity; then he dies at thirty-seven on what seems to be the threshold of a greater career. That is the story as Wolfe has told it (except for the ending) in his novels; and the letters—with the subsequent biography by Andrew Turnbull—confirm what we had more than suspected: that most of his fiction was fact. But they also change the values of the story, giving it a logic that had seemed to be lacking, so that it becomes a problem in human geometry, with axioms, postulates, and a solution, QED. Given a certain type of literary ambition, given a high level of talent and an intense devotion, what comes afterward?

1   Wolfe was determined to be a great writer, like many other boys of his generation, but his determination was more obsessive than that of others—except perhaps Hemingway—and it was based on a special type of emotional need. It also led to a special program, which is most clearly announced in one of the early letters to his

Thomas Wolfe boarding a streetcar in Berlin, 1936.

159 WOLFE: HOMO SCRIBENS

mother. The letter started calmly, with news of the play he had written for Professor Baker's 47 Workshop at Harvard and a hint that Baker thought he would have a brilliant future. Then, growing excited as he wrote, Wolfe spoke of his plans. "I intend to wreak out my soul on paper," he said, "and express it all. This is what my life means to me: I am at the mercy of this thing and I will do it or die." The next sentence reveals the nature of the "all" that he was going to express at the risk of his life. "I never forget," he said, "I have never forgotten. I have tried to make myself conscious of the whole of my life since first the baby in the basket became conscious of the warm sunlight on the porch, and saw his sister go up the hill to the girl's school on the corner (the first thing I remember)." That happened when Tom was eighteen months old, and one finds it recorded in *Look Homeward, Angel*: ". . . the second Spring, one warm day, he saw Daisy go off to school up the hill; it was the end of the noon recess, she had been home for lunch." And so it was with many other tumultuous memories recorded in that letter to his mother. If the remembered events took place before he left North Carolina, they would reappear in *Look Homeward, Angel*; if afterward, they went into *Of Time and the River* or the posthumous novels. None of these was a novel in the ordinary sense; all were taken from an immense store of conscious memories.

"This is why I think I'm going to be an artist," he said at the end of the letter after setting down his catalogue of impressions. "The things that really mattered sank in and left their mark." Then came the program he would follow at any cost, even that of shortening his life. "I will go everywhere and do everything. I will meet all the people I can. I will think all the thoughts, feel all the emotions I am able, and I will write, write, write."

He was starting with a better than usual equipment for carrying out such a program. His ambition was matched by an unflagging energy that is a talent in itself, indispensable for his type of writing, and the energy was supported by a strong physical constitution. He had the build of an All American tackle: he was six feet seven inches tall, long armed and barrel chested, with a powerful heart. He could endure hunger, cold, and sleeplessness like an Arctic explorer, could gorge himself on meat like an Eskimo, and could withstand savage doses of coffee, tobacco, and alcohol. He had a good mind in the conventional use of the term; that is, he made high marks at school and college, which he finished before he was twenty, and later at the Harvard Graduate School. He reasoned clearly and—a curious point about an author who depended so much on sensation—he won special distinction in a course in logic. More important is the fact that his mental operations were almost completely verbalized, so that he seldom groped for a word. Many of his letters dashed off at top speed are careless masterpieces of eloquence.

He was a teachable person, in the sense that he had a rather uncommon capacity for being helped by his elders. There were four of these, outside the family, who played a decisive part in his career. The first was Mrs. Margaret Roberts, who, with her husband, ran the boys' school that Tom attended in Asheville. In one of his letters he addresses her as "you mother of my spirit who fed me with light." The second was a father figure, George Pierce Baker of the 47 Workshop, who believed in the integrity of Wolfe's talent and kept telling him, "Write! Write! Do nothing else." The third was Aline Bernstein, whom he met on a boat returning from Europe in the summer of 1925; she was a little round woman, kind and practical, who had become a successful stage designer and was nineteen years older than Wolfe. As he said of his autobiographical hero Eugene Gant, "something always turned him to older women." Mrs. Bernstein introduced him to her wealthy friends, taught him to be more nearly at ease in company, and, in their five years together, I suspect that he acquired from her some of the gentleness and consideration that were mingled with his wildness.

Maxwell Evarts Perkins, his editor at Scribners, was the last and closest of those elder friends. Wolfe regarded him as a spiritual father, while Perkins—who had five children, all daughters—treated Wolfe as an only son. At last the son broke away from the father, in a letter of twelve thousand words—most of Wolfe's decisive steps were taken by writing letters—but he continued to depend on Perkins and express his gratitude. Indeed, he was grateful to all his foster parents, even when he quarreled with them, and before the end he was reconciled with all except Baker, who had died too soon.

But more than he relied on his capacity for learning from others—and the lessons had to be those he wanted to learn—more than he relied on his energy or strength or intelligence, Wolfe relied on his memory, or rather on a peculiar quality of his memory. He says in that fascinating little book *The Story of a Novel* (1936):

> The quality of my memory is characterized, I believe, in more than ordinary degree by the intensity of its sense perceptions, its power to evoke and bring back the odors, sounds, colors, shapes, and feel of things with concrete vividness. . . . I would be sitting, for example, on the terrace of a café watching the flash and play of life before me on the Avenue de l'Opéra and suddenly I would remember the iron railing that goes along the boardwalk at Atlantic City. I could see it instantly just the way it was, the heavy iron pipe; its raw, galvanized look; the way the joints were fitted together. . . . Or again it would be a bridge, the look of an old iron bridge across an American river, the sound the train makes as it goes across it; the spoke-and-hollow rumble of the ties below . . . or it would be, most lonely and haunting of all the sounds I know, the sound of a milk wagon as it enters an American street just at the first gray of the morning, the slow and lonely clopping of the hoof upon the street, the jink of bottles, the sudden rattle of a battered old milk can, the swift and hurried footsteps of the milkman, and again the jink of bottles, a low word spoken to his horse, and then the great, slow, clopping hoof receding into silence.

Besides the intensity and exactness of such impressions, there was another feature of his memory, or rather of the experiences preserved in it, that gave an urgency to his writing. Many of the experiences had a background and color that had never been portrayed in literature. There were tender-minded persons at the time who believed that events had to reach a certain order of seemliness or dignity before they were worthy of being treated in drama or fiction. Wolfe had quite a different feeling. "There is nothing so commonplace, so dull," he had told his mother, "that is not touched with nobility and dignity." He knew that his mother would understand, because he had been talking about events in their own household. They belonged to a family of "good people," in the Southern phrase, which means hard-working people, self-respecting and without pretensions. The name Wolfe was Pennsylvania German, and

Tom's father was a stonecutter born near Gettysburg. The Westalls, his mother's family, were Scotch-Irish from the Carolina mountains. On both sides they were eloquent talkers, but they had never tried to preserve their talk on paper. Tom was the first writer among them, or in the little city where they lived, and his voice had more power because he was conscious of speaking for the silent generations and of giving them a sort of posthumous nobility. Like Dreiser in this respect, he was a new man, speaking for a new order of society, in a country that was still new in literature.

2 ⚞ "I would sit there," he says in the same passage of *The Story of a Novel*, "looking out upon the Avenue de l'Opéra and my life would ache with the whole memory" of his own country; "the desire to see it again; somehow to find a word for it; a language that would tell its shape, its color, the way we have all known and felt and seen it. And when I understood this thing, I saw that I must find for myself the tongue to utter what I knew but could not say." If there is a central criticism of Wolfe's writing, it is that he found the language too easily. It contains new words, such as "stogged" and "jink," but most of it consists of words and phrases remembered from his voracious reading. There are new impressions and effects, but they are weakened by his talent for rapid verbalization. He did not stop to look for the one adjective that would be both right and surprising; if in doubt he set down three adjectives, because they came faster and because he trusted that each of them would supply the deficiencies in the other two. Sometimes the habit made him sound absurd, as in a letter addressed to his publisher's reader, which he submitted with the two-foot-thick manuscript of *Look Homeward, Angel*. "Generally," he said with a touch of pleonasm, "I do not believe the writing to be wordy, prolix, or redundant."

He wrote obsessively, "like a fiend"—the phrase keeps recurring in his letters—or "as if pursued by devils." "It may be before I am through," he told Margaret Roberts, "that I shall say something important—that in the mad rush to get it down, something of high worth may come out." Meanwhile he kept quoting production figures, like the manager of a busy mine from which words were being drilled and blasted like chunks of ore. Thus he reported in 1926: "I am writing about 3,000 words a day, which I hope to increase to 4,000. The novel will be Dickensian or Meredithian in length, but the work of cutting—which of course means adding an additional 50,000 words—will come later." In 1933: "I have written over a million words in manuscript the past four years, which make a box five feet long by two and one-half feet wide piled to the top." In 1934: "I have written 75,000 words or more the last three weeks, which ought to be some sort of record."

Of course it was by no means a record in respect to mere wordage. Upton Sinclair, when he was a young man employed to write half-dime novels, used to produce thirty thousand words every week with the help of two secretaries, a morning secretary who typed in the afternoon and an afternoon secretary who typed the next morning. In the 1930s one of the radio moguls emitted—one could hardly say that he wrote—a hundred thousand words in a single week with the help of a dictating machine, but those were the limp words of three soap operas. Wolfe, on the other hand, was working at high tension in the effort to preserve his inmost feelings. The seventy-five thousand words that he claimed to have written in three weeks of June 1934—by actual count there were less than one-half as many—were the account of his father's death that appeared in *Of Time and the River*, and they were among the best words of his brief career. To produce them in three weeks, or in twice that time, might still be regarded as some sort of record.

In July of that same year he told a friend, "The sheer physical labor has been enormous. I can't use the typewriter, and have to write every word with my hand, and during the last four years, as I estimate it, I have written about two million words." Wolfe's reports of production were always on the hopeful side. Another estimated two million words—in a packing case that he turned over to his last editor, Edward C. Aswell of Harpers, before setting out on a trip to the West—were actually a little more than one million. The thirty thousand words of notes that he claimed to have made on the trip were 11,400 when counted. Those errors in themselves revealed his rage for production at any cost, including that of accuracy.

What was behind the rage? In different cases the will to write may be explained as the result of different emotional needs (beyond the simple wish to be rich and famous that writers share with people in other professions). There are some writers who aim primarily to instruct or persuade or dominate; they want to be shepherds of the public. Often they excel in rhetoric, the art of persuasion. Other writers are obsessed with the idea of creating perfect objects that will outlast their creators; such men are the makers or builders, the masters of form, and sometimes the journeymen carpenters. Wolfe had both those purposes, together with the desire for fame, but they were subordinated in him to a primary need for pouring out the contents of his mind. The special gift he had was for self-expression, not for persuasion or construction. He thought of himself not as a shepherd or prophet, not as a craftsman producing artifacts, but rather as an active force of nature: a mountain torrent, a geyser, or a volcano in almost constant eruption. His last postcard to his friend Hamilton Basso was mailed from Yellowstone Park; it was a picture of Old Faithful, with the note: "Portrait of the author at the two million word point."

He wanted to pour out everything he remembered in one torrential flood, but he also wanted to increase his reservoir of memories by going everywhere and doing everything. He wanted to absorb the whole world into his mind; Wolfe himself might have said that he wanted to *devour* the world with everything it contained —persons, books, landscapes, joys, sorrows—and then digest it into written words. "The world is a large, large oyster," he wrote to George Pierce Baker, "but I do not think that I will choke when I swallow it." His letters are full of alimentary images. Writing to Margaret Roberts about his voracious hunger for books, "I suppose I make a mistake," he said, "trying to eat the plums all at once." Later he told her that the desire to write had become "almost a crude animal appetite." He made similar remarks to other correspondents: "I am devouring the German language in gluttonous gobs. . . . I had indigestion from seeing and trying to take in too much. . . . If you ever hear the sad news of my sudden and tragic extinction, which God forbid you won't, I want you to remember that I was not a man who starved to death but a man who died of gluttony, choking to death on an abundance of food, which surpassed everything but his hunger."

The hunger was actual as well as figurative; in Wolfe's last year he used to dine on two large steaks every evening. Yet one suspects that his talk of swallowing the world partly served to conceal an instinct that lay deeper in him, setting him apart from other writers of the period and from all but a few writers of any period: an instinct for acquiring property. When he imprinted an experience on his mind, it was rescued from time the destroyer and became his lasting possession. When he transformed it into words on paper, it became a tangible possession, almost like family silver; or it might better be compared to bills of sale and warranty deeds that testified to his ownership of so many places, so many persons, so many emotions—an imperial domain that he held in secret and without a rival.

No wonder he made a point of saving everything he wrote. As each episode was completed, it would be tied in a bundle like stock certificates and dropped into the big packing case that served as his safe-deposit vault. Only the unpublished manuscripts went into the case; the others had become public property, so to speak, and Wolfe gladly sold them to collectors for what they would bring. Eventually there were three of the big pine boxes, all standing in the center of his parlor at the Hotel Chelsea, in Manhattan. Besides manuscripts they contained unmailed letters, receipted bills, cooking pots, old shoes and hats, and an electric iron that somebody had given him. Wolfe hated to buy things for himself, but when he acquired them by gift or accident, he couldn't bear to throw them away.

His mother was like that too. He said in *Look Homeward, Angel* that her room "was festooned with a pendent wilderness of cord and string; stacks of old newspapers and magazines were piled in the corners; and every shelf was loaded with gummed, labeled, half-filled medicine bottles." With money saved from her boarding-house, the Old Kentucky Home, Mrs. Wolfe bought real estate first in Asheville, then in Florida during the boom. She lost her little fortune because, though she loved to buy, she waited too long to sell; what she enjoyed was the sense of possessing a great deal of property. Her youngest son took after her in an unexpected fashion. His money "melted away like snow," as he kept complaining; it dripped through his fingers for grand meals, for wine and tips and taxis (seldom for clothes and almost never for furniture); but still he had his precious hoard in the packing cases; he was a millionaire of words.

"You can say that I have come through the great depression," he wrote to Kyle Crichton, then on the staff of *Scribner's Magazine*, "with over a million words of manuscript and a large, hard wart on my second finger, as my tangible accumulations." To his brother Fred he wrote, before setting out on his last trip to Asheville in the summer of 1937, "My main concern is, of course, my manuscript. There is an immense amount of it, millions of words, and although it might not be of any use to anyone else, it is, so far as I am concerned, the most valuable thing I have got. My life is in it— years and years of work and sweating blood—and the material of about three unpublished books." He was eager to have the books published; that was his normal desire for fame and influence over the minds of others; but he was also afraid to have them published, because that would rob him of his accumulated hoard. It would expose the hoard to critical strangers, some of whom would be certain to say that it wasn't gold at all, but brass, while others (especially Bernard De Voto) would claim that it hadn't been honestly earned, but was all owed to the help of "Maxwell Perkins and the assembly line at Scribner's."

Wolfe's sense of loss and his fear of criticism were both stronger than his desire for fame, with the result that the publication of each novel drove him into a fit of black despair. After *Look Homeward, Angel* appeared in England, he wrote from Europe to John Hall Wheelock of Scribners, "There is no life in this world worth living, there is no air worth breathing, there is nothing but agony and the drawing of the breath in nausea and labor, until I get the best of this tumult and sickness inside me." He said to Max Perkins in a letter of the same day, "I shall not write any more books." After *Of Time and the River* was published in the spring of 1935, he again went to Europe and was out of his mind for several days. "In Paris I couldn't sleep at all," he wrote to Perkins. "I walked the streets from night to morning and was in the worst shape I have ever been in my life. All the pent-up strain and tension of the last few months seemed to explode and I will confess to *you* that there were times when I really was horribly afraid of going mad—all the unity and control of personality seemed to have escaped from me— it was as if I were on the back of some immense rackety engine which was running wild and over which I had no more control than a fly."

In the same letter to Perkins, he tried to rationalize his regret that *Of Time and the River* had been published. "The great length of the book will be criticized," he said, "but the real, the tragic truth is that the book is not too long but too short. I am not talking of page-length, word-length, or anything like that—as I told you many times, I did not care whether the final length of the book was 300, 500, or a 1000 pages, so long as I had realized completely and finally my full intention—and that was not realized. I still sweat with anguish—with a sense of irremediable loss—at the thought of what another six months would have done to that book—how much more whole and perfect it would have been." It was Perkins, a truly inspired editor (and an even better one for Wolfe than he was for Fitzgerald and Hemingway), who had told him in December 1933 that the first draft of the novel was ready for revision. It was Perkins who had worked with him on the manuscript every evening for the better part of a year and who had taken it out of his hands chapter by chapter. The last part of the novel had gone to the printer in December 1934 while Wolfe was in Chicago and could not hold it back; otherwise he would have kept adding episodes for another six months . . . another . . . and another. Partly the letter asserts the desire for perfection of any artist who loves his handiwork, but partly it reveals another feeling, almost like that of a landowner when the mortgage has been foreclosed and he is turned away from his own door. The "irremediable loss" Wolfe had suffered was that of his dearest possession, "the most valuable thing I have got," the best of his hoarded millions of words.

3 ✍ During his early days in New York, Wolfe used to write in bound ledgers opened on top of the icebox, so that he stood at his work like a factory hand. Later he wrote at a table, using ordinary sheets of manuscript paper, but more of them than almost anyone else with normal vision except Hemingway. Ninety penciled words to the page was the average for both of them, but Hemingway worked slowly, while Wolfe wrote at top speed, never hesitating for

a word, as if he were taking dictation. The moment a sheet was filled he would push it aside to drop on the floor, without stopping to read it over or even to number it. In the course of his filling thousands of sheets with millions of words, the wart he developed on the second finger of his right hand became "almost as large and hard," he said, "but not as valuable, as a gambler's diamond." He was not so much an author of books as a member of that much less familiar species the writing man, *Homo scribens*. His life was spent in conjugating a single verb—*scribam, scripsi, scriptum est*—with the result that his working habits and problems are more interesting to study than the works themselves. Indeed, they reveal the works in an unexpected light and help to explain why their real virtues were achieved at an inevitable cost to the writing man and his readers.

The first of his problems was how to maintain a steady flow of words from the vast reservoir of his conscious memories to the moving tip of his pencil. Before the flow could be established he would go through weeks or months of self-torture, walking the Brooklyn streets at night, fleeing to Europe, staying drunk for days on end. Once the flow started it might continue for months, during which his pencil sprayed out words like water from a hose. "You forget to eat, to shave, to put on a clean shirt when you have one," says Wolfe's autobiographical hero George Webber in *You Can't Go Home Again*. "You almost forget to sleep, and when you do try to you can't—because the avalanche has started and it keeps going night and day. . . . You can't stop yourself—and even if you could you'd be afraid to because there'd be all that hell to go through getting started up again."

Revision formed part of his system too, but not the usual sort of revision that consists in making interlinear changes, then having the draft retyped. "When he was dissatisfied with a scene or character," said his last editor, who had watched him working, ". . . he would put it aside, and rewrite it some different way from start to finish." In other words, he had to start the flow over again and continue until he had reached the end of an episode. He would remember new details and incidents the second time, so that his rewritten manuscripts were longer—often several times longer—than the first drafts. After being copied by a typist, they were, as I said, bundled and put away in one of the big pine packing boxes. Then, in another frenzy of production, he might go to work on a new episode, often one remembered from a different period of his life.

His friends wondered how it was that he could reach into a packing box and, after a little fumbling, produce the desired episode, even if it had been written months or years before. I think the answer must be that he had his own filing system, chronological by subject matter. If the episode belonged to his boyhood, it would go below the episodes relating to his studies at Harvard, which in turn went below his years of teaching at Washington Square College and his love affair with Aline Bernstein, which went below his struggles to write a second novel. All were parts of "the book" into which he planned to transcribe his life and world and time as a continuous flow of memories. His ambition, announced by George Webber, was "to use myself to the top of my bent. To use everything I have. To milk the udder dry, squeeze out the last drop, until there is nothing left."

Unfortunately the book of his life was too big to be published or even to be written. His memories would have to be divided into separate books, or novels, and each of these would have to be more than a chronological succession of events; it would also have to possess its own structure and controlling theme. That was the problem of changing flow into form, one that always puzzled him and for which he found a solution only in his first novel, as if without trying.

Look Homeward, Angel has a natural unity because, as Wolfe said in a letter to Margaret Roberts, it is "the story of a powerful creative element"—the author as a boy—"trying to work its way toward an essential isolation; a creative solitude; a secret life— its fierce struggles to wall this part of its life away from birth, first against the public and savage glare of an unbalanced, nervous, brawling family group, later against school, society, all the barbarous invasions of the world." As always with Wolfe, it is a book of memories, but these are shaped and controlled by a theme close to the author's heart, the familiar theme of the young artist in a hostile environment. It has a natural beginning, which is the artist's birth, and a natural end, which is his escape from the environment.

Moreover, it has the advantage of having been conceived with a literary model in mind. As Wolfe said of himself while pretending to speak of George Webber, "He was still very much under the influence of James Joyce, and what he had written was a *Ulysses* kind of book." The confession seems puzzling. On the face of it *Look Homeward* is not a *Ulysses* kind of book, but another portrait of the artist as a young man. Almost the only hints of *Ulysses* are a few stylistic devices, a few borrowed mannerisms, and an implied equation: Asheville equals Dublin. It seems strange that Wolfe should acknowledge those debts with humility.

There is, however, a simple explanation. Like most readers in the 1920s, who were approaching a difficult new work without the help of commentators, he had missed a great deal of what Joyce was trying to do: for instance, the meaning of Bloom's adventures, most of the parallels with the *Odyssey,* and the reason why different styles are used in different chapters. What he admired in *Ulysses* and tried to emulate was a mixture of other qualities: its accuracy and completeness—for Joyce too had remembered everything—its bawdiness, its defiance of literary conventions, and its presentation of lower-middle-class life in Dublin with a mixture of revulsion and loving care, so that the characters become archetypes, each with a kind of animal integrity. I called *Ulysses* his model, but it was more like a door through which he passed into an exciting new world of literary freedom.

What could he do after writing *Look Homeward*? "I've got too much material," George Webber tells his friend Randy Shepperton. "It keeps backing up on me . . . until sometimes I wonder what in the name of God I'm going to do with it—how I'm going to find a frame for it, a channel, a way to make it flow. . . . Sometimes it actually occurs to me that a man may be able to write no more because he gets drowned in his own secretions." Then after a pause George says, "I'm looking for a way. I think it may be something like what people vaguely mean when they speak of fiction. A kind of legend, perhaps."

In 1930, the year after the publication of *Look Homeward,* Wolfe was looking for a legend into which he could fit everything he had felt and seen after leaving Asheville. Since he was in Europe at the time, and since his strongest emotion, outside of the desire to write another book, was longing for the home he had lost—irretrievably, so he thought, for Asheville people had threatened to lynch him if he came back—he fixed upon the Antaeus legend of the giant born from the marriage of Earth and Water. He gave the legend a special turn, however, to fit his circumstances. In a letter to Max Perkins he explained that the argument of his new book would be

> . . . of the Lybian giant, the brother of Polyphemus, the one-eyed, and the son of Gaea and Poseidon, whom he hath never seen, and through his father, the grandson of Cronos and Rhea, whom he remembereth. He contendeth with all who seek to pass him by, he searcheth alway for his father, he crieth out: "Art thou my father? Is it thou?" and he wrestleth with that man, and he riseth up from each fall with strength redoubled, for his strength cometh up out of the earth, which is his mother. Then cometh against him Heracles, who contendeth with him, who discovereth the secret of his strength, who lifteth him from the earth whence his might ariseth, and subdueth him. But from afar now, in his agony, he heareth the sound of his father's foot: he will be saved for his father cometh!

Of course the giant born of earth was Eugene Gant again, or Wolfe in person. His brother Polyphemus was intended to stand for the sterility that hates life; probably he was to be represented by Francis Starwick, the homosexual dramatist who appears in *Of Time and the River*. Gaea or Earth was to be introduced in the same novel as Mrs. Esther Jack, but the manuscript chapters about her were omitted from the published book and filed away; later they would figure in *The Web and the Rock*. Heracles the antagonist was to be the city of New York. As for the father, Wolfe's plan was that he should never be seen. But in a final chapter called "Pacific End"—later Wolfe thought of it as a final complete book, though he never got round to writing it—Antaeus was to hear "the thunder of horses on a beach (Poseidon and his horses); the moon dives out of clouds; he sees a print of a foot that can belong only to his father, since it is like his own; the sea surges across the beach and erases the print; he cries out 'Father' and from the sea far out, and faint upon the wind, a great voice answers 'My Son!'"

It was a magnificent conception, if slightly overblown, and this time it does suggest *Ulysses*—where we know that Stephen Dedalus stands for Telemachus, Molly Bloom for Penelope, and other characters for Nausicaa, Circe, Polyphemus (again), and the Lotos Eaters. I said that Wolfe hadn't grasped the strict parallels between *Ulysses* and the *Odyssey*, but I was thinking about his first reading of the novel. Before Wolfe formed his project for a second book, Joyce had explained some of his intentions to Stuart Gilbert, who had published hints of them. In an article printed in *The New Republic* (later revised for *Axel's Castle*), Edmund Wilson had offered the first complete interpretation of *Ulysses*, and Wolfe seems to have been fired by reading it. Much more than *Look Homeward, Angel*, his project for writing a second novel reveals his dream of writing "a *Ulysses* kind of book."

Be he was not in the least a Joyce kind of author, that is, a combination of architect on the grand scale and artisan haunted by a dream of minute perfection. He was not a constructivist but an expressionist, in the proper sense of the word, and his need for expression kept changing as his pencil raced over page after page. Soon the Antaeus legend became mixed with others, and the hero—without ceasing to be Thomas Wolfe—was called upon to play the successive parts of Orestes, young Faustus the student, Telemachus, Jason, and Faustus in love. The more Wolfe worked on the book, the farther he seemed from its "Pacific End." By the fourth year after the publication of *Look Homeward*, he had written a million words, on his own estimate, and the great conception was buried as if under lava. Of course it was Perkins who saved him, by suggesting how he might make a novel out of one segment of the material, while saving the rest for other books. Even then almost half the segment had to be pared away before *Of Time and the River* could be published (1935) in 912 pages.

The plan he evolved for a third big novel was less Joycean or Wagnerian. As he described the book in a letter to Aswell, his new editor, "It is about one man's discovery of life and the world, and in this sense it is a book of apprenticeship." The hero's name would be changed from Eugene Gant to George Webber, and his height would shrink from Gant's six feet six to five feet nine; Wolfe was looking for a protagonist whose angle of vision did not duplicate the author's, so that his world could be treated more objectively. Webber would be the eternal innocent on his painful way to knowledge—another Candide or Wilhelm Meister—and the lessons he learned would be summed up in the title, *You Can't Go Home Again*. That meant, Wolfe explained,

. . . back home to one's family, back home to romantic love, to a young man's dreams of glory and of fame, back home to exile, to escape to "Europe" and some foreign land, back home to lyricism, singing for just singing's sake, back home to aestheticism, to one's youthful ideas of the "artist," and the all-sufficiency of "art and beauty and love," back home to the ivory tower, back home to places in the country, the cottage in Bermuda away from all the strife and conflict of the world, back home to the father one is looking for—to someone who can help one, save one, ease the burden for one, back home to the old forms and systems of things that once seemed everlasting, but that are changing all the time—back home to the escapes of Time and Memory. Each of these discoveries, sad and hard as they are to make and accept, are described in the book almost in the order in which they are named here. But the conclusion is not sad: this is a hopeful book—the conclusion is that although you can't go home again, the home of every one of us is in the future: there is no other way.

Here was another grand conception, and one better suited to Wolfe's working habits than that of his second novel had been, for it was loose enough so that one episode after another could be fitted into the scheme. But already, as he worked on it, the episodes had proliferated and some of them had grown almost to the length of separate books. His immense store of memories was imposing its own pattern on the narrative, or its lack of pattern. The bandy-legged figure of George Webber was being presented less and less objectively until it became indistinguishable from the author's figure; George seemed to grow taller as one looked at him. By the spring of 1938 Wolfe had once again written more than a million words—two million by his own count—and turned them over to Aswell. Most of the words—too many of them—were published after his death in *The Web and the Rock* (1939), *You Can't Go Home Again* (1940), and part of *The Hills Beyond* (1941). It was Aswell who put the material together. No one can say how Wolfe himself would have finished "the book," or group of books, or in how much time, or how and whether, if he had lived, he could have brought himself to relinquish all that wealth of words.

But although he was incapable of solving the larger problem of form, he did solve a lesser problem in a way that is often overlooked. Wolfe's unit of construction was the episode, not the scene or chapter or novel. He always had trouble connecting the episodes, some of which, as I said, were almost the length of books. Two of the best are "The Web of Earth" and "A Portrait of Bascom Hawke," both of which were printed in *Scribner's Magazine,* although the "Portrait" was afterward taken apart and fitted into *Of Time and the River.* Other fine episodes are the long passage about the death of old Gant, written for inclusion in the same novel while Wolfe and Perkins were revising it; the account of the students in Professor Hatcher's (or Baker's) famous course in the drama; the disintegration of Francis Starwick; the story of Nebraska Crane (partly in *The Web and the Rock* and partly in *You Can't Go Home Again*); and the visit to Nazi Germany called "I Have a Thing to Tell You." If these had each been published separately, in versions based on the original manuscripts, Wolfe might have gained a different reputation, not as an epic poet in prose, but as the author of short novels and portraits, little masterpieces of sympathy and penetration. But with his mania for bigness, one can't be sure that he would have enjoyed that other kind of fame.

4 ✍ Most of Wolfe's faults as a writer were closely and fraternally connected with his virtues; both resulted from his method of composition. Take for example the fault most frequently and justifiably urged against him, that he was unable to criticize his own work, that he couldn't distinguish what was good in it from what was absurd or pretentious, and that he wouldn't take criticism from others. Wolfe acknowledged the fault even when he was a very young man. At twenty-two he said in a letter to Professor Baker, "I admit the virtue of being able to stand criticism. Unfortunately it is a virtue I do not happen to possess." It wasn't that he was lacking either in humility of a sort or in critical talent. One couldn't talk to him about books for ten minutes without finding that he was perceptive and discriminating about other people's work, if he had read it. He didn't apply that type of discrimination to his own work not

through inability to do so, as he sometimes said, but chiefly as a matter of policy.

In a sense he chose to be only half of an author. The usual author is two persons or personalities working in partnership. One of them says the words to himself, then writes them down; the other listens to the words, or reads them, and then silently exclaims, "This is good, this is what you wanted to say, but *this*! Can't you say it again and say it better?" A result of the dialogue between the writer and the reader within is that the usual manuscript moves ahead spasmodically—a sentence or two, a pause while another sentence is phrased and rejected and rephrased, then a rapidly written paragraph or two, then another pause while reader and writer argue silently (or even aloud) about what has been said, then the sound of a page crumpled and dropped into the wastebasket, then a day's interval, perhaps, then other pages that go better. . . .

With time always pressing him, Wolfe couldn't afford to stumble ahead by a process of inner dialectic. There had to be that uninterrupted flow of memories from mind to paper; if he once questioned the value of the memories or changed the words that came to him, the flow halted for the day or night or perhaps for weeks. The solution he found instinctively, but later supported with arguments, was to suppress the critical side of his nature, or at least to keep it silent until an episode was finished; then if the inner critic objected to what he had written, he would do it over from the beginning, again without allowing the critic to interrupt. It was an effective system for producing words—very often accurate and truly inspired words—but it involved a great deal of wasted effort for the writer and wasted time for the reader of his published work.

Another fault urged against him is his use of formulas, including stock phrases, paired nouns or verbs where only one is needed ("grief and anguish," "sneered at and derided"), as well as the inevitable and therefore useless epithet. Here again the fault results from his system of writing and is closely connected with virtues that it helped him to achieve. Wolfe composed his novels, or rather the episodes that went into his novels, much as ancient bards, standing before a company of warriors, composed their epic poems. Like them, if for different reasons, he had to maintain an unbroken flow of words, with the result that there had to be moments when his pencil moved automatically while his mind was preparing the next powerful effect. I couldn't help thinking of Wolfe when reading a passage in Moses Finley's illuminating book, *The World of Odysseus*:

> The repeated formula is indispensable in heroic poetry: The bard composes directly before his audience; he does not recite memorized lines. In 1934, at the request of Professor Milman Parry, a sixty-year-old Serbian bard who could neither read nor write recited for him a poem of the length of the *Odyssey*, making it up as he went along, yet retaining meter and form and building a complicated narrative. The performance took two weeks, with a week in between, the bard chanting for two hours each morning and two more in the afternoon.
>
> Such a feat makes enormous demands in concentration on both the bard and his audience. That it can be done at all is attributable to the fact that the poet, a professional with long years of apprenticeship behind him, has at his disposal the necessary raw materials: masses of incidents and masses of formulas, the accumulation of generations of minstrels who came before him.

Wolfe was perhaps the only American author of this century who could have duplicated the feat of the Serbian bard. That was because he had the same sort of equipment: partly an enormous store of characters and incidents (drawn from his own experience, not from the traditions of the race), and partly a supply of epithets, metaphors, and synonyms (this time remembered from his early reading) that could be applied to any human situation. His writing was a sort of chant, like the declamation of a Homeric bard. Poetry of a traditional sort can be written faster than prose, and Wolfe kept falling into traditional poetry. His books, especially *Of Time and the River*, are full of lines in Elizabethan blank verse:

Were not their howls far broken by the wind?

huge limbs that stiffly creak in the remote
demented howlings of the burly wind,

and something creaking in the wind at night.

Page after page falls into an iambic pattern, usually a mixture of pentameters and hexameters. Other passages—in fact there is a whole book of them called *A Stone, a Leaf, a Door,* selected from Wolfe's writing by John S. Barnes—are a rather simple kind of cadenced verse:

> *Naked and alone we came into exile.*
> *In her dark womb*
> *We did not know our mother's face.*

Often there are internal rhymes and half-rhymes: "October is the season for *returning*: the bowels of youth are *yearning* with lost love. Their mouths are *dry* and bitter with *desire*: their hearts are *torn* with the *thorns* of spring." Again there are phrases almost meaningless in themselves, but used as musical themes that are stated and restated with variations, sometimes through a whole novel. "A stone, a leaf, a door" is one of the phrases; others are "O lost" and "naked and alone" in *Look Homeward* and "of wandering forever and the earth again," repeated perhaps a hundred times in *Of Time and the River.* All these patterns or devices—cadence, meter, rhyme, assonance, refrains—are those into which the language naturally falls when one is trying to speak or write it passionately and torrentially. They are not the marks of good prose—on the contrary—and yet in Wolfe's case, as in that of a few other natural writers, they are the means of achieving some admirable effects, including an epic movement with its surge and thunder. They also help Wolfe to strike and maintain a *tone,* one that gives his work a unity lacking in its structure, a declamatory tone that he needs for his effort to dignify a new race of heroes and demigods, to suffuse a new countryside with legend, and to bring new subjects into the charmed circle of those considered worthy to be treated in epic poems.

His persistent immaturity—still another fault that is often urged against him—was not so much a weakness of character as it was a feature of his literary policy. He had to play the part of an innocent in the great world. He had to have illusions, then lose them painfully, then replace them with others, because that repeated process was the story he wanted to tell. He had to be naïve about his emotions in order to feel them more intensely and in order to convey the impression—as he does in his best work—that something as commonplace as boarding a train or writing a book is being experienced not only for the first time in the author's life but for the first time in history. If he had learned from the experience of others he would have destroyed that sense of uniqueness. If he had said to himself with the wisdom of middle age, "There must be a catch somewhere" in his exultation, or, "You'll feel better about it tomorrow" in his bottomless despair, he would have blunted the edge of both feelings and made them less usable as memories.

God says in a Russian proverb, "Take what you want and pay for it." That might have been the motto and moral of Wolfe's collected works and of his private life as well. Determined as he was to find words for every experience, he denied himself many of the richest experiences because they might have interfered with his writing, or simply because he had no time for them. He never had a real home after he was seven years old; he never owned so much as a square foot of the earth he loved (even his grave is in a family plot); he never planted a tree or a garden, never married, never fathered a child. Much as he loved good company, he spent most of his time alone in dingy lodgings or roaming the streets at night. He played no games, took part in no sports, displayed no social accomplishments. Indeed, he had few amusements: eating and drinking were the first two, and afterward came travel, making love, and conversation, in about that order of importance. He didn't enjoy music, or much enjoy art (except the paintings of Breughel and Cranach); he stopped going to the theater after his quarrel with Mrs. Bernstein; and though he liked to talk about books, I suspect that he was only a sporadic reader after he left Harvard. His real avocation was the physical act of writing; his one preoccupation was preparing for the act. He said in a letter to Mrs. Roberts, written a few months before his death:

> . . . there is no rest, once the worm gets in and begins to feed upon the heart—there can never after that be rest, forgetfulness, or quiet sleep again. . . . After this happens, a man becomes a prisoner; there are times when he almost breaks free, but there is one link in the chain that always holds; there are times when he almost forgets, when he is with his friends, when he is reading a great book or poem, when he is at the theatre, or on a ship, or with a girl—but there is one tiny cell that still keeps

working; even when he is asleep, one lamp that will not go out. . . .

As far as I am concerned, there is no life without work—at least, looking back over my own, everything I can remember of any value is somehow tied up with work.

The price Wolfe paid in his life was not the price of his debauches, which were intense while they lasted, like all his other activities—once he landed in jail and another time in a German hospital with a broken head, richly deserved—but which were occasional or intermittent. He paid more for his one great virtue than for all his vices. He paid for his hours of steady writing, for his sleepless nights, for his efforts to remember and interpret everything that happened, to find a key to it all, to give form to his memories. The price was partly in terms of health, for he was drawing sight drafts against his constitution without stopping to ask whether there was still a credit balance. But there was also a price in mental health that most of his critics have been too considerate to mention, even long after his death. His alternating moods of exuberance and despair became more extreme; especially the periods of despair were longer and deeper. Some physicians would say that in his last years he was a victim of manic-depressive psychosis.[1]

He also developed paranoidal symptoms, as do many other manic-depressives. There were ideas of reference and delusions of persecution and grandeur. At times he thought the whole literary world was leagued in a conspiracy to keep him from working. "As

---

1. But most psychiatrists would prefer to call him "deeply neurotic." In their professional language, "psychosis" is a strong word applied to the state of those who lose touch with reality over a long period. Wolfe remained capable of handling his own affairs, and handling them well. In psychiatric terms, a persuasive diagnosis is the one given by William U. Snyder in the next-to-last chapter of *Thomas Wolfe: Ulysses and Narcissus* (1971). "While it would not be appropriate to call him a victim of manic-depressive psychosis," Professor Snyder says, "he certainly can be classified as a psychoneurotic with severe labile and cyclical emotional features. In addition, he exhibited many evidences of paranoidal behavior; again, this was probably subpsychotic in intensity most of the time, although even Wolfe himself spoke of having been 'mad' on a number of occasions. . . . But his overall problems of adjustment did not keep him from being a very creative person, and may, in fact, have contributed to his creative drive."

for that powerful and magnificent talent I had two years ago," he wrote to Perkins in January 1937, "—in the name of God is that to be lost entirely, destroyed under the repeated assaults and criminalities of this blackmail society under which we live? *Now* I know what happens to the artist in America." His farewell letter to Perkins was a magnificent piece of sustained eloquence—130 of his manuscript pages—but in places it was a crazy man's letter. One fine sentence is often quoted: "And I shall wreak out my vision of this life, this way, this world and this America, to the top of my bent, to the height of my ability, but with an unswerving devotion, integrity and purity of purpose that shall not be menaced, altered or weakened by anyone." But the following sentences, which reveal his state of mind, are usually slurred over:

> I will go to jail because of this book if I have to. I will lose my friends because of it, if I will have to. I will be libeled, slandered, blackmailed, threatened, menaced, sneered at, derided and assailed by every parasite, every ape, every blackmailer, every scandalmonger, every little Saturday Reviewer of the venomous and corrupt respectabilities. I will be exiled from my country because of it, if I have to. . . . But no matter what happens I am going to write this book.

That is impressive as eloquence, but not as a statement of the facts. Wolfe was working on a book that might have hurt a few persons, notably Mrs. Bernstein and some of the staff at Scribners, but not so much as several of his Asheville neighbors had been hurt by *Look Homeward, Angel*. Nobody was trying to keep him from writing it. For the author it would involve absolutely no danger of prison, blackmail, ostracism, or exile. "I am a righteous man," he said in the letter, with an undertone of menace, "and few people know it because there are few righteous people in the world." There are many with delusions of righteousness, which they use as an excuse for being unjust to others. Wolfe was becoming one of them, as he realized in part of his mind—the Dr. Jekyll part, as he sometimes called it. At this point, as at some others, he was losing touch with reality.

His fits of despair sometimes left him moping in silence, but at other times they led to quarrels, broken furniture, and a torrent of spoken and written words. The fits did not recur at regular intervals and they were not induced by mere pretexts; on the contrary they had understandable causes, usually connected with his work. As Wolfe said to Alfred S. Dashiell of *Scribner's Magazine* in one of his many letters of apology,

> The effort of writing or creating something seems to start up a strange and bewildering conflict in the man who does it, and this conflict at times almost takes on physical proportions so that he feels he is struggling not only with his own work but also with the whole world around him, and he is so beset with demons, nightmares, delusions and bewilderments that he lashes out at everyone and everything, not only people he dislikes and mistrusts, but sorrowfully enough, even against the people that he knows in his heart are his friends.
>
> I cannot tell you how completely and deeply conscious I have been of this thing and how much bloody anguish I have sweat and suffered when I have exorcised these monstrous phantoms and seen clearly into what kind of folly and madness they have led me.

In some ways the problem went back to his childhood, but most of it, I feel, started later with his gift for feeling joys and sorrows more intensely than others did. He chose to cultivate the gift because it helped him in his writing, and gradually it transformed his character. At first he was proud, if in a rather sheepish fashion, of sometimes losing control of himself. He wrote to his sister Mabel in May 1929, "Don't be afraid of going crazy—I've been there several times and it's not at all bad." It was indeed an almost normal state for a romantic artist forcing himself, provoking himself, beyond the natural limit of his emotions. Soon he began to feel the sort of dismay he expressed in the letter to Dashiell, but it was becoming too late to change his professional habits. There were always occasions in the literary life for those fits of manic exultation and, increasingly, of despair—the sense of loss on publishing a book, the insults of a few reviewers (notably Bernard De Voto), the strain of getting started again, the fatigue that followed months of steady writing, the disappointment when Perkins felt that his latest work wasn't quite his best, the injustice of a suit against him for libel—and all those hurts became more painful as he brooded over them in solitude or drank to forget them, until at last he couldn't help interpreting them as signs that his talent was threatened by a vast conspiracy. His psychosis, if we call it that, was not organic or toxic, nor was it functional in the usual sense of being an illness due to unsolved emotional conflicts. Like the oversize wart on the second finger of his right hand, it was a scar he had earned in combat, a professional deformation.

5 ✿ In the summer of 1936 Wolfe paid a last visit to Germany, where he was entertained almost in the fashion that Americans had entertained the Prince of Wales. There were political motives for the publicity and hero worship, though Wolfe was not aware of them. Most of the famous American writers had taken a public stand against Hitler, and their books could no longer be published in his realm. By praising Wolfe the Germans were saying, in effect, "We too have a great American friend." But they also sincerely admired his first two novels, which had *Angst* and *Sehnsucht* and other qualities dear to German readers, besides a youthful vigor that seemed to them truly American. Wolfe for his part liked the Germans better than any other European people, and he richly enjoyed the visit. He thought for a time of marrying Thea Voelcker, a newspaper artist with whom he spent a week at Alpbach, in Austrian Tyrol. On his return to Berlin, however, he became more and more disturbed by marchers in uniform, by Hitler's voice on the radio, and by the frightened looks of German friends who were suspected of having a radical past or a Jewish grandparent. He started to write his first political story, "I Have a Thing to Tell You," about the persecution of the Jews. Soon after reaching New York he paid back an advance from a German steamship line for which he had promised to write two short articles about his travels. "I want to be scrupulous now," he told an official of the line, "not to abuse your generosity or to make any commitments that would not be in full accordance with certain deep and earnest convictions of my own."

It was almost the first sign that Wolfe had any such convictions outside the one field of his life in art. But the trip to Germany had given him a new perspective—as he told Thea Voelcker in a curiously formal letter that said nothing about marriage—and he was beginning to worry about the state of the world. There were personal worries too, including dentists' bills, attacks in the press, and suits for libel, with the result that he fell into a state of depression that lasted, this time, for more than a year. In his calmer moments he resolved to become a different man. He looked at himself with less tenderness and even with the beginnings of self-ridicule. He tried to cure himself of nostalgia for his boyhood, and he even abandoned his long search for a spiritual father; that may have been the chief meaning of his breakaway from Max Perkins, though it was compounded with other meanings and accusations. One reason for choosing Edward Aswell of Harpers as his new editor was that their relation could not be paternal on either side. Aswell and himself, he was delighted to learn, had been born in the same week of the same month of the same year.

With this change in his life went a change in his work, or at least in his ambition for the work. Now he wanted it to be more objective, based more on observation and invention, somewhat less on memory—though he still intended "to use my own experience absolutely—to pour it in, to squeeze it, to get every damn thing out of it that it is worth." He began to revise in manuscript, something he had been unable to do in earlier years. "I have something I'd like you to see," he said in a letter to the novelist Hamilton Basso, "but it ain't wrote good yet. You wait—I'll learn 'em!" He said in a sort of prospectus for his new book that it "marks not only a turning away from the books I have written in the past, but a genuine spiritual and artistic change. . . . I have sought, through free creation, a release of my inventive power." When he gave the rough manuscript to Aswell early in May 1938, he explained that the book would take a year or more to complete, but that he was not asking for assistance. "I do not believe," he said, "that I am in need of just the same kind of editorial help at this moment as Mr. Perkins so generously gave me in 1933, 1934. At any rate, since the whole process [is that] of trying to learn, like little Duncan," Aswell's son, "to stand erect, to toddle, and then to walk by myself, it might be better for me to go on by myself for a while, and see what happens."

In high spirits now that he had accumulated what he reckoned as two million words of manuscript, and found a new publisher, and received an advance of ten thousand dollars, he set out on the trip to the West that he planned as a vacation after months of driving labor. He gave a lecture at Purdue May 19, was entertained in Chicago, Denver, and Portland, made an automobile tour of the national parks, then contracted pneumonia July 6 on a boat ride to Vancouver. The next two months were spent in and out of hospitals in Seattle, where people were still arguing a dozen years later about whether he might have survived with a different sort of medical attention. Early in September his sister Mabel took him East by train. An operation at Johns Hopkins, and later an autopsy, showed that his bout of pneumonia had reopened a tubercular lesion in one lung and that the infection had spread to the brain. His last letter, written in Seattle against the doctor's orders, was to Max Perkins. "Whatever happens—I had this 'hunch,'" Wolfe said, "and wanted to write you and tell you, no matter what happens or has happened, I shall always think of you and feel about you the way it was that Fourth of July day three years ago when you met me at the boat, and we went out on the café on the river and had a drink and later went to the top of the tall building, and all the strangeness and the glory and the power of life and the city was below."

Perkins was at the hospital when he died on September 15, but arrived too late to see him. His last words were those a nurse heard him mumble in a coma: "Mama, I have been a bad boy. All my life I have been a bad boy."

The question that remains is about the meaning of his death and whether it was an accident or a tragedy. Most of his friends regarded it as both of these and also as a blow to the future of American letters. "That is the real tragedy—for us," Aswell says in a sorrowful memoir. "He had just come into the fullness of his powers when he died." Elizabeth Nowell's introduction to the volume of letters ends in the same fashion: "The tragedy, of course, is that the story is unfinished—that his death at the age of thirty-seven has left us only to speculate on what he might have come to, had he lived." But is "tragedy" the right word for an unfinished story and for a death that intervened—as these friends seem to imply—like a bolt of lightning on a sunny day? The end of a tragedy is written in the beginning. The death of a tragic hero is the result of a choice he has made, in which he persists at the price of his own destruction.

There are some indications, though not conclusive ones, that Wolfe's career was a tragedy in this more accurate sense of the word. His letters of 1937 and 1938 abound in confidence that he has found a better path—"I am more full of faith and hope and courage than I have been in years," he told Mrs. Roberts—but there is another note in them too, of utter exhaustion. "I am desperately tired and need a rest," he says in letter after letter. In June 1937, before his last visit to Asheville, he explained to his brother Fred that writing is "a desperate, back-breaking, nerve-wracking and brain-fatiguing labor. . . . I am not merely saying I am tired, I am not just pretending I am tired—I am, actually, honestly and genuinely, physically and mentally." The summer in Asheville gave him no relief. "I went home a very tired man," he reported later, "not only with all this trouble of Scribner's gnawing, but the pressure and accumulation of everything that has happened in the last two years. And when I left home I was as near a breakdown as I have ever been."

After days and nights at his desk, week after week, he had earned the right to complain of nervous fatigue. But also there were hints of another feeling that he must have hesitated to confess: the fear that not only his strength but his subject matter was being exhausted. "No matter how great a man's material may be, it has its limits," he said in one of his unmailed letters to Perkins. ". . . You say that you have been worried about my being able to control my vast masses of material. May I tell you that in the past year one of my chief and constantly growing worries has been whether I shall have any material left that I can use if you continue to advise against my present use of it." There was this much truth in this other complaint, that any sort of critical disapproval, even the mildest, was likely to shut off the torrential flow of words to paper that was the basis of his literary activity. Yet even if nothing halted the words, they came from a reservoir, not a river, and it might never be refilled.

In growing older he was moving further from the sources of his inspiration, as other writers have done. When I first read the series of interviews with famous novelists that appeared in *Paris Review*—including those reprinted in the first volume of *Writers at Work*—I was impressed by the fashion in which one after another spoke of his childhood as the basis for all his writing, past and future. Said François Mauriac, "It is as though when I was twenty a door inside me had closed forever on that which was going to become the material of my work." Said Graham Greene, "The creative writer perceives his world once and for all in childhood and adolescence, and his whole career is an effort to illustrate his private world in terms of the great public world we all share." Wolfe was lucky in that his adolescence, with its keen sensual perceptions and sharp memories, lasted much longer than with most writers. But sooner or later the common fate would overtake him—there are signs that it was already overtaking him—and his perceptions would become a little blunted, his memories less poignant. Then he could only have looked for other resources, have tried to make new combinations of remembered events, have depended more on patience or skill and less on immediate sensations. He would have been forced to illustrate his private world, as Greene said, "in terms of the great public world we all share."

Wolfe did make an effort in this direction, as we have seen, but it came late in his career and there is some question whether he would have succeeded in it even if granted a longer life. In the huge manuscript turned over to Aswell, he is less objective and inventive than he had hoped to be. Once again the big novel he planned had broken apart into a series of mostly remembered episodes. Some of these are much better than others, but none is quite on the level of his best early work. Curiously the most objectively conceived of the episodes is one of the weakest; it is "The World That Jack Built," printed on pages 149–322 of *You Can't Go Home Again* and long enough to be a novel in itself. Here Wolfe was writing his version of the "big party," attended by famous guests on the edge of bankruptcy, that became an obligatory feature of novels about the 1920s—the going-to-pieces party that was described by Dos Passos at the end of *U. S. A.*, by Fitzgerald in *Tender Is the Night,* and, in a Chicago Irish version, by James T. Farrell in *Studs Lonigan.* The mention of those other names suggests how little Wolfe does by comparison in handling the same material, which he fails to make his own. He writes about stockbrokers and fashionable artists as if he had watched them but never more than half-listened to what they said; then he tries to depict a contrasting world of servants and elevator operators and falls into proletarian clichés.

Perhaps the best of his late writing is the open letter to Fox Edwards (or Max Perkins) that is printed as a final chapter of *You Can't Go Home Again.* Here there is no attempt at objectivity; Wolfe is talking about himself. He keeps asserting that he is strong and confident, but the letter has a valedictory tone, as if he were saying good-by to others besides his foster father and closest friend. At the very end he says:

> Dear Fox, old friend, thus we have come to the end of the road that we were to go together. My tale is finished—and so farewell.
>
> But before I go I have one thing more to tell you.
>
> Something has spoken to me in the night, burning the tapers of the waning year; something has spoken in the night, and told me I shall die, I know not where. Saying:
>
> "To lose the earth you know, for greater knowing; to lose the life you have, for a greater life; to leave the friends you loved, for greater loving; to find a land more kind than home, more large than earth—
>
> "—Whereon the pillars of the earth are founded, toward which the conscience of the world is tending—a wind is rising, and the rivers flow." [2]

Wolfe had been talking about his aspirations for a newer and better America—that would be "the land . . . toward which the conscience of the world is tending"—but at this final point his hopefulness became confused with another feeling, deep in himself, that his unwritten work would never be written, that his tale was ending in the only way it could end. At most the feeling was intermittent; it was in conflict with other feelings, notably his determination to write more and more; but at any moment of crisis or illness it would weaken his will to live. Death was not only the rest he never seemed to get; it was a new adventure he was seeking, not altogether subconsciously. Like Baudelaire in his most ambitious poem, he thought of dying as taking a ship for unknown countries:

> *O Death, old captain, it is time! Raise anchor!*
> *Out of the commonplace, O Death! Set sail!*

---

2. Incidentally the farewell letter to Fox Edwards is revised from the letter Wolfe wrote and mailed when parting from Max Perkins. But the lines beginning with "Something has spoken to me in the night" first appeared as the end of Wolfe's fine story, "I Have a Thing to Tell You," which was also fitted into the loose framework of *You Can't Go Home Again*.

This other, and I think we might call it tragic, interpretation of his early death is in part confirmed when we examine the careers of other writers who have tried to live and work in the same tradition. There have indeed been others; Wolfe was unprecedented, but he offered a precedent that younger men have tried to follow. I am not thinking of those who imitated his unbuttoned style or echoed his hymns to the American earth; at one time there were hundreds of those hopeful disciples. More interesting are the other writers who were seized upon by Wolfe's ambition to possess a whole world by transforming it into words. There are not so many of these because the ambition requires Wolfe's vigor and his obsessive memory to be carried very far; but a dozen or more appeared in the years after his death and each of them has written a long and rich novel about his coming of age or his native place. What did they do afterward?

I don't like to mention their names, since I suspect that their later achievement has not been brilliant. That sort of writing is an intense strain on the author, and not many of the others have had Wolfe's extraordinary stamina. Some of the younger men had nervous or alcoholic breakdowns or lapsed into inferior work. One name safer to mention is that of Ross Lockridge, author of *Raintree County*, a novel of 1066 pages crowded with characters and incidents; critics complained that nothing was left out. The book had a popular success that Lockridge did not live to enjoy, for, as we read in the supplement to *Twentieth Century Authors*,

> . . . the strain of many years of work on the book began to show. An intense man, burning with what a friend described as "a boyish eagerness that never relaxes," he suffered a nervous breakdown. In March of 1948, only two months after his book was published, and only a few weeks before his thirty-fourth birthday, he committed suicide.

Wolfe outlasted him by four years and three novels, just as his books will outlive those by his younger followers. Reading them again—while skipping pages, I confess—and reading the letters that record his career from the beginning, I feel a new respect for his single-minded devotion to his aim. He was one of the explorers who not only opened a new path but followed it to the end. He had always dreamed of becoming a hero, and that is how he impresses us now: perhaps not as a hero of the literary art on a level with Faulkner and Hemingway and Fitzgerald, but as *Homo scribens* and *Vir scribentissimus*, a tragic hero of the act of writing.

IX HART CRANE
A Memoir

1 ✿ I knew him for nearly a year before we felt any great
sympathy for each other. We had first met on a warm evening in
August 1923. I had lately come back to New York after two years
in France and was working again as a copywriter for Sweet's
Catalogue Service. Hart, who had arrived from Cleveland in March
of that year, was in the copywriting department of the J. Walter
Thompson agency. We had written for the same little magazines,
including *Broom* and *Secession,* and had exchanged letters about
poetry. At last he paid me a visit in the old house on Dominick
Street, almost in the shadow of the downtown skyscrapers, where
my first wife and I were living in two upstairs rooms.

He was twenty-four years old, a solidly framed and apple-
cheeked young man dressed in a brown suit to match his prominent
eyes. Gesturing with a dead cigar, he tramped up and down the
living room announcing that he was sick of being a copywriter; that
advertising appealed to nothing but the acquisitive instinct. I had
never liked that sort of sweeping declaration. Advertising, I said,

appealed to a whole collection of human characteristics or weaknesses or whatever you wanted to call them: sex and greed and social emulation and romantic dreams of the future. I doubted whether there was any such thing as a human instinct.

Hart flushed and his mouth turned down at the corners. "You don't know what you're talking about," he growled in a Midwestern voice. He shook hands on leaving, after shifting the dead cigar to his mouth, but he stamped out of the house almost as if he were shaking the dust of it from his feet.

I saw him several times that fall. At the end of October he resigned from J. Walter Thompson's, saying that he was caught there like a rat in a trap, and we spent a weekend together at Eugene O'Neill's country house, with disastrous results for O'Neill when we tapped a cider barrel and set him to drinking again. In the spring of 1924 Hart was jobless, roomless, and dependent on the hospitality of friends. I told him about an opening at Sweet's Catalogue Service and he got the job—at forty dollars a week, or ten dollars more than he had previously been earning. Our desks were beside each other and we had lunch together two or three times a week, yet still there was a shadow of constraint between us.

"Hart isn't very bright," I told Peggy one evening at dinner.

I meant that he hadn't the quick competence I had come to expect of my friends, most of whom had been scholarship boys in college. Hart had not finished high school, and although he read intensely, rather than widely, there were immense gaps in his knowledge of things we took for granted. When one explained to him how a certain piece of copy was to be handled, he sometimes had a look of sullen incomprehension. I hadn't yet learned to appreciate his single-minded devotion to writing poems, or his capacity for working at each of them week after week until it had assumed the exact new shape of which he dreamed.

It was Allen Tate who brought us together. He had been exchanging letters with Hart, and when he made what I think was his first visit to New York, in June 1924, it was Hart who introduced him to most of my friends. I had forgotten the circumstances of my first meeting with Allen until he mentioned them in a letter. There was a party, he says, in the Greenwich Village apartment of James Light, a director of the Provincetown Playhouse. "I remember," the letter continues, "that I appeared neatly dressed in a dark suit, carry-

Hart Crane and Peggy Cowley in the garden of the house he rented at Mixcoac, near Mexico City (early spring of 1932).

ing a preposterous walking stick and wearing a Phi Beta Kappa key. I was completely unsophisticated. You were already a man of the world—had been to France and known the Dadaists, etc. You remarked, 'We no longer wear our Phi Beta Kappa keys.' And you picked up somewhere an old stick—not a cane—and carried it the entire evening."

That is Allen's story, not mine, for I didn't feel then like a man of the world and he never impressed me as being unsophisticated. I thought, then or later, that he had the best manners of any young man I had known, in America or France. I thought he used politeness not only as a defense but sometimes as an aggressive weapon against strangers. But he couldn't have been offensively polite to me that evening, in spite of my jibes, and we must have arranged to meet again at Hart Crane's on the following Tuesday.

That second meeting with Allen I do remember, and I even found the date of it in a letter: June 24, in the late afternoon. Hart had recently moved to Brooklyn Heights, where he had rented a back room with a magnificent view of Brooklyn Bridge. After exclaiming at the view, we talked about poetry. Hart gestured, as always, with a dead five-cent cigar while he declaimed against the vulgarity of Edgar Poe. Allen and I had reservations. Seeing a volume of Poe on the shelf, I opened it and read "The City in the Sea":

> While from a proud tower in the town
> Death looks gigantically down.

Hart exclaimed that it was good to hear a poem read aloud. We left his room, all three of us talking excitedly, and wandered through the streets lined with red-brick warehouses until we came to the end of a scow at the end of a pier at the Brooklyn end of the bridge. There we sat talking, more slowly now, while we looked across the river at an enormous electric sign—WATERMAN'S FOUNTAIN PENS—and all those proud towers beyond it with the early lights flashing on. Suddenly we felt—I think we all felt—that we were secretly comrades in the same endeavor: to present this new scene in poems that would reveal not only its astonishing face but the lasting realities behind it. We did not take an oath of comradeship, but what happened later made me suspect that something vaguely like that was in our minds.

It must have been late in the summer that Allen moved to

New York. William Slater Brown was there too, a former ambulance driver whom I have mentioned in the chapter on Cummings, his fellow prisoner in the Enormous Room. Bill had lately married one of my high-school friends, Sue Jenkins, who was capably editing a pulp magazine called *Telling Tales*. Allen became her assistant at a salary of thirty dollars a week, then the beginning rate for assistant editors. I think that was after he married Caroline Gordon, who was introduced to us as a newspaper woman from Tennessee; "You'll like her," Sue said. Matthew Josephson, who had been the editor of *Broom*—at no salary whatever, in the last months of the magazine—was now a customer's man in Wall Street, but he found a good deal of time for his impecunious friends. Even Kenneth Burke had deserted his New Jersey farmhouse to spend a winter in the Village. That was the good winter, or so I have always thought of it, when we met after work at the Poncino Palace to drink hot rum toddies at the kitchen table, and when we had dinner together once or twice a week at John Squarcialupi's restaurant, then on Perry Street.

> *All of an age, all heretics,*
> *all rich in promise, but poor in rupees,*
> *I knew them all at twenty-six,*
> *when to a sound of scraping shovels,*
> *emerging from whatever dream,*
> *by night they left their separate hovels*
> *as if with an exultant scream,*
> *stamped off the snow and gathered round*
> *a table at John Squarcialupi's,*
> *happy as jaybirds, loud as puppies.*

At the time we were planning the first (and last) issue of an angry little magazine to be called *Aesthete 1925*, and that gave a sort of direction to the dinners, with contributions to be shouted up and poems to be read aloud, but soon the evenings would dissolve into anecdotes and horseplay. Kenneth Burke was the arguing man and the noisy analyst of human follies, including his own. Allen revealed a gift for comic inventions and pure impishness. Hart, after banging away at the big upright piano while shaking his bristly head to the beat of "Too Much Mustard," always made more than his share of the jokes, laughed louder, if possible, than anyone else, and drank more of John Squarcialupi's red wine. Later in the evening, though, he might be as morose as a chained bear in a Russian tavern. Once he upset a bottle of wine on the tablecloth, pushed back his chair, and plunged out of the door without saying a word.

"Where is he going?" I asked.

"Don't you know?" said one of the girls, who made a point of knowing almost everything. "He's going to Brooklyn to pick up a sailor."

I had indeed known that he was homosexual, though I forget how I learned about it; probably Hart himself had told me, as he usually ended by doing with a new friend; or he had told someone else who passed the news along. I regarded it as an item of personal gossip, as if I had been told that he had a birthmark on his back or suffered—as he did—from constipation. He did not look or talk like a homosexual; he looked like a country boy masquerading in a business suit, and his speech was northern Ohio except for a few big words and a larding of waterfront obscenities. "I never could stand much falsetto," he used to say. Instead of being delicate, his poems were solidly built and clumped on heavy feet, like Hart himself; and his social behavior—as much of it as I had a chance to observe—seemed aggressively masculine. Hart liked women, and his favorites were not of the thwartedly maternal type sometimes known as fairy godmothers; he liked girls of his own age, the prettier the better, and usually they liked him in return. Some of them made laudable attempts on his vice, and Hart abetted them, up to a point. The situation became comic when, as sometimes happened, he snatched a girl from the roving hands of a heterosexual friend. But most of his friends were intensively married, and Hart seemed happy in their company.

There was, however, one obvious sign of alienation to be noted even in that best of winters. At some moment in the evening, after the hilarious stage and the stage at which he repeated one phrase obsessively, Hart's face would assume that sullen look, and he would begin glancing toward the door. It may have been that, as Gorham Munson said, he felt subtly excluded from the domestic concerns of the others. Kenneth Burke once told me: "I remember a party at the Browns'. Party had got to humming, and Hart had got to the stage where he felt it was time for him to become angry.

I happened to be near the door when I saw him stamping across the room, all ready to leave in a huff. I said, 'What's the matter, Hart?' He began muttering about how awful 'all these people' were. Whereat I, being in a good-naturedly impish stage, decided to spoil his rhythm. I pointed out that he had no reason to be indignant. Everybody here was his friend, we all thought him a great poet, nobody's fighting—so what more did he want? He turned back, muttering, and got lost in the general turmoil. A little later, the same pattern, Hart storming toward the door in a mighty rage. So I went through my part of the routine again. I said I simply could not understand why he felt so resentful when everybody thought so highly of him, etc. Why 'these awful people'? Hart went back a second time. Of course there was a third time too, with Hart storming out and my plaintive, mollifying interruption, 'Now wait a minute, Hart, what's the matter now?'

"Hart turned, pointed, and shouted at the top of his voice, 'I can't stand that damned dog!' "

Always there was something Hart couldn't stand, people or dogs or "all those cats tramping up and down the stairs," and during the spring of 1925 his particular aversion was working for Sweet's Catalogue Service. This time I was more than a little offended, for I had found him the job and regarded it as a pleasant sort of refuge. If I was planning to leave the refuge too, that was because I could earn a living by free-lance writing. Hart, on the other hand, was a poet with no facility in writing prose for publication. His letters were marvelous if he dashed them off, but he suffered from writer's block when faced with the simplest book review. The only trade he knew was copywriting, at which he never acquired great competence, but he was safe at Sweet's as long as he cared to stay. The copy chief liked him and accepted his implausible excuses when he stayed home with a hangover. The salary was low even for those days, but most of us felt that a poet shouldn't demand much money; what he should look for was a job that kept him alive without consuming his ambition or his vital energy. Copywriting for Sweet's Catalogue was merely stating the facts about honest products, and except for two months before the annual publication date, there was no feeling of pressure. Hart was able to write some fine poems during his year at Sweet's, including all but the first and last of the six "Voyages"; he even found time to work on them in the office. It was a friendly office too, but still he began talking again of being caught like a rat in a trap.

At the end of May he demanded that his salary should at once be doubled. When the demand was refused, as Hart expected it to be, he resigned on two weeks' notice, without money saved or much prospect of earning it. Meanwhile Bill Brown, who had received a small legacy, was buying land in the hills seventy-five miles north of Greenwich Village. On the land was an old house that had to be painted, and Hart offered his services as a painter's helper. That was the beginning of a new era for all of us.

2 ✍ I first saw the Browns' house at the Fourth of July party they gave that summer. It was an eighteenth-century cottage facing the two stone fences of a post road that had been abandoned for at least a hundred years. Beyond the fences was an old orchard and then a wilderness of overgrown fields. The Browns' land, eighty acres of it, lay in the township of Pawling, New York, near the southern end of a high ridge that paralleled the Connecticut state line. Later when I moved into the neighborhood—as Allen Tate did for a time, and Robert M. Coates the novelist, and Matthew Josephson—I learned something about its history. The ridge along the state border had always been the haunt of outlaws and hermits; during the Revolution it was the last refuge of the local Tories, called "robbers" by the farmers. A band of them had been surrounded and shot down or captured at Robbers' Rocks, a jumble of boulders near the Browns' property. Tory Hill, as the Browns called the neighborhood, still had its share of men who lived outside the law. There were several bootleggers, including a Wall Street bankrupt and a cashiered army officer named Wiley Varian, and there was a character known as the Russian Wolf, who used to brew himself glasses of tea while robbing an unoccupied house.

Most of the houses on the back roads were inhabited by childless couples or old bachelors or widows living alone. The second-growth woods crept over the stone fences and crowded into the dooryards. Tory Hill was a decaying, even desolate neighborhood, but it had dirt roads for walking, blueberries in the unpastured fields, deer in the woods, trout in the brooks that tumbled through secret glens, and never a game warden or a No Trespass sign. October and November were the season when wagonloads of apples went jolting across the state line to the cider mill in Sherman. There was the smell of fermenting cider on all the back roads, and before the deep snows fell, old people came out of their houses for a sort of saturnalia. One passed groups of them by the roadside, hairy men in rags who sang in cracked voices or shouted obscenities. Once I saw Hart among them, reeling and shouting with the others.

We newcomers in the neighborhood—"Dear Tories," as Hart addressed us in his letters—had our saturnalias too, usually on national holidays when friends could join us from the city. The first of our big parties was on that Fourth of July in 1925. The Fourth was a Saturday, but the festivities started the day before, as Hart described them in a letter to his mother. "Nothing could beat the hilarity of this place," he told her, "—with about an omnibusful of people here from New York and a case of gin, to say nothing of jugs of marvelous hard cider from a neighboring farm. You should have seen the dances I did—one all painted up like an African cannibal. My makeup was lurid enough. A small keg on my head and a pair of cerise drawers on my legs!" I remember his pagan ecstasy as he capered on a stone fence built by God-fearing Yankee farmers. "We went swimming at midnight," he continued, "climbed trees, played blind man's buff, rode in wheelbarrows, and gratified every caprice for three days."

It was on Saturday that Hart did his cannibal dance. Afterward, with the nail keg still perched on his head, he sat by the lilacs in the dooryard, meditatively emptying a box of salt on the phonograph. Sometimes he glanced up at a tree that seemed to be rooted in the dazzlingly blue sky. Caroline Tate, pregnant and stark sober, heard him repeating time and again: "Where the cedar leaf divides the sky . . . where the cedar leaf divides the sky . . . I was promised an improved infancy." On Sunday afternoon, the third day of the party, Hart finally attained the state of exultation in which he was able to write, or put together, one of his more difficult poems. A drizzling rain had driven us indoors from the hummocky lawn that served as an obstacle course, or law court, for our hard-argued games of croquet. Hart went into his room, next to the big kitchen where we were telling stories, and for the next hour we could hear him pounding the typewriter while his phonograph, now cleaned of salt, blared away at full volume. Sometimes the phonograph ran down, the pounding stopped, and Hart fell to declaiming what seemed to be lines of verse, although we couldn't hear the words through the closed door. At last the door opened. Hart came stamping out, his eyes blazing, with a dead cigar in one hand and two or three sheets of heavily corrected typescript in the other.

"Rread that," he growled exultantly, like a jungle cat standing over its kill. "Isn't that the grreatest poem ever written?"

It was "Passage," an intoxicated vision that is hard to understand even in its final draft. That early form of it was nearly incomprehensible, except for a few magical phrases, but we nodded our heads and said yes, yes, it was marvelous, it was a great poem; any milder praise, at the moment, would have driven Hart into a sullen anguish. An hour later most of us started back to the city. Hart stayed on Tory Hill to finish painting the house—"That old dry wood just *drrinks* it up," he kept repeating—and also to revise the poem, a process that required days or weeks of sobriety. "Aside from this one blowout," he told his mother, perhaps truly, "I have not had a drop since I have been here."

That summer Mrs. Crane sold the big house in Cleveland where Hart had passed most of his boyhood and adolescence. She summoned him there to help dispose of the furniture, and he was gone for two months. From his tower room he gathered all his possessions—"5 cases of books; 1 trunk (filled with blankets, china, pictures, etc.); 1 desk; 1 chair."—and shipped them by freight to the Browns'; but Hart didn't follow them, since the cottage was too small to accommodate a permanent lodger. Instead he spent most of the autumn in New York, not writing much and looking desperately, by then, for any sort of job.

Meanwhile the Tates had moved to Tory Hill. They couldn't buy a farmhouse, not having received a legacy, but they rented eight semifurnished rooms from Mrs. Addie Turner, who lived with her aunt in a barnlike house half a mile from the Browns' cottage by a path that wound through abandoned fields. As compared with the cottage it had conveniences: a pump in the kitchen, a mailbox outside the door, and a telephone less than a mile away. The rent for the rooms was only eight dollars a month, but I wondered how the Tates were going to keep warm and pay for their groceries.

Much later Allen told me that while they were living at Addie Turner's the monthly income of the family—mostly from book reviews—was forty dollars or less. But potatoes were cheap that year, and Allen warmed himself twice, in Thoreau's phrase, by sawing and splitting his own firewood.

They were living as cheaply as possible in order to buy time. For Caroline—whose mother had offered to take the baby—it was time to finish a novel, the second she had attempted. Allen had no such definite project, and I think he was trying to preserve something precious to poets; Scott Fitzgerald called it an "inner hush," but it is closer to being an inner monologue, a trickle of words directed to an inner audience, which silently approves the words or demands that they be repeated and revised. Sometimes new conceptions or magical phrases occur in the midst of the monologue, and then it is time to seize upon them, to work over them patiently, to shape them into a poem. But I know Allen felt, as I did too, that real poems did not come from a deliberately chosen subject; they had to be waited for; they could not be willed into being. The problem was how to achieve a continual readiness to accept and shape the poems when they did appear, while refusing to commit oneself to any lesser and time-consuming purpose such as earning more money, for example, or eating meat every day.

In the midst of their poverty the Tates were planning to solve Hart's financial problem and thus make it possible for him to finish the long poem he had been talking and dreaming about for nearly three years. Hart had a greater thirst for fame than the rest of us, and it made him less patient in the face of hardship. "For the last six weeks I've been tramping the streets," he said in a letter to his wealthy father, from whom he was estranged, "and being questioned, smelled and refused in various offices. . . . My shoes are leaky, and my pockets are empty; I have helped to empty several other pockets, also. In fact I am a little discouraged." The Tates wrote to New York and invited him to share their living quarters. He would need very little money, they told him; there would be no distractions from writing, and he would have a big room to himself. Hart eagerly accepted their offer, but before he took the train to Patterson, New York, which was the nearest station to Addie Turner's, there was a dramatic change in his fortunes. He had written to the financier Otto Kahn, asking for the loan of a thousand dollars to help him write *The Bridge,* and Kahn—after consulting with Waldo Frank and Eugene O'Neill—not only gave him the money but promised him another thousand if he needed it. Hart finally reached the Turner house on Saturday, December 12, after several nights of celebration. Instead of being despondent and empty-handed, he arrived with liquor, fancy groceries, a new pair of snowshoes, and extravagant plans of work for the coming year.

Considering the strongly marked personalities of all three writers and the cramped quarters in which they were living—only three of the eight rooms could be heated above freezing—and considering the difference in economic status, with Hart now spending six times as much on himself as the Tates were spending together, anyone might have predicted that his visit would end in a quarrel; the proof of good will on both sides is that everyone lived in comparative harmony for nearly four months of a hard back-country winter. There is a pretty full record of those months in *The Letters of Hart Crane,* which of course should be read with the understanding that the letters present only one side of the story. For two or three weeks Hart was happy putting his room to order and collecting his old and new books in one place for the first time in years. January proved to be colder than usual, even for the hill country along the Connecticut border, and he complained of chillblains from sleeping alone in a frigid room. He said that his hands were so stiff from chopping wood that he could scarcely hold a pen, but nevertheless he was "at work in an almost ecstatic mood" on the last or "Atlantis" section of *The Bridge.* Downstairs at the kitchen table, Caroline was working at her novel hour after hour. Allen was meditating poems as he tramped through the woods with a single-barreled shotgun called the White Powder Wonder; once he shot a squirrel. Hart finished a draft of "Atlantis" toward the end of the month and made a hasty visit to his mother in Cleveland. Soon after his return the deep snows fell, and the Turner house was as effectively isolated as a lighthouse on a Maine island. There were six weeks when the mailman couldn't get through and when Hart used his snowshoes to carry home mail from the farmhouse a mile away that had a telephone. Still, everything was harmonious because everyone was working. Hart had started on the first section of *The Bridge;* then he formulated a new scheme for the whole cycle of poems. "One's original idea has a way of enlarging steadily," he said, "under the spur of concentration on minute details of execution."

The trouble with that sort of minute concentration is that it can be continued only for a certain time. The trouble with back-country winters is exactly opposite: they go on and on without consulting the calendar. Hart had finished his new outline for *The Bridge* by the middle of March and had summarized it in a letter to Otto Kahn, but snow was still falling at the end of the month. When it melted at last, the roads were deep in mud, and the Turner house was as effectively isolated as it had been in February. For the first time Hart's letters assumed a querulous tone, now that he found himself incapable of working. "A life of perfect virtue, redundant health, etc.," he said, "doesn't seem in any way to encourage the Muse, after all. . . . I drone about, reading, eating and sleeping." But Hart was never able to drone about for days on end. He would feel a sudden need to unburden himself, or would think of a funny story that had to be told, and a moment later he would come bursting into the room where Allen was trying to finish a review, or else he would clump across the kitchen while Caroline was puzzling over a difficult scene, and then, if he was greeted with something less than heartfelt warmth, he would clump back to sulk in his study. There had to be an explosion, and it came in the middle of April, before the first spring weather. After that the only communication between "Mr. Crane's part," as Addie Turner called his rooms, and "the Tates' part" was by means of notes slipped under doors.

The Tates stayed in the Turner house all summer and raised a garden. Then, having been offered a basement on Perry Street, they went back to the place where money had to be spent, but where it was a great deal easier to earn. Hart had left at the end of April, bound for the Isle of Pines with Waldo Frank, but his possessions remained at Mrs. Turner's, in his own quarters. No matter how far he wandered during the next few years, he always came back to Tory Hill. Mrs. Turner's house was the nearest thing he had to a home.

Addie Turner was a grass widow of sixty with a whining voice and a moderately kind heart. Her barn of a house had once served as dormitory for a boys' academy that briefly existed in the neighborhood. Besides "Mr. Crane's part" and "the Tates' part" (later occupied as a studio by Peter Blume), it also included *"my* part," as Addie called it, and "my aunt's part." The aunt was a woman of eighty who never spoke to strangers; she spoke to God. Once we heard her saying as she washed her two dishes, *"Great Expectations*—I've read that book twenty times and I still don't like it." "Mr. Crane's part" was two rooms on the second floor, one of them a big study. It was always neat when I saw it, the drop-leaf oak desk bare of papers, the books on their shelves, and the snowshoes crossed on the wall, not far from a carved wooden panoply of African arms that Hart had also bought with his check from Otto Kahn. Mrs. Turner "did" for him and cooked most of his meals, which they ate together. Sometimes when Hart felt good and the phonograph was playing, he put both arms around her oversize waist and whirled her across the room until she dissolved in simpers.

Hart was at home in the country without belonging to the country. He did not go trouting in the spring, or plant a garden, or have a dog to follow him, or gather apples for his own cider, or saw and split a winter's supply of wood. Sometimes he helped the Browns with their country chores, but only as a child might help them, for the fun of it. Like Addie Turner and the hairy old men, he never owned a car or learned to drive one. He spent the mornings in his study, then late in the afternoon he tramped the roads, perhaps with an empty cider jug to be filled on Birch Hill. In the evening he usually visited the Browns, but sometimes he roamed much farther. When we were living five miles from Tory Hill, Hart came to see us fairly often. I remember one occasion when Peggy and I drove home from a fairly gay evening at the Browns' and went to bed at midnight. It must have been hours later when I woke to find a heavy arm resting on my shoulder. Hart was lying face downward between my wife and me, embracing both of us. Without saying a word, we disengaged ourselves. Hart rose, also without a word, and dressed in the faint glow of starlight from the window; then he groped and grumbled his way down the breakneck stairs. We never asked him how he got home.

Hart, Hart. . . . He did so much that was outrageous, but so much that was unaffectedly kind or exuberant and so much that kept us entertained. Nobody yawned when Hart was there. He liked to dance—aggressively, acrobatically, without much knowledge of steps, but with an unerring sense of rhythm; he swept his partner off her feet and usually she followed him with a look of delicious terror. He liked to do solo dances too, including one that he called the Gazotsky because it was vaguely Russian. He liked anything sung by Sophie Tucker or Marlene Dietrich and burst into admiring chuckles as he listened. He liked to hear nonsense poems, the bawdier the better, and wrote a few of them. I remember one about Sappho that he used to recite:

> Said the poetess Sappho of Greece,
> "Ah, better by far than a piece
>   Is to have my pudenda
>   Rubbed hard by the enda
> The little pink nose of my niece."

Somebody repeated Hart's lines to Norman Douglas, in a slightly altered version, and he promptly included them in his famous anthology of dirty limericks. I forget what Hart said when he saw the book.

There is so much I forget about him, as if part of my own life had been erased, and so much I remember too. Hart, Hart. . . . He had a streak of puritanism and liked to punish himself for his vices. He also had a snobbish streak that was revealed when he talked about rich or titled acquaintances. Sometimes he promoted a friend— Harry Crosby, for instance—to the status of millionaire without consulting Dun and Bradstreet's. In spite of a robust constitution he suffered from a number of recurring ailments, including acidosis, urethritis, urticaria (or plain hives), constipation, crabs, and rose fever. These he treated with home remedies, chiefly canned tomatoes, larkspur lotion, and an enema bag. He tried to stay away from doctors, possibly because he was afraid of being given the obvious advice: Stop drinking.

Much as he liked plays, he did not go to see them unless somebody gave him free tickets. He seldom went to movies, and I do not remember seeing him with a newspaper in his hand; in fact I never heard of his reading for entertainment. He read classical authors, slowly and intently; his favorites were Dante, Rabelais, Marlowe, Shakespeare, Melville, Whitman, and Rimbaud. I think he approached them almost as if they had written the standard textbooks of advanced engineering; he was looking for models that would help in designing his Bridge. When he dipped into magazines, it was chiefly to see what other poets of the time were doing. Almost everything in his life was directed toward one end, that of writing great poems, and he permitted himself few distractions. Working in advertising agencies was a distraction from poetry, so he couldn't stand much of it. But drunkenness, dancing, frenzied conversation, and sexual orgies were not distractions for Hart, since he regarded them as means of attaining a heightened consciousness and hence as essential parts of the creative process.

3 ⚹ As I think back on his brief career and its bitter end, they seem to me as foreordained as the results of a demonstration in a laboratory: take this and that, do this and that, and here is what happens. Hart, of course, had special gifts combined with liabilities, and there was something in the mood of the age that encouraged special types of frenzy, but otherwise the operation might almost have proceeded in a vacuum. Philip Horton was mistaken in the sub-title he chose for his fine early biography of Hart: "The Life of an American Poet." Hart was a poet and an American, but putting the two words together produces a sentimental effect, as if Horton were saying, "This is what happens to poets in America; they are driven to madness and suicide." Or again it is as if he were saying to Hart's relatives (most of them dead), and the magazines that did not print his work (but many of them did), and the publishers who hesitated over his books, and the critics who attacked them, and Hart's friends who had patience with him, but perhaps not enough (or too much) —as if he were saying, "You failed to understand him, all of you, and hastened his end."

The fact is that Hart might have lived in any country and the result would have been the same: for example, he might have been called Mayakovsky or Yesenin. When he went to France in 1929, he met with less comprehension from the *agents de police* than he ever did from Irish cops in Brooklyn. The French kicked and beat him, threw him into jail, and "the dirty skunks in the Santé wouldn't give him any paper to write poems on, the bastards," as Harry Crosby wrote in his Paris diary. Hart didn't talk much about the experience. What he wouldn't admit to others or even to himself—except in moments of cold self-knowledge that he never ceased to have—was that he could scarcely have written the poems even if the bastards had given him plenty of paper and a private cell. By 1929 the operation had gone beyond the point of fruitful returns.

John Unterecker's later and more circumstantial biography (*Voyager: A Life of Hart Crane*, 1969) makes it clear that family circumstances—the divorce of his parents and, in particular, the mother's neurotic demands on him—were largely responsible for launching him on the course he would follow. But once he was launched on the course, I doubt whether any amount of understanding could have done more than delay the end of it. The immediate forces that led to the tragedy were more internal than external, and they were literary before they were moral. They had their source in Hart's single-minded determination to write great poems of a special type, and even more in the process he found for writing them.

The process started when Hart chose, or was chosen by, the subject for a poem. We do not know exactly how or when that happened—whether it was in a moment of drunken exaltation or during lonely hours at his desk—but almost everything that followed has become a matter of record. His first step, after the subject imposed itself, was to make a collection of words and phrases that might be used in the poem. He liked words that had an unusual sound or shape, and "thesaurized" them, as the French say, almost like a magpie collecting bits of glass. Some of the best words came from his rereading of Melville and Whitman. Almost all the phrases were invented—with what a heaped-up wealth of images!—but a few of them were overheard in waterfront speakeasies or in the Seventh Avenue subway: "I'm a Democrat, I know what time it is." "Fandaddle daddy, don't ask for change. If you don't like my gate, why do you swing on it?" He made note of the phrases, whether invented or overheard, on the backs of envelopes he carried in his pockets, and sometimes he tested their effect by reciting them to a group of friends. "One must be drenched in words, literally soaked in them," he told Gorham Munson, "to have the right ones form themselves into the proper pattern at the right moment."

That first stage in the creative process might last for weeks or months—it lasted five years with "Cape Hatteras"—or the words might be collected for a poem that would never be written, as in the case of a projected "Calgary Express" for which he was still taking notes in 1929. Once the right words had formed themselves into something like the proper pattern, there came a stage of revision that again might last for weeks or months. Hart was like the sorcerer of a primitive tribe; he was trying to produce not poems only, but incantations or mantras that would have a magical power, evoking in the reader the same hallucinated visions that the poet had seen. Such incantations cannot exert their full effect unless every pause is calculated and every word is in its inevitable place; not a syllable can go to waste; everything has to be patiently tested, sharpened, enriched, and clarified. "What made the first part of my poem so good," Hart said truly in another letter to Munson, "was the extreme amount of time, work and thought put on it."

But that was the third stage, not the second, and something had to intervene between the collection of shining phrases and their assignment, one by one, to their final places in a pattern. The pattern itself had to take shape, at the right moment—or rather, for Hart, there had to be a "new level of consciousness," as he called it, at which he saw a vision of what the poem should be as a structure in time. The vision might be a momentary thing, but it was absolutely essential to Hart, and he would make any sacrifice to achieve it. When he was a boy writing his first poems, he found that smoking strong cigars was one means of inducing visions—"I used to feel myself being wafted right out of the window," he said. Later he decided that drinking wine was an easier way. "If I could afford wine *every* evening," he said in a letter written from Cleveland in 1922, "I might do more"—that is, write better poems. "My carousing on New Year's Eve," he said a few months later, "had one good outcome; it started the third part of 'Faustus and Helen' with more gusto than before." "The Wine Menagerie," which grew out of a similar experience, begins with the lines:

> *Invariably when wine redeems the sight,*
> *Narrowing the mustard scansions of the eyes,*
> *A leopard ranging always in the brow*
> *Asserts a vision. . . .*

The first drafts of almost all his poems, after 1922, were composed in the same fashion, sometimes after years of waiting for the right moment. That moment, on which he pounced like a leopard, was a state of nervous exaltation usually induced by alcohol, but also provoked at times by rage or sexual frenzy; and it could be prolonged and intensified—so he soon discovered—by listening to music with a heavy beat (usually blues or rumbas or Ravel's *Bolero*). Therefore he got drunk night after night, always hopefully; therefore his typewriter stood close to an Orthophonic Victrola, then the newest thing in portable wind-up phonographs; and therefore he cruised the waterfront looking for obliging sailors. All his carousals had an element of self-sacrifice, almost of self-flagellation; they were undertaken partly and primarily as a means of driving himself to write great poems. As Rimbaud had done half a century before him, he was trying to make himself a seer "by a long, immense, and calculated derangement of all the senses."

Rimbaud abandoned the effort at the age of twenty; he said of it afterward, "All *that* was bad." For the rest of his life, which was somewhat longer than Hart's, he wrote nothing but letters and a few travel articles. How many other poets have tried that method of self-induced frenzy—and how many sham poets, each pretending to believe in his talent as an excuse for his vices, or simply for cadging drinks. I used to watch their performances at the Café du Dôme, and later I would see them slumped over the sidewalk tables with their long hair dribbling in a sticky pool of rum; they were a troupe of bogus failures, all hating one another. But the method has been followed by genuine poets too, and sometimes it has led to remarkable achievements, as in Hart's case and a very few others; the trouble is that nobody has enough talent or a strong enough constitution to follow it for more than a few years. Dissipation, which has been a means to an end, soon becomes an end in itself. The critical sense, which is a sober faculty, has little chance to be exercised. There is less capacity for sustained revision, and therefore the incantations lose the rightness on which they depended for their magical power. As regards the essential visions, they can no longer be evoked by a strong cigar or a flask of wine in an Italian tenement; they must be aroused by more brutal stimulants—and are they visions then, or merely hallucinations? The "leopard ranging always in the brow" asserts itself in acts of destruction or self-destruction.

That was Hart's story in brief. His recipe for writing poems was relatively successful for only five years—from 1923 to 1927—and it was completely successful for only five weeks, in the summer of 1926, when he was on the Isle of Pines. During those weeks of frenzied labor he completed more than half the poems in *The Bridge,* including all but one of what nobody should hesitate to call the great poems. The following summer, on Tory Hill, he wrote "The River," which seems to me the greatest of all, and soon afterward a draft of "The Hurricane," which was his last attempt to create a new idiom; but that was close to the end of his development as a poet. The three long poems that he wrote in the fall of 1929 in a desperate effort to finish *The Bridge*—they were "Indiana," "Cape Hatteras," and "Quaker Hill"—proved to be sentimental or bombastic and, as I think Hart realized, they weakened the effect of the work as a whole. He would have done anything to revive his talent, and he even tried the expedient of staying sober for three months, while visiting his father at Chagrin Falls, near Cleveland, but it was not a success. "If abstinence is clarifying to the vision, as they claim," he wrote to Waldo Frank during that period, "then give me back the blindness of my will. It needs a fresh baptism." It received not only a baptism, in the following year, but a total immersion in folly.

During that final year in Mexico, Hart told Katherine Anne Porter "that he was no longer capable of feeling anything except under the most violent and brutal shocks: 'and I can't even then deceive myself that I really feel anything,' he said." Nevertheless he proved capable of having one completely new experience, a tender and passionate love affair with a woman, and under that stimulus he stayed sober long enough to finish a poem about Mexico, "The Broken Tower," that was almost worthy to be placed with the best of the poems he had written in 1926. In other circumstances it might have been the beginning of a new symphonic cycle. But he no longer had enough confidence in himself to be sure the poem was good without assurance from friends, which was slow in coming; and it had required such exhausting efforts that he doubted whether he could write another.

Hart lived for only a month after finishing "The Broken Tower" at the end of March 1932. There were many reasons for his suicide, including his frenzied drinking, his sexual quandary, his lack of money—or prospects of earning it—and his feeling that poets had no place in American life, at least during those early years of the Depression. He used to fling up his arms and shout, "What good are poets today! The world needs men of action." But the mood would have passed if only he could have been sure that he was still a poet. Writing poetry—not poems written, but those to come—was the motive and justification for all his vices, for life itself. He would never be an old man using his picturesque decay as an excuse for getting drinks on the house. With no more poems he could be confident of writing, now that his method had betrayed him, he had no reason for being. Wherever he turned or ran, he was caught like a rat in a trap, and the trap was himself.

4 ✍ The last time I saw Hart was six miles from Tory Hill, on the next-to-last Sunday of March 1931. Peggy and I had separated, painfully but amicably, and she was planning to go to Mexico for a divorce. I was living in New York, working hard for *The New Republic*. Peter and Ebie Blume, who were spending the winter in Sherman, in the Josephsons' not-much-remodeled farmhouse, had asked me up for the weekend. When I arrived on Saturday afternoon I was surprised to find Hart there. He greeted me shyly at first, as if he thought I might be angry at him, and then with boisterous good humor.

"They've given me a Guggenheim, what do you think of *that?*" he said.

I thought it was splendid, but wondered what would happen next. Since his return from Paris, Hart had been running through friends and admirers like an heir through his rich estate. One usually tolerant companion had said of him, "People will love Hart when he's dead." They loved him when he was living, too, but he was making it hard for them. After a famous Labor Day at Amawalk in 1929, his friends had stopped inviting him to big parties. That was when he smashed Montgomery Schuyler's collection of records and tried to throw the phonograph out of a second-story window. Then he shouted to Monte, "My father is a millionaire. Who is *your* father?" Matty Josephson had a story to tell from New York. "All right, so we give a party," he said, "and Hart is there, and along about one o'clock he gets to the violent stage where he wants to smash the furniture. So we throw him out. We don't hold it against him, it's just the way he was. But we were in a rented place and we couldn't have the furniture smashed. When the party is finally over, we go to bed. Then along about four in the morning Hart has progressed to the contrite stage. So he phones, waking you up to apologize. That's the stage you can't forgive."

In the spring of 1930 Addie Turner had become terrified of his violence. Once when he stormed into the night to buy another jug of cider, she locked the door against him, but he broke it down when he got back and broke a window too; then he went reeling from room to room with a lighted lamp. "Oh, Mr. Crane," she wailed. At the beginning of July Addie told him to take what he owned and leave the house. "Mr. Crane's part" stood empty that summer, and Hart stayed in neighboring farmhouses, wherever he was invited for a week or a month. There were two weeks when he lived in a tent, but not in sin, with a girl he called Little Miss Twidget. His possessions were scattered in two or three places. Now in March, after his sober but unproductive winter in Chagrin Falls, he was back to collect the possessions, by which he set great store— the snowshoes, the books, the panoply of African arms, and a silver-bronze "Sea Gull" by Gaston Lachaise—and leave them in charge of the Blumes, with whom he was on good terms. He had decided that this would be his last visit to the neighborhood.

That afternoon he passed out gifts to everybody, with a warmth and thoughtfulness that made them precious. To Peter he gave a suit of evening clothes, handed down from his father; to Ebie, a pea jacket and a striped French sailor shirt; to Muriel Maurer—a friend of the Blumes—the broad red-flannel sash he had never dared to wear; and to me, a belt embossed with a large brass anchor. I felt as though we were Roman soldiers casting lots for his garments. At dinner the Blumes served one drink to each of us, then took the bottle away. Hart watched it go in unaccustomed silence.

Sunday, the last of the days I spent with Hart, might have been the epitome of many other days. In the morning, while Peter worked on a painting—it was "South of Scranton," now at the Metropolitan—Hart and I went for a walk on the frozen road, under the gray March sky. Hart was thoughtful; he seemed to have acquired the tired wisdom about himself that is sometimes revealed by dissipated men (as notably in Byron's letters). He talked without bitterness about the critics who had condemned *The Bridge* and wondered if they weren't partly right; "But——" he said, and left the word hanging. His difficulty now was that he didn't know what to do next. In asking for the Guggenheim he had spoken of going to France, but he was dismayed by the thought of the months he had wasted there.

"What about Mexico?" I said.

I had spent October in Mexico, and I talked about its somber landscapes, its mixture of Spanish and Indian cultures, and its cheapness as compared with Europe. Cheap rum, cheap cigars that were good to smoke, houses that rented for practically nothing, and a man to take care of the house—a *mozo*—for ten dollars a month. Some of the *mozos* were said to offer additional services, and I had heard that the sexual customs of the Aztecs were much like those of the Arabs.

Hart took a few steps in silence. "Maybe I'll go to Mexico," he said, "if the Guggenheim people don't mind."

Suddenly he started talking about the long poem on Cortez he had planned to write. He recited four lines of the poem—I think they were the only ones ever written, but they seemed to open gates for him. At lunch there was nothing to drink and Hart didn't complain. His face, instead of being pale as it was in the morning, had gone beet red under his now completely gray hair. He talked excitedly about Mexico and then, without a pause, about Marlene Dietrich, whose voice, he said, came straight from Tutankhamen's tomb. Ebie, usually attentive to her guests, made only a pretense of listening. Once she went out to the pantry and came back with a worried look. I learned afterward that Hart had found and carried off the bottle that the Blumes had produced at dinner. It wasn't the first time he had displayed the drunkard's talent for finding hidden liquor and hiding it somewhere else.

That afternoon was a party for Hart, even if the rest of us were sober, and it proceeded like all his parties, by inexorable phases. First came the hour when he was full of honest warm affection for everyone present and had so many good things to say about each of us that we must have all been blushing. He spoke with the same affection of his friend Harry Crosby, publisher of *The Bridge,* who had committed suicide while on a visit to New York the year before; then he insisted on reading us one of Harry's long poems, which described a voyage down the Nile in a dahabeah.

The poem had a refrain, and Hart shouted it at the top of his voice, pounding his fist on the table:

> Let the sun shine!
> And the sun shone.

It seemed the dark living room was flooded with hot Egyptian sunlight. Hart excused himself for a moment, I suppose to visit the hidden bottle. When he returned, he was in the second phase, that of brilliant monologue. Everything reminded him of something else: landscapes, of musical compositions; poems, of skyrockets or waterfalls; persons, of birds, animals, or piles of grimy snow; he could abstract the smile from a woman's face and make us see it in the design of the mantelpiece. His now immense eyes glowed in the first lamplight; they seemed to have burned the vitality from his other features and turned his hair to ashes. Soon he was launched on a stream of words repeated more for their sound than for their meaning. I was going to say that nobody ever made a record of Hart's monologues, but that isn't quite true: Hart himself recorded a few of them when he was drinking alone, and there were times when he must have hammered away at his typewriter as if he were addressing a crowded room. I found one of those jottings among my papers. Part of it reads: "They say my digits fidget, that I'm but a follicle of my former fratricide. . . . What shall I do? I masticate firmly and bite off all my nails. I practice invention to the brink of intelligibility. I insult all my friends and ride ostriches furiously across the Yukon, while parrots berate me to the accompaniment of the most chaste reticules. By all the mysteries of Gomorrah, I ask, what can a gaping gastronomist gather in such a gulch of simulation?"

That was how he talked for part of the late March afternoon, but then there began to be periods of silence, while Hart glared into the shadows as if in search of enemies. I may have heard him utter the word "betrayal." It was the phase at which one might have expected broken furniture, but luckily he was a little afraid of Peter, who had put an end to one of his drunken rages by throwing him down and sitting on his chest, until Bill Brown came to sit on his thrashing feet. This time the dangerous moment passed and dinner was served. Hart said little during the meal, and less while he was packing, although there was an interlude when he had us searching the house for his bottle of larkspur lotion. We found it sitting on the mantelpiece, where he had left it; then we set out in an open touring car for the twenty-mile drive to the station. Hart crouched against Muriel's thick-piled coat and shivered violently, while his eyes followed the headlights as they picked out now a white farmhouse, now a line of heavy white posts at a curve in the road. He began wailing, "Oh, the white fences . . . oh, the interminable white Connecticut fences"—as if he were giving voice to some inner anguish, buried for years, and as if the fences were an expression of everything that had hindered him from creating a myth for America.

Hart slept in the train, then roused himself as it crawled into Grand Central Station. He said good-by to me in the concourse, warmly but decisively, while his eyes kept glancing away. He had entered the last phase of his party—a familiar phase, though I never saw more than the start of it—when he cruised the waterfront looking for sailors and sometimes ended by being beaten or jailed. As I watched him almost running with his two bags toward the taxi stand, I thought that he was obeying the iron laws of another country than ours, and I felt that his weekend had been a sort of furlough from the dead.

X HEMINGWAY
The Old Lion

1 ✍ When Hemingway came back from the wars for the last time, in March 1945, he was the most famous writer in the world and he had chosen—or the public had chosen for him—the most obdurate problem he could bring himself to face. He must, the public said—and his friends took for granted, and Hemingway himself seems to have felt—he must write a novel about World War II that would be bigger in every way than his novel about the Spanish Civil War. For this he had more than enough material, all gathered at first hand, but there were obstacles to the writing of which the public and even his friends had no conception.

In the beginning and in the end, too, the worst obstacle was physical and mental at the same time. Hemingway was always taking risks, was always getting knocked on the head, and during the war he had suffered two serious concussions. One of them, in a London blackout, also involved a scalp wound that had to be closed with fifty-seven stitches. Back in Cuba, Hemingway complained to his physician, Dr. José Luis Herrera, about the aftereffects, which he listed as "terrible headaches, slowness of thought and speech, loss of verbal memory, a tendency to write syllables backwards, sporadic ringing in the ears, and partial impairment of hearing." Herrera said, according to Hemingway's biographer Carlos Baker, that the bad liquor Ernest had drunk during the campaigns in France and Belgium was the worst possible treatment for subdural hematoma. He advised gradual retraining of the injured brain, with limited intellectual activity each day.

For some months, Baker reports, Hemingway severely restricted his drinking. He devised a literary program for himself: he would get back into the swing of writing, first with personal letters, then with simple short stories, then with complex short stories, and at last with a novel. Gradually the symptoms disappeared, but they were replaced in time by other obstacles to completing any novel, let alone a big one. Among the obstacles was his still growing fame, which crowded his house, the Finca Vigía, with editors, interviewers, hangers-on, international sportsmen, and jolly drinking companions. Hemingway himself had created his public image, but now it was enforcing a pattern of conduct that did not encourage meditation. Another obstacle was his restless vitality, which drove him farther and farther afield on expeditions that consumed his time and exposed him to the danger of new accidents. The two airplane crashes in East Africa, early in 1954, not only revived his old symptoms, with complications such as double vision, but gave him internal injuries from which he never recovered. On his return to the Finca, however, he went back to his routine of writing for several hours each morning.

It was more than a routine: it was a duty and a painful discipline. No matter how late he had gone to bed or how long he had lain awake, he went to his writing table early, usually by eight o'clock. He started by reading over what he had written already; if he was working on a novel he went back to the beginning—unless he had accumulated too much manuscript—and in any case he read the last two or three chapters to immerse himself in the action; then he was ready to carry it one step forward. He wrote in pencil, in a big, round, legible hand, with the lines sloping downhill; ninety of his words (as with Thomas Wolfe, but the words were shorter) filled a manuscript page. At twelve or twelve-thirty he was finished for the day. "The best way to stop," he said, "is when you are going good and when you know what will happen next. If you do that every day when you are writing a novel, you will never be stuck." The truth seems to have been that he was stuck more often as time went on, but he kept going back to the persistent, sometimes frustrating, struggle with words. He also said on more than one occasion that he made a point of not thinking consciously about his work except when he was at his writing table, so as to give more scope to his subconscious mind. Half of his work was done there, he told his friends; things had to happen in the subconscious before they could go on paper. But he did not make the mistake of accepting everything the subconscious offered. After things were on paper he began to revise and reject, that is, to exercise his sharp talent for criticism.

As might be expected from this disciplined routine, Hemingway accumulated a great many written words during the sixteen years after his return from the wars. Besides two published novels—*Across the River and into the Trees, The Old Man and the Sea*—and besides a quantity of shorter pieces, some of them still uncollected, he also produced five book-length manuscripts. The shortest was *A Moveable Feast,* which was more or less finished, though not to the author's satisfaction, and which appeared in 1964. Three others were *The Garden of Eden,* a novel about a strange honeymoon in the south of France; *The Dangerous Summer,* a report on his travels in Spain with Antonio Ordóñez, the matador; and an untitled account, half-factual, half-fictional, of his last disastrous safari. Those three manuscripts are all in a somewhat inchoate state and, after dipping into them, I should doubt whether they will ever be printed except for scholars. There are effective passages in all of them, however, and embedded in *The Garden of Eden* are two extraordinary stories that I hope can be published separately. The longest and most worked-over of the manuscripts was the one that Hemingway's friends, without having read it, used to call "the sea novel" and that appeared in 1970 as *Islands in the Stream.*

The manuscript had a complicated history. While following the American armies in France—and sometimes going before them—Hemingway had conceived of writing a trilogy about the war, with one volume each devoted to sea, air, and land. The sea novel was to come first, but it would seem—Ernest was secretive about what he was writing—that he didn't start work on it until late in 1947;

The public figure: Hemingway being interviewed after a bullfight during his last good summer (1959). **WIDE WORLD PHOTOS**

then he continued it at intervals until 1952. Gradually his conception of the book changed: instead of his writing it as a continuous novel, it was to be a collection of three long stories—or perhaps four; there was a time when he thought that *The Old Man and the Sea,* written in January and February 1951, might serve as an epilogue. But wisely he decided to publish *The Old Man* as a separate book, and then, after further revision of the other three stories, he declared that they were finished and put them into a bank vault in Havana.

It was a curious way to treat them, one that had something to do with income taxes, as Hemingway explained at the time. But also he may have felt doubts about them, never expressed, and they weren't quite finished except as separate stories; if they were to appear as parts of the same novel, adjustments would have to be made. Hemingway never went back to them. His widow and his publisher, Mary Hemingway and Charles Scribner, finally undertook to prepare the book for the printer, though after a regrettable delay. Having read most of the original manuscript, I can say that their later decisions were wise ones: first to keep the stories together, then to omit some passages—the longest of which is an interlude in Florida, good enough in itself, that would have made the book less unified—and finally to make no other changes except in Ernest's erratic spelling and punctuation. One is grateful for having the book in its present form.

Islands in the Stream consists of three episodes in the life of Thomas Hudson, a famous, so one gathers, painter with three sons by two marriages, both of which have ended in divorce. In the first and longest episode, Hudson is living alone on the island of Bimini and looking forward to a visit from the sons, who are his closest tie with life. The visit is idyllic (and beautifully told), but soon after it ends, Hudson is notified by wireless that the two younger sons and their mother have been killed in a motor accident. The second episode takes place in Havana a little more than a year after Pearl Harbor. Hudson has armed his fishing cruiser as a Q-boat, a decoy for German submarines, but the northeast gales have forced him to spend a week ashore. Now he learns that his oldest son has also been killed, flying a Spitfire in England. He is briefly reconciled with his first wife, whom he still adores, but they quarrel again and soon Hudson is ordered back to sea. "Get it straight," he says to himself in Hemingway language. "Your boy you lose. Love you lose. Honor has been gone for a long time. Duty you do."

In the final episode, which takes place the following summer, Hudson and his nondescript crew are pursuing the well-armed survivors of a bombed German U-boat. The Germans have come ashore at an isolated fishing village, have slaughtered the inhabitants, and then have sailed westward along the coast in two harmless-looking turtle boats. With a prescience that he shares with other Hemingway heroes, Hudson is sure that he will be the first to die when his crew catches up with them, but still he stands on the bridge, a fair target, and does his duty to the end.

One might speculate that *Islands in the Stream* made it still more difficult for Hemingway to undertake the other two novels he had planned to write about the war. It is longer than he had probably intended it to be, it took more time in the writing, and the hero's death on the last page would make it necessary to invent another hero before going on with the story. In itself the book is not one of his major novels, except in length, but the dialogue is lively, the landscapes are solid and palpable—as in his earlier work—and there are several admirable scenes. There is, for example, Hudson's colloquy with Mr. Bobby, the bartender on Bimini who tells him how to paint an immense picture of the Last Judgment. There is young David Hudson's daylong fight with a giant broadbill, a rite of initiation (and all the scenes with the three sons are handled in a tender fashion new to Hemingway). There is Hudson's cat Boise, lording over the big draughty house near Havana, and later there is Hudson drinking at the bar of the Floridita with Honest Lil, the dean and deaconess of the Havana whores. The sea chase of the last episode should be the best sequence of all, and in fact it demands comparison with the bombing of the bridge in *For Whom the Bell Tolls,* but it loses by the demand. Hudson's glum sense of duty seems a pallid emotion when set beside Robert Jordan's tangle of fierce desires. Eager for life and happy in love, the hero of the other novel is dying for a vision of man's future. "If we win here we will win everywhere," Jordan says to himself in his last moments. Hudson, with no such vision, is dying, the reader feels, essentially because he has lost the will to live.

The author himself had lost the sense of commitment that sustained him during the Spanish Civil War; once he compared it to "the feeling you expected to have and did not have when making your first communion." That was a loss shared by all the writers who had been deeply engaged in the political struggles of the 1930s, and some of the others—Dos Passos, Erskine Caldwell, and Steinbeck, to name only three—suffered as much from it in their work as Hemingway did. The loss might help to explain what is weak in the novel, though a better explanation would be that Hemingway's subconscious, on which he depended as always, had failed to come forward with the help he implored.

During his early period the subconscious had seldom betrayed him. Time and again his "luck," as he called that inner resource, had enabled him to produce apparently simple works that have an amazing resonance, appealing as they do to subconscious feelings in others. Time and again he had descended to a level of emotion, call it prelogical or prehistoric, at which natural objects are symbols without ceasing to be solidly real; at which homely actions acquire a ritual value and events are presented in a fashion that makes them archetypes of human experience. The hero of Hemingway's early novels, whom we are privileged to regard as one person—whether his name is Frederic Henry or Jake Barnes or Robert Jordan—becomes a hero like those of ancient myths. That is, he is marked out for admiration and envy; he rebels against organized society (in *A Farewell to Arms,* where he also undergoes a symbolic death and rebirth); he wanders impotent through a wasteland (in *The Sun Also Rises*); he encounters heralds and precursors, then finally rejoins his people (in *For Whom the Bell Tolls*) and gives up his life after leading them in a brilliant exploit. That last novel has more than one suggestion of the Christ story: Maria is Mary Magdalen, Pablo is Judas, and when Jordan rides out to die at the bridge, he is followed by exactly twelve disciples.

But what would Hemingway do after the hero was dead? How would he resurrect him and present his later career, once again in a pattern as bold as that of a prehistoric myth? Those were questions that bothered me for years, and only once did they receive a satisfying answer. Of course it was in *The Old Man and the Sea,* where the subconscious once again came to his help and enabled him to write a story that had the simplicity and resonance of his early work—that had too much simplicity, I thought at first, but the resonance was unmistakably present. Santiago the fisherman was a new archetype for Hemingway, the hero as a hapless but unbroken old man. "But man is not made for defeat," the fisherman says to himself. "A man can be destroyed but not defeated."

Instead of becoming a hero of legend, Thomas Hudson is the hollow center of the sea novel. He seems to be based on Hemingway himself, as the other heroes had been—with the two exceptions of Santiago and the Harry Morgan of *To Have and Have Not*—but in most ways he represents only one aspect of the author. Brave, omni-competent, intensely male; a superb fisherman, a hunter of men, a captain adored by his crew of ruffians, and a heavy drinker able to hold his liquor, he stands mostly for the image that Hemingway projected to the public. Almost the only hint he gives of Heming-way's "shadow side," as Carl Jung would have called it, is a feeling of despair that he tries to overcome by not thinking about it. For this despair the author brings forward a simple explanation: it was caused, he gives us to understand, by the death of Hudson's three sons. Not every reader has accepted the explanation. Some have felt, as I confess to doing, that Hudson's despair is of longer standing, that it mirrors something deep in the author's psyche, and that the three sons have been offered up as a blood sacrifice to the exigencies of fiction.

All that is the weaker side of *Islands in the Stream*. One must add that it is a bold, sometimes tender, often funny and swash-buckling narrative that no one but Hemingway could have written. It has less depth and power than his earlier novels—so much is un-deniable—but it also gives proof, sentence by sentence, of the skill he cultivated during his later years of disciplined effort.

2   Early and late in life, Hemingway was an extraordinary person. Even the first photographs, after those in baby clothes, reveal the unusual power he had of projecting himself. He looks straight at the camera, he smiles that warm smile of his, and his older sisters— as later his companions in fishing or skiing—fade into the back-ground; everyone fades except his big, smiling, square-faced mother, who had something of the same power. Perhaps his lifelong grudge against the mother was based on early rivalry, for Hemingway had

a passionate desire to be first in everything. If he couldn't be first in a sport, he abandoned it, as he abandoned football after his senior year at Oak Park High School, where he didn't star on that year's championship team; the prospect of having to play more football was one of the reasons he gave for not going on to college. He had been first, however, in writing for the school paper, and writing was to be the trade he followed for the rest of his life.

There are other early traits to be mentioned. Besides writing stories, he told others to his classmates as if they were adventures of his own. Sometimes they really were, but at other times they were more vivid and memorable than true. He had a weakness for boasting, usually with the deprecatory air that makes boasts more effective. He didn't boast about his studious mind, but in fact he applied himself more diligently than others did to any subject that attracted his interest, and, as I said in connection with his Paris years, he learned almost anything with amazing speed. He was imaginative, enthusiastic, and persistent; also he had more energy than other boys of his age, a talent in itself, and perhaps he already required less sleep than others.

After being wounded in Italy, he was to spend many sleepless nights. That wound proved to be a decisive event in his career, and he was to make it an event in the lives of a whole generation of writers. It took place on the night of July 8, 1918, a month after he reached the Italian front in a Red Cross ambulance unit and less than two weeks before his nineteenth birthday. "There was one of those big noises you sometimes hear at the front," Ernest told a friend much later. "I died then. I felt my soul or something coming right out of my body like you'd pull a silk handkerchief out of a pocket by one corner. It flew all around and then came back and went in again and I wasn't dead any more." An ash can, as soldiers called them, fired by an Austrian trench mortar, had exploded beside him in a forward trench. Badly wounded as he was—later the surgeons counted 237 steel fragments in his legs—Ernest hoisted a still more badly wounded Italian on his back and plodded off toward the dressing station. On the way he was wounded twice again, by slugs from a heavy machine gun, but somehow he reached the station before he collapsed. It was an exploit for which he was awarded the Italian silver cross.

"In the first war I was hurt very badly; in the body, mind, and spirit and also morally," he told me thirty years later. "The true gen is I was hurt bad all the way through and I was truly spooked in the end." Perhaps that was the origin of a contrast between the public and the private Hemingway that was to persist all through his life. Publicly he was a war hero and a real one, too, considering the courage and instinctive presence of mind he had shown in an emergency. He thoroughly enjoyed the role and played up to it like an old trouper. Privately, though, he was and for a long time would remain a frightened man. It was not until the Spanish war—perhaps, so he told me, not until some crazy airplane rides over occupied China in the spring of 1941—that he overcame his fear of being blown up at night. Till then he had concealed the fear and had challenged himself time and again by deliberately walking ahead into new dangers.

I have a grievance against the enormous and very useful life of Hemingway by Carlos Baker. It tells us what he did and what he said to whom during his long career, but it gives hardly any notion of the immense charm he exerted on his friends, on women, and on older persons he respected. Partly the charm was owed to his physical presence: he was tall, handsome, broad-shouldered, with heavy biceps, yet carried himself with a curiously diffident and reassuring air; meeting him was like being led into the box stall of a huge, spirited, but surprisingly gentle stallion. More of the charm depended, though, on his habit of paying undivided attention to each of several persons in turn. He looked in one's eyes, then he turned his head to listen carefully: "Most people never listen," he used to say. Very old men and women, some of them later his enemies, remember with nostalgia his early times in Paris. His first wife, later Mrs. Paul Scott Mowrer, said of him forty years after their divorce, "He was then the kind of man to whom men, women, children, and dogs are attracted. It was something."

About Hemingway's public image a great deal has been written—rhapsodically by journalists and disapprovingly by men of letters beginning with Edmund Wilson—but it has never been studied with any seriousness. Why shouldn't it be studied?—considering that the image has played an important part in fifty years of cultural history. As a matter of fact, it had a history of its own and retained some constant elements while growing through different phases as if it were a person instead of a persona. One phase was that of the young writer living in exile and speaking for the postwar generation with absolute integrity. Another was that of the sportsman, traveler, and discriminating drinker, often photographed with a glass in his hand beside the carcasses of enormous fish and mammals. Still other phases were those of the committed man defending the Spanish Republic, of the war correspondent ranging through France with a private army, and, in the final years, of the square-faced, grizzly-bearded veteran watching paternally over his flock of young admirers: Mr. Papa.

The image in all its phases—after the first suburban episode of the war hero dazzling his neighbors in Oak Park—played its part on an international stage. Always it was rendered more persuasive by Hemingway's zest for living, by his energy, his passionate desire to be first, and his inborn gift for projecting himself. In one phase, that of the sportsman and bon vivant, the image had a discernible effect on a number of commercial enterprises. Years ago when I was gathering material for a profile, I talked with Jakie Key, a charter-boat captain in Key West. "If you want to say something bad about Hemingway," he told me, "don't talk to me. Hemingway made this charter-boat business—he brought the fishermen down." Yes, he brought the fishermen to Key West and Bimini, and bands of hunters to the high African plains, and American college students by hundreds, then by thousands, to the festival at Pamplona. Ski resorts in Tyrol and Idaho, bullfights all over Spain, restaurants in Venice, Milan, Paris, Havana: he had good times at all of them, he told with gusto what they had to offer, and the crowds came streaming after.

Of course the real importance of the Hemingway image has been its effect on literary history. It appeared at exactly the right time: in the early 1920s, when a new generation of American writers was coming forward. Although those writers were of almost the same age and strongly shared a feeling of being different from older persons, as late as 1925 they still lacked a collective name, a set of beliefs jointly held, and a code of literary conduct. It should be noted once again that Hemingway gave them the name, after seizing upon a remark of Gertrude Stein's: "You are all a lost generation," she had told him. The younger men adopted the name—which Hemingway himself soon disowned—but they were looking for other things that would make them a generation in spirit as well as in biological fact. They especially needed a sort of older brother on whom they could model themselves as a step for each of them toward achieving a separate identity. Hemingway gave them the older brother too, in heroes like Nick Adams and Jake Barnes—who quickly became confused with his personal image—and the stories gave them a code of conduct. Like Hemingway the other new writers would project themselves as being simple, unaffected, tough-spoken, versed in the language of boxing and the bullring, contemptuous of outsiders—especially of those who wrote for money—and brave in an uncomplaining way while suffering from a secret wound.

Once again I have to make a distinction of age. The Hemingway image had an effect on some writers of his own age group, notably Fitzgerald and Faulkner (more effect in the latter case than has been widely recognized), but Cummings, Edmund Wilson, Dos Passos, Hart Crane, and most of the others had already shaped their literary personalities. His strongest immediate influence was on writers beginning with Steinbeck who were too young to have served even briefly in the Great War. The influence continued to spread, and it is all-pervasive in the hard-boiled novelists of the 1930s. When still younger novelists wrote about their adventures in the Second War, they produced Hemingway dialogue and Hemingway scenes of action. Often their heroes seemed to be reflections of Robert Jordan among the Spanish guerrillas or of Frederic Henry caught up in the retreat from Caporetto. The Hemingway image was more vivid for them than their own adventures in a different war.

It must be remembered that the image is an essential part of the truth about Hemingway. Not only did he project an idealized picture of himself, but he usually succeeded in living up to it. He had aspirations toward goodness, toward something close to saintliness. When he fell short of his ideal in a fit of professional jealousy or one of his black rages, he blamed himself and sometimes offered contrite apologies. He was truly a leader of men, foresighted in laying plans for them, incisive in judgment, resourceful and cool-headed in a crisis. He was an outstanding sportsman, that is, an accomplished fisherman, a fair boxer, a good marksman in spite of his impaired vision, and a superb wing shot. He was truly generous to others with his time, and later in life with his money. Beside or beneath these qualities, however, were others that Hemingway tried to expunge from the picture. They were his shadow side, to use Jung's term again, and this included sudden rages, hypochondria, fears of death that became a longing for death, and fits of depression that he called "black-assed melancholy." Often he was boastful, truculent, quick to take offense, and he nursed his grudges for a long time. He could no more tolerate rivals—literary rivals in particular—than could an old lion.

After reading *Green Hills of Africa* in 1934, I wrote a little poem—"Ernest," it was called—that I wish had been less prophetic.

> *Safe is the man with blunderbuss*
> *who stalks the hippopotamus*
> *on Niger's bank, or scours the veldt*
> *to rape the lion of his pelt;*
>
> *but deep in peril he who sits*
> *at home to rack his lonely wits*
> *and there do battle, grim and blind,*
> *against the jackals of the mind.*

But what were the dangers that Ernest faced at home?

According to Jung, "A man cannot get rid of himself in favor of an artificial personality without punishment. Even the attempt to do so brings on, in all ordinary cases, unconscious reactions in the form of bad moods, affects, phobias, compulsive ideas, backslidings, vices, etc." I quote from Jung not because I have any notion of becoming a Jungian critic, but for the special reason that his formulations cast even more light on Hemingway's problems than do those of Freud. All sorts of Jungian terms seem to apply: not only persona and shadow side, but anima, archetype, and collective unconscious. Moreover, Jung took a special interest in the problems of aging men and women. We read in an article about his theories:

> Many neuroses, particularly in people during the second half of life, derive from an exaggerated use of one or another function to the exclusion of the others. [Jung has named the four functions as thinking, feeling, sensation, and intuition.] An extraverted thinking type, such as a businessman or an engineer, may enter the second half of life having attained all of his rational goals, including financial success and recognition. Nonetheless, these successes and his work no longer bring him the

pleasure they once did, and he begins to feel moody and depressed. Jung feels that previous goals have lost their power to mobilize psychic energy and what the individual needs to do is to realize some other side to his personality, particularly the feeling side.[1]

Such was the diagnosis, with a suggestion for therapy, that Jung seems to have offered to some of the unhappy American tycoons who came to consult him at Bollingen. What would he have said to Hemingway? In those later years Hemingway had attained most of his rational goals: he was rich, admired, imitated, and almost universally read. Writing well had always been his central ambition, and now he was, as I said, the most famous writer in the world; the statement would be confirmed by a count of the columns and inches that the press devoted to his exploits and remarks. After the two plane crashes in East Africa, he was granted the almost unique privilege of reading his own obituaries, which compared in length with the later tributes to Winston Churchill. That same year, 1954, his position was so to speak sanctified by the award to him of the Nobel Prize, yet most of the time he was feeling as moody and depressed as the tycoons who made their pilgrimages to Bollingen and begged Jung to help them. Would Jung have offered him the same sort of diagnosis?

In Jung's catalogue of types, Hemingway as a public figure—though not in private—was clearly an extraverted man of sensation. Would Jung have said that he was tired of his persona; that it had ceased to mobilize his psychic energy; that the persona had begun to weaken the subjective force of his writing by substituting itself for his proper heroes (as it had done in the case of Thomas Hudson)? Would he have advised Hemingway to cultivate some repressed side of his personality, for example, the side on which he was clearly an introverted intellectual? One has a brief vision of Hemingway's retiring into solitude to write a handbook of fiction or an *Apologia pro Vita Sua*. It is a fascinating picture, but hardly one for which Hemingway would have been willing to sit as model.

After the disaster in East Africa, it was too late in any case

---

1. The quotation is from David Elkind, "Freud, Jung and the Collective Unconscious," *The New York Times Magazine,* October 4, 1970.

for simple therapeutic measures. It was even too late for a return to the Catholic Church, a step that Jung might have advised him to take as a means of surmounting his inner problems. Hemingway had lived too hard and it would seem that he was older physiologically than by the calendar. He had suffered too many internal injuries, he had been battered on the head as often as an old boxer, and he no longer had enough resilience to go back to an old faith or adopt a new style of life or undertake a new approach to writing. Besides all that, he was committed to his public image. He was also tired of it, perhaps, but it still had immense rewards to offer him.

What proved to be the greatest of these, and the last that he truly enjoyed, was a triumphal visit to Spain in the summer of 1959. This time Hemingway toured the country with Antonio Ordóñez, who was competing *mano a mano* with his brother-in-law Luis Miguel Dominguin for recognition as the number-one matador. Antonio was the son of Cayetano Ordóñez, who had been portrayed in *The Sun Also Rises* as the heroic Pedro Romero, and Ernest felt a paternal interest in him. Everywhere he went with the younger Ordóñez, they were cheered by the crowds. At Pamplona, where they spent the week of the *feria,* July 6 to 12, the crowds were bigger than ever and Hemingway was mobbed by younger admirers, including pretty girls. He found time, though, for picnics on the Irati River, where the trout had come back and some of the virgin beech forest was still standing. "Make it all come true again," he had prayed at the end of *Death in the Afternoon.* Most of it came true during that week in Pamplona, with adulatory crowds in the background. "You know," he said to Aaron Hotchner, who had become his confidant, "it's all better than *The Sun Also Rises.*"

Later, at Málaga, there was his sixtieth birthday party, which lasted for twenty-four hours, with champagne from Paris, Chinese foods from London, fireworks from Valencia, and a shooting booth from a traveling carnival. Ordóñez and the Maharajah of Cooch Behar stood meekly in the booth while Ernest shot cigarettes from their lips; then Ernest organized the guests into a *riau-riau* that snaked through the shrubbery. A rocket lodged in the top of a royal palm and blazed there until the fire department arrived in a truck that it must have borrowed from a Mack Sennett comedy. The guests stayed for breakfast. It might have been all the grand parties of the 1920s packed into one, and it was Ernest's valedictory. Afterward everything turned bitter. The competition between the two great matadors ended when Dominguin was badly gored. Ordóñez spent a month in jail for using picadors who had been suspended. Hemingway went back to Idaho to write a story of the trip for *Life* magazine. The story got out of control and became a rambling, boastful manuscript three times as long as the forty thousand words that *Life* had agreed to print. Hemingway kept struggling with it, but found himself unable to cut it down to size or bring it up to his own standards. Finally the revisions had to be made by others.[2]

During the year that followed his last grand summer, Hemingway's body was visibly dwindling away and his mind suffered even more. One might apply Jung's words to him and say that the traits of character he concealed from the world and repressed into the unconscious were rising again to haunt him in outlandish forms. Always suspicious of people's motives, he now began to dream of a vast conspiracy against him in which most of his friends had involved themselves after selling out to the FBI. He would leave a restaurant in the middle of dinner if he saw two strangers drinking together. "Those two FBI men at the bar—" he would say in a low voice after looking hard at two traveling salesmen. ". . . Don't you think I know an FBI man when I see one?" He had other fears of dying in penury or of being clapped into jail for mild infractions of the game laws. His lifelong aggressiveness and his killer instinct were being turned against himself, the last of his possible trophies.

Still, after relinquishing the manuscript of *The Dangerous Summer,* he went back to his writing table every morning in the effort to finish another book that might, in this case, be truer than life. Still he regarded writing as a trade that was never to be mastered, and he said more than once, "I'm apprenticed out at it until I die."

The manuscripts that Hemingway left behind him, especially *Islands in the Stream* and *A Moveable Feast,* give one a new respect for the efforts and incomplete achievements of his later years. Handicapped as the old lion was by injuries and admirers, tormented by demons from the subconscious, he continued almost to the end a double life, playing the great man in public—even at the Mayo

---

2. Chiefly by A. E. Hotchner, who gives a moving account of those last years in *Papa Hemingway* (1966).

Clinic, where he played the part superbly for the doctors—then standing alone at his writing table, humble and persistent, while he tried to summon back his early powers. In the spring before his death he was planning to revise *A Moveable Feast,* but found that he had been too deeply wounded to write even a single line. "I can't finish the book. I *can't,*" he confided over the telephone to Hotchner. "I've been at this goddamn worktable all day, standing here all day, all I've got to do is this one thing, maybe only a sentence, maybe more, I don't know, and I can't get it. Not any of it. You understand, I *can't.*" That confession of failure came almost at the end; for every practical purpose it *was* the end. As we retrace the story, Hemingway's private or writing self becomes distinct from his shadow side, and it seems to us more appealing than his admired and debated persona. There is one respect and only one in which he resembled Hart Crane, who was born on the same day and whom he outlasted by nearly thirty years. Both of them felt that if they couldn't write, they didn't want to live.

XI Taps for the Lost Generation

". . . by a generation I mean that reaction against the fathers which seems to occur about three times in a century. It is distinguished by a set of ideas, inherited in moderated form from the madmen and outlaws of the generation before; if it is a real generation it has its own leaders and spokesmen, and it draws into its orbit those born just before it and just after, whose ideas are less clear-cut and defiant."

—From "My Generation," by F. Scott Fitzgerald, first printed in *Esquire*, October 1968.

1   There are no happy endings, but still, everything considered, it was more a lucky than a lost generation. Fitzgerald and his contemporaries were lucky, first of all, in the time they chose for being born, when the country was emerging from the long depression of the 1890s and when almost everyone looked forward to the miracles

that were certain to be wrought by a new century. As little boys they witnessed the early miracles: self-propelled vehicles among the carts and carriages (or drawn up at the curb for repairs) and the first movie houses, admission five cents, where they could pass an enchanted hour. Cities were growing as everything grew, but still the countryside began at the end of a five-cent streetcar ride, and it would always be there, always with fields to race across and woods to gather chestnuts in. So at least they felt as boys, and they were to be the last generation—except in the South—that could not help feeling close to the land.

They were lucky to grow up in a period that Van Wyck Brooks found the right name for: "The Confident Years." Under a rumbustious President, the country was flexing its muscles and sending its fleet around the world. Oh, there were lots of things wrong with the country, including trusts, political bosses, and slums (what were they?) in the back streets, but there was nothing in its future that middle-class boys had to worry about; nothing that wouldn't mend itself automatically if the boys grew up to be honest and if each of them worked hard for personal success. They all had a Protestant ethic drilled into them, even if they were Catholics like Fitzgerald. Later, after he lost his faith, the Protestant ethic remained with him. "All I believe in in life," he was to say in a letter to his daughter, "is the rewards for virtue (according to your talents) and the *punishments* for not doing your duty, which are doubly costly." It is an old-fashioned belief, but he was lucky to have it, and the stamp of it went into his stories, as into the work of his contemporaries.

They were most of them lucky in their early education, as compared with the boys and girls who followed them into high school fifty or sixty years later: that is, they weren't "exposed to a learning experience." Instead they were taught, and abhorred the teaching, and still were left with a residue of skills. They were taught such irrelevant subjects as ancient history (not social studies), English literature (with poems to be memorized), syntax, composition, and Latin grammar. They confronted English grammar, too, and rebelled against it, but at least they knew when they were breaking the rules. At some point in their high-school or college years, they were introduced to recent European literature.

Perhaps the introduction was made by a gifted teacher such

as Dean Gauss at Princeton or John Crowe Ransom at Vanderbilt; perhaps by an older friend such as S. Foster Damon at Harvard or Phil Stone in Oxford, Mississippi, who lent young Faulkner the books he carried off to read. That reading was a crucial event in the lives of Faulkner and others. It led to a series of discoveries: first that there were subtler methods and more difficult standards in literature than those of *The Saturday Evening Post*; then that there was something later to be called the modern sensibility, which was ironical, introspective, and self-questioning; then finally that the production of great works expressing that sensibility was an aim to which one's life might be devoted. The aim might even become— and did become for many of the future writers—a sort of religion with its own moral precepts. These included the Protestant or middle-class ideal of earning success by hard work done honestly—as regards the work itself—but they bore no other resemblance to the morality of churchgoing citizens. "An artist," Faulkner was to say late in his career, ". . . is completely amoral in that he will rob, borrow, beg, or steal from anybody and everybody to get the work done." He might have been repeating a lesson implied by books he had read before going off to the Great War.

It was a nice war, so Gertrude Stein used to insist to those who sat at her feet. In a longer perspective than hers, it was a disaster that ended the most hopeful era in Western history, but still it was a lucky war for the young American writers who served in it briefly. It immensely widened their horizons, it sharpened their enjoyment of life by the real or imagined nearness of death; then unexpectedly it was over before they had time to become truly disheartened. They went home, as Fitzgerald said, with an unexpended store of nervous energy, enough to carry them through the next ten frantic years.

But my theme here is the luck of the generation, not its familiar adventures in New York and Paris. It continued to be lucky in the decade after the war, when most of its writers published their first books. The new age proved to be one of success for beginners in all fields. An older generation feeling unsure of itself, perhaps a little guilty, was eager to learn what the youngsters were thinking and doing. Fitzgerald spoke up for the youngsters, and his first novel, published when he was twenty-four, made him an instant celebrity. Thereafter he would help to hold the generation together by his feeling, expressed time and again, that all his contemporaries were friendly rivals playing on the same bound-to-be-winning team.

The generation was lucky again in having Edmund Wilson as its young Sainte-Beuve. From his editorial desk first at *Vanity Fair*—where he shared it with John Peale Bishop, a gifted friend from Princeton—then after 1926 at *The New Republic,* he scanned the horizon for new talents and wrote perceptive comments on each of them. Sometimes his comments were the first, as those he made on Hemingway. He took almost as much interest as Fitzgerald in writers of his own generation, and he did a great deal to shape the critical image of Fitzgerald, Dos Passos, Wilder, Cummings, and others including the Nashville poets of the *Fugitive* group.

Curiously he hadn't planned to be a critic primarily; he had dreamed of having all literature as his imperium. Perhaps he wanted most to be a dramatist, but he also hoped to distinguish himself as a novelist, a poet, a publicist, a historian, and, in general, a man of letters. That he became a critic was largely by popular demand. His contemporaries realized quite early that he read more books more attentively and had more opinions about them than anyone else in the country. Writers listened to him as they did not often listen to other critics, and many of them tried to meet his difficult standards. At Princeton (class of '16) Dean Gauss had inspired him with the ambition to create "something in which," as he says in his tribute to Gauss, "every word, every cadence, every detail, should perform a definite function in producing an intense effect." That effect was what he hoped to find in new writers, and he scolded them, if in reasonable terms, when they fell short of producing it. He helped to keep Fitzgerald and his other brilliant contemporaries up to scratch.

By the late 1920s men of the generation were being published in Europe, and there again they profited from special circumstances. The new European writers who might have overshadowed them had died by age groups at Verdun and on the Somme. The new Americans had something of their own to say and part of it was a message that pleased the European public. That public resented the wealth and complacency of the empire across the Atlantic, but was impressed by it, too, and was waiting to learn whether its new literature would be as rugged and efficient as its motor cars. When some of the literature appeared in translation and when Europeans found that it was largely, so it seemed to them, a protest against wealth and complacency, presented in scenes of violence and abject suffering, they were rather quick to accept the new authors. Dos Passos, Hemingway, Wilder (who appealed to a different audience), and Wolfe were all international figures at thirty. Even Faulkner—though Europeans felt that he was more foreign than the others—was enthusiastically read in France during the Depression years, when his work was being disparaged at home.

Most of these writers suffered less from the Depression itself than did the younger men who followed them after 1930. Established in their profession, they didn't have to waste time in employment agencies or sit moldering in lunch wagons, and not many of them marched in those United Front parades that furnished a collection of names to the FBI. Hollywood was a source of income for some, including Faulkner and Fitzgerald, whose books then had a disappointing sale. Still, these and others continued writing the books, and they were becoming the dominant age group in American letters before this country entered World War II.

That was not a lucky war for the younger writers who came after them. The younger men suffered more casualties, they served in uniform for as much as five years, during which they had little time for writing, and they returned to civilian life without any great residue of stored-up energy. (All the more credit, one must add, to Bellow, Mailer, Styron, Jarrell, and others who did admirable things after World War II without any special favors from fortune.) Writers of the World War I generation were luckier once again, but still this wasn't their war. Crane, Wolfe, and Fitzgerald were dead before we entered it. Most of the others had done their best work, as would later be discovered, but they continued to rise in public estimation. One after another was invited, as it were, to sit in the high-backed chair at the head of the table, where Hemingway had already sat after *A Farewell to Arms* and Dos Passos had sat in the middle 1930s. Wolfe enjoyed an extraordinary posthumous reputation during the war, when it seemed that every literate young man in the army camps was reading his novels. Then it was Hemingway's turn again; then Faulkner's after his Nobel Prize in 1950—critics paid him triple honors in recompense for the years of neglect; and Wilson's turn came round in his later years. After 1950 a special chair had been installed for the glittering shade of Fitzgerald.

All these presided in turn or jointly over the long table without having their places seriously threatened by younger writers. It is not at all that talent was lacking among those who came shortly after them. To mention names, if only a few, Steinbeck, Cozzens, Farrell, West, Warren, O'Hara, Roethke, and Welty were all born between 1902 and 1909 and all produced good work from the start, but they did not form a cohesive age group. Some were drawn into the orbit of the Lost Generation—as notably Nathanael West and, in his early books, O'Hara—while the others did not rebel against it. With some exceptions the same statement holds true for writers of talent born between 1910 and 1925. All this might suggest that a generation, in historical terms, is no more a matter of dates than it is one of ideology. A new generation does not appear every thirty years, as Pío Baroja and other theorists have maintained, or "about three times in a century," to quote Fitzgerald; it appears when writers of the same age join in a common revolt against the fathers and when, in the process of adopting a new life style, they find their own models and spokesmen.

According to Baroja's scheme—and Fitzgerald's too—a new literary generation should have appeared in the 1950s, but the young writers who came forward then had no apparent sense of group identity.[1] Frank Conroy, one of the more talented, was asked to describe his contemporaries in the same issue of Esquire—October 1968 —that first printed Fitzgerald's article "My Generation." "It is clear that most of us now in our early thirties," Conroy says, "were not a generation in any self-conscious sense. We had no leaders, no program, no sense of our own power, and no culture exclusively our own." He says of his high-school classmates, "Our clothing, manners and life styles were unoriginal—scaled-down versions of what we saw in the adults"; this time there would be no instinctive revolt against the fathers. In college his contemporaries were called the Silent, the Cautious, or the Apathetic Generation, another way of implying that they were not a generation at all, in Fitzgerald's sense of the word.

---

1. And what about the so-called Beat Generation? That was in fact a small rebel band, one that hoped to speak for the new writers of its time, but found that most of these were a different breed of duck with a different sort of quack. Some of the Beats, however—notably Jack Kerouac (b. 1922) and Allen Ginsberg (b. 1926)—were among the "madmen and outlaws" who served as models for the real generation that was later to appear.

Conroy says of their college reading, "The New Critics had filled us with an almost religious awe of language. We read Leavis, Edmund Wilson and Eliot as well, taking it all very seriously, worrying over every little point as if Truth and Beauty hung in the balance." Those last remarks bring to mind an important feature of the 1950s: that the New Critics—and some fewer older ones—were doing more original work at the time and exerted more influence over bright young people than did new writers of fiction and poetry. The critics paid little attention to new work in any field except their own. They practiced their art of exegesis on the masterpieces of older writers, including several of the World War I generation: Faulkner especially, but also Fitzgerald, Hemingway, Cummings, and Hart Crane. Students admired the masterpieces and dreamed of the age in which they were written, a time when nobody, so it seemed, was silent or cautious or apathetic and nobody was tempted to ask the anguished question "Who am I?" The result was that members of the Lost Generation were lucky once again, basking, as it were, in a late afternoon of adulation and nostalgia.

Hemingway and James Thurber died in 1961, Faulkner and Cummings in 1962. Those four deaths in a little more than a year changed the whole order of precedence in the literary world. *The New York Times Book Review* printed the results of an inquiry— one can hardly say "inquest" in this connection—into opinions about who would take their places at the long table. The six critics queried by *The Times* had dozens of authors to mention, but reached no agreement as to which of them ranked highest. There was in fact a three-year interregnum in the kingdom of letters. Then suddenly in 1965 a new generation came to public notice, ten or fifteen years behind schedule, but complete by then with its leaders and spokesmen, its costumes, its music, its new style of life, and moving with disciplined indiscipline toward a general assault on the fathers. It had political opinions, too, and poured them forth in something that was close to being a new language, a free-swinging mixture of jive and pedantry. The new men had no patience at all with the religion of art or with lives sacrificed to the dream of ultimately producing masterpieces; "Now! Now!" they kept demanding. If more of its members had survived, the Lost Generation might have felt lonely and puzzled in the new atmosphere. One might say that its luck had continued to the end, with many of its members choosing the right time to die.

2 ✍ I have tried to present the generation in terms of eight representative figures each of whom had an effect on American writing in his time and after. All were born in the years from 1894 (Cummings) to 1900 (Wolfe). That choice of years has reasons behind it and explains the absence of other representative figures, for instance, Katherine Anne Porter, Elizabeth Madox Roberts, Henry Miller, Djuna Barnes, Archibald MacLeish, and Edna St. Vincent Millay, all a little older, and Steinbeck, Cozzens, and Nathanael West, among others a little younger. There are no women among the eight, a fact being that the admired writers of the generation were men in the great majority. The time of famous women storytellers and poets was, in this country, either a little earlier or twenty years later. I feel a lasting gratitude for the work of Caroline Gordon, Louise Bogan, Dawn Powell, and one or two other women of the generation, but they have been less widely read than male contemporaries of no greater talent.

The famous Jewish novelists of later years were little boys or babies in the 1920s. So were the famous Black writers except Richard Wright, who was in his teens, and there are no representatives here of ethnic groups. It has to be said that the men of the Lost Generation were white, middle-class, mostly Protestant by upbringing, and mostly English and Scottish by descent, with Fitzgerald to stand for the Irish and Wolfe, through his father, for the Pennsylvania Germans (Dos Passos had a Portuguese grandfather). In other words, these writers had what would come to be regarded as a privileged background, though the notion would have seemed preposterous to most of them when they were twenty. Only Cummings and Wilder (and of course Wilson) came from families belonging to the Establishment, as it would later be called. Most of the others were Midwesterners or Southerners and all except Wilder were in full revolt against the social and literary standards of the Eastern seaboard.

The eight writers will have to stand for others whose work I might have discussed at length. I am sorry for not having devoted a chapter to Edmund Wilson, who had a substantial influence on his contemporaries. He died before this book was finished and I then wrote a tribute for *The New Republic,* which had published the best of his early work, but I did not feel able at the time to do a longer study; that will be for later. I should have noted that in the 1940s Wilson gradually stopped writing about his own generation. He had joined the staff of *The New Yorker* and was taking full advantage of the opportunity it gave him to pursue his interests in many fields. One followed the magazine to see what in God's name he would be doing next. He traveled through postwar Europe and sent back opinionated reports; then, after mastering Hebrew, he wrote about the conclusions to be drawn from the Dead Sea Scrolls; then he went from reservation to reservation gathering material for articles (and once more a book) about the sorrows of the Iroquois; then, after a bout of reading, he made a survey of recent Canadian poetry and fiction. For a long time he had been studying the literature, so-called—not much of it has literary interest—that centered on the Civil War. Many of those studies went into *The New Yorker,* too, before being expanded into *Patriotic Gore* (1962), his last monumental work of scholarship. Meanwhile he was fighting some epic battles mostly reported in other magazines: with the Internal Revenue Service after refusing to pay his income tax; with his quadrilingual rival Nabokov over their respective translations of Pushkin; and with the Modern Language Association over its new editions of the American classics.

He was no longer the Sainte-Beuve of a new literature, but something at once bigger and less definite; perhaps one might think of him as a mixture of Dr. Johnson, Carlyle, and Burton the traveler. His new work was rigorously done, but sometimes his heart wasn't in it. He noted in his journal after *Patriotic Gore* that he was glad to be finished with those Civil War worthies; they weren't people he could write his best about. There is a difference in quality between his literary pieces for *The New Yorker* and those collected in *The Shores of Light* (1952), a book consisting chiefly of his earlier work for *The New Republic.* The earlier essays and reviews are sometimes less mature in judgment, as is to be expected, but they are warmer and more compelling.

"I find that I am a man of the twenties," Wilson says in the last of his books published during his lifetime, *Upstate* (1971), which is also the most intimate. "I am still expecting something exciting: drinks, animated conversation, gaiety, brilliant writing, uninhibited exchange of ideas." The men of the twenties had such good times that later some of them—as Hemingway, for example—fell into a frozen attitude of regret for the irrecapturable past. Wilson was one of the few who continued to grow, chiefly by extending his scholarly interests—during his last years he was studying Hungarian literature in the original—but still he lost something by partly severing his ties with his generation; those had been a sort of umbilical cord that nourished him with convictions and enthusiasms. He judged his contemporaries and liked most of them. "What will Edmund think about this?" they sometimes asked themselves when making a moral decision. At his most influential he had served as a literary conscience not only for Fitzgerald but, in some measure, for the generation as a whole.

So I should have had a full chapter about Wilson, and I also might have given more space than I did to Allen Tate. He too has been a man of letters in the broad sense, although he has not ventured into reporting, where Wilson excelled, or into the drama, where the other kept going astray. Tate is a poet primarily and then a critic narrower in subject matter and more philosophical than Wilson, but he has also written biographies and an impressive novel about the Civil War (*The Fathers*, 1938). His background and his Southern pieties might have led to mention of the Southern Agrarians, more or less an outgrowth of the *Fugitive* group, and this in turn might have led to a longer discussion of the modern sensibility— Tate would call it modern solipsism—in its impact on a traditional order. Lewis P. Simpson of *The Southern Review* believes that this impact was a principal cause of the Southern literary renaissance in the second quarter of the century. That is a plausible theory, and in fact the conflict between tradition and sensibility is richly illustrated by *The Fathers* as well as by Tate's most admired poem, "Ode to the Confederate Dead." [2]

---

2. Tate says of the "Ode," "That poem is 'about' solipsism, a philosophical doctrine which says that we create the world in the act of perceiving it; or about Narcissism, or any other *ism* that denotes the failure of the human personality to function objectively in nature and society. . . . Narcissism and the Confederate dead cannot be connected logically, or even historically. . . . The proof of the connection must lie, if anywhere, in the experienced conflict

Books, pencils, galley proofs, a manuscript: Edmund Wilson just after he wrote *Memoirs of Hecate County* (1946).

There should have been something about James Thurber. "I'm a funny man by profession," he used to say, and critics have a way of neglecting funny men unless they have been canonized. The public admired Thurber's work for sound reasons. In his "pieces," as he always called them, for *The New Yorker*—they might be short stories or memories or parodies or Aesop redone for our time—he created a world of his own that was full of imagined misconceptions and discomfitures, a dream world resembling that of the surrealist poets. He was also a stylist, the best in his field since Mark Twain. A stylist has to be a patient man, and Thurber might write and reject as many as fifty thousand words before completing a "piece" of fifteen hundred. "Get it right or let it alone," reads the moral appended to one of his fables. "The conclusion you jump to may be your own." In his later years he became a reformer of sorts: he was fighting to save the English language from a malignant disease that he called "carcinomenclature." "Once the political terminologists of all parties began to cross-infect our moribund vocabulary," he said in one of his pieces, "the rate of degeneration became appalling. Elephantiasis of cliché set in, synonyms atrophied, the pulse of inventiveness slowed alarmingly, and paraphrase died of impaction. Multiple sclerosis was apparent in the dragging rhythms of speech, and the complexion of writing and of conversation began to take on the tight, dry parchment look of death." Thurber suggested that the emergency required a new branch of medicine, in the hands of experts whom he proposed to call psychosemanticists. "Their job," he said, "will be to cope with the psychic trauma caused by linguistic meaninglessness . . . and to save the sanity of persons threatened by the onset of polysyllabic monstrosititis."

"Psychosemanticist" might be one of the terms applied to Kenneth Burke, who has attacked the problem of language from many angles, including the Freudian, the Marxian, and the Aristotelian. I should have written about Burke and could have done so more easily if he were not my oldest friend. We first met when Kenneth was four, I was three, and both our families were living in Pittsburgh. At the time my father was the Burkes' family physician

---

which is the poem itself." (*Essays of Four Decades,* pp. 595–97.) It is to be noted that Faulkner experienced a similar conflict and embodied it in many or most of his novels.

and he took my mother and me along with him on one of the visits he made in his black buggy. Mother used to tell me that I went around the Burke parlor touching everything in reach while Kenneth followed repeating apprehensively, "Don't touch. Mustn't." One is tempted to read patterns and meanings into those childhood meetings, and it is true that in our high-school days I was more venturesome than Kenneth, getting into more scrapes, but later our relation was reversed. As a critic he has been the one who went touching everything from floor to chandelier, while at times I have scolded him by letter for not observing the critical rules handed down from the Elders.

By touching, by asking himself questions, and by looking for hidden principles, he came to be one of the truly speculative thinkers of his American era. He didn't start that way. He started in what appeared to be the conventional fashion by publishing a book of stories (*The White Oxen*, 1924), but the stories revealed a special cast of mind. Each was conceived as a problem in formal structure, as if it were a sonata, and each attacked a different problem; he kept moving on. His usual movement was from concrete to abstract, from specific works to general principles. In his first book of essays, *Counter-Statement* (1931), he propounded a general definition of form that came to be widely accepted: "Form in literature," he wrote, "is an arousing and fulfillment of desires. A work has form in so far as one part of it leads a reader to anticipate another part, to be gratified by the sequence."

Having formulated the principle, he found himself incapable of writing realistic fiction. "I'm tired of getting people in and out of doors," he explained. His first and only novel, *Towards a Better Life* (1932), was presented as "a series of epistles, or declamations," in which the author's intention was not to tell a story, but rather, as he explained in an introduction, "to lament, rejoice, beseech, admonish, aphorize, and inveigh." *Towards a Better Life* is an extraordinary book that had its reviewers and critics, even a few enthusiastic ones, but had almost no other readers at the time. Its effect on the author was to intensify his search for hidden principles: which of these had resistlessly impelled him to write the book? After some years and a number of exploratory treatises (*Permanence and Change*, 1935, *Attitudes toward History*, 1937), he came up with the radical statement that literary documents of all sorts are to be viewed as modes of symbolic action. Thus, his one novel had been, in essence, a ritual of rebirth.

This is no place to expound the system of interpretation to which he was led by the statement and to which he gave the name of Dramatism. Burke himself has expounded it, particularly in his two longest books, *The Grammar of Motives* (1945) and *The Rhetoric of Motives* (1950). He is sometimes hard to follow, but he is not afflicted with polysyllabic monstrosititis. Briefly, Dramatism starts with the definition of man as "the symbol-using animal," whose actions are to be distinguished from the mere *motions* of natural objects. It then says that every action involves five elements: act, scene, agent, agency, and purpose. (Later Burke was to add a sixth term, attitude—or incipient action—thus transforming his famous pentad into a hexad.) From this simple beginning—and from the early stress on literary criticism—the system ramifies into a great number of fields, including aesthetics, religion, sociology, semantics, politics, anthropology, and theory of communications. Its author used to tell graduate students that he didn't know *what* he was teaching—"Perhaps I'm flunking my required course in Advanced Burkology." [3]

For a long time Burkology was hardly discussed at all, except by angry critics wounded in their preconceptions. The author had carried some of his notions to extremes at which they were open to attack ("Don't touch. Mustn't.") But he seems to have had sympathetic readers even in the early 1950s, for one began to notice that many of the terms to which he had given special meanings—"strategies," "symbolic action," "perspective by incongruity," "discounting," "the demonic trinity"—were appearing almost surreptitiously in critical essays by others, not to mention works on the social sciences. In the 1960s all his books were republished, even those long out of print. He began to accumulate prizes, foreign disciples, honorary degrees, and other paraphernalia of recognition. In the 1970s, not quite mellowed by late success, he has been codifying his methods, indulging in controversy (he bristles at the word "behaviorism"), and writing sharp, original, doggedly unprofessional poems. He has lived

---

3. It was his friend the critic Stanley Edgar Hyman who had invented that last term. "Burke has no field," Hyman had written, "unless it be Burkology."

for fifty years in a still precariously rural section of New Jersey, in a farmhouse that for the first forty-seven years was without running water.

Yes, I should have written at length about Burke and about a few others as well—E. B. White, John Peale Bishop, Robert M. Coates, Matthew Josephson, Ramon Guthrie—all born in those years from 1894 to 1900 and each having his own way of being uncorrupted. If I had found space for them it would have become evident that the generation was more varied in its achievement than I have made it seem by writing about novelists and poets. It also included critics, dramatists, reporters and publicists, familiar essayists, fabulists, historians, biographers, funny men, and philosophers—for almost the first time, in this country, a full complement in every branch of writing and one that was marked, in almost every branch, by the pervasive spirit of the age.

3 ✍ I knew them all and some have been my friends over the years, but I saw less of them after 1942 or thereabouts. By that time a few of them were dead and the Second War was scattering the others. I was a deaf man living in the country, hoeing my garden. Some of them I saw on weekly visits to New York, which was still the center of literary life—but it was rather less of a center than before and chiefly one, it seemed to me, for younger age groups. Among middle-aged writers the political arguments of the 1930s—over the New Deal, Trotsky, the Spanish Civil War, and the Russian purges —had left fissures some of which were never to be closed (as for instance the one between Hemingway and Dos Passos). That may be part of a pattern in writers' lives: at first they are happy to roam in bands, then year by year they retire from the herd like old bull elephants. Still, the famous writers of my own age and others who deserved to be famous were reassuring though invisible presences. Pleased by each public sign of recognition, I did what I could to explain features of their work that I thought had been missed. They were our spokesmen, after all, and every glittering success they made reflected on the rest of us. Fitzgerald was not the only one to feel that we were all playing on the same team.

Now most of the team is gone and the survivors are left with the sense of having plodded with others to the tip of a long sandspit where they stand exposed, surrounded by water, waiting for the tide to come in.

In later years I have wondered whether certain types of criticism are possible except in relation to authors of one's own age group. Those types are not the highest ones, I suspect; they do not often lead to universal principles and they are not as persuasive in the classroom as the reinterpretation of an older work for a new age. The text of the older work remains and every critic has the privilege of reading it attentively. But there are values in the text, there are images and associations, that can be grasped intuitively by those who grew up at the same time as the author; "empathy" is the abused word. In reading Hemingway's Michigan stories I remember—as he obviously did—walking through first-growth hemlock timber and feeling the short, warm, dry, a little prickly needles under bare feet. "One year," he was to write, "they had cut the hemlock woods and there were only stumps, dried tree-tops, branches and fireweed where the woods had been." I remember that too, if not from Michigan. In reading some of Faulkner's novels I remember the first automobile that chugged through the village in a cloud of dust and running boys, while men in overalls craned forward from the bench in front of the general store; that was in Belsano, where I was born, but it might have been in Frenchman's Bend. Such memories enforced the feeling of both novelists that they had lived in two worlds and that the earlier one was better in many ways, perhaps in most, but "You could not go back." Critics who did not know the earlier world sometimes offer reinterpretations—I have read them by the dozen—that are inspired, compelling, and completely wrong in their sense of values.

I confess to sharing the weakness I imputed to members of the generation, Dos Passos and Hemingway in particular, that of living too much in the past. "But we had such good times then," I find myself saying with others. We thought of ourselves as being wise, disillusioned, cynical, but we were wide-eyed children with a child's capacity for enjoyment. Did other generations ever laugh so hard together, drink and dance so hard, or do crazier things just for the hell of it? Perhaps some did—most certainly they did—but they did not leave behind such vivid records of their crazy parties and their mornings after. Those records testified to a bargain struck with themselves by writers of the generation. They had taken more liberties than other people, and in return they had accepted the duty of portraying their new world honestly, in all its exultation and heartbreak.

The good writers regarded themselves as an elite, a word that later came to be a sneer. They were an elite not by birth or money or education, not even by acclaim—though they would have it later—but rather by such inner qualities as energy, independence, vision, rigor, an original way of combining words (a style, a "voice"), and utter commitment to a dream. Those qualities they grouped together as their "talent," about which they spoke as if it were something precariously in their possession, a blooded animal, perhaps, to be fed, trained, guarded carefully, and worked to the limit of its power, but not beyond. At a time when Faulkner needed money, he refused a tempting commission to write a nonfiction book. "I'm like the old mare," he wrote me, "who has been bred and dropped foal 15-16 times, and she has a feeling that she has only 3 or 4 more in her and cant afford to spend one on something outside." I have quoted elsewhere a remark made by Wolfe to his editor Max Perkins: "As for that powerful and magnificent talent I had two years ago," he said, "—in the name of God is that to be lost entirely . . . ?" He seemed to regard his talent as a proud stallion that could be stolen or crippled by his enemies. Hemingway had a different comparison: he said that his talent was like a gas flame that he kept turning lower and lower until there was an explosion. Fitzgerald wrote to his daughter the spring before he died, "I am not a great man but sometimes I think the impersonal and objective quality of my talent and the sacrifice of it, in pieces, to preserve its essential value has some sort of epic grandeur."

That last was too big a phrase and Fitzgerald apologized. "Anyhow," he concluded, "after hours I console myself with delusions of that sort." But the earlier phrase "impersonal and objective" was not delusive when applied to the talent of all those writers. For one thing, they tried to be accurate observers of their age; for another, they regarded their talent as something apart from their ordinary selves. Hence, their efforts to preserve the talent were selfless, after a fashion, or at least ran counter in many cases to their material interests. A question they asked themselves was "How can I best live in order to produce the books that are in me?" It was a *professional* question, and the adjective reminds me of a brief scene in *Tender Is the Night*. The scene is from the section of the novel that presents Dr. Richard Diver as a brilliant young psychiatrist. While studying in Zurich he has met Nicole Warren, beautiful, rich, and a patient, at the time, in Professor Dohmler's psychiatric clinic. Nicole falls in love with Dick, and the experience leads to a partial cure of her psychosis. The Swiss doctors are afraid that Dick will either jilt her and cause a relapse or else marry her and ruin his career.

"I have nothing to do with your personal reactions," Professor Dohmler says. "But I have much to do with the fact that this so-called 'transference' must be terminated."

"It's certainly a situation," Dick says.

The eminent professor raises himself, Fitzgerald tells us, "like a legless man mounting a pair of crutches." "But it is a professional situation," he thunders quietly.

And so it is with many of the situations recorded in this book (or not recorded and left to the biographers). Marriages, divorces, friendships made and broken, bouts of drinking, follies of various sorts—not to mention "strategies," as Kenneth Burke would call them, such as creating a persona to serve as the imaginary author of one's books—even fits of madness in one case and suicides in two others—were they not largely the result of professional decisions made in the hope or despair of producing masterpieces?

Writers of the generation were intensely ambitious, but only in the professional field. Hemingway was an exception here: he was cursed with that passion to excel in every field, but writing came first for him, in the beginning as in the end. The others—not counting Fitzgerald in the time of his early success—were rather modest in their demands on life. No, they didn't in the least object to earning money, but they devoutly planned to earn it in such a way as not to forfeit their independence or diminish the future value of their talent. They also didn't object, as a general rule, to living in comfort, to having rich or prominent friends, and to being looked at admiringly by beddable young women (a prerogative of success to be observed in many fields, but perhaps in the literary field more than in others outside the performing arts). Sometimes they pretended to be indifferent to such things, and money too, and the pretense led to a number of farcical situations. But their taste, such as it might be, for worldly rewards was never a "dirty little secret," as Norman Podhoretz was to call it in speaking of his own contemporaries. I am trying not to idealize the picture. There were acts of generosity toward rivals, and there were also jealousies galore, backbitings and scratchings, and jabs to the kidney in a clinch. It has to be said with emphasis, however, that the good writers of the generation were not bent on "making it" in the later sense of the phrase: that is, they didn't want to acquire power over others in the contemporary world or to be the boss man of an organization. Those ambitions would have seemed to them cheap and conventional, like the dream of owning a chauffeur-driven Cadillac. Their dream was of having place and power in a more lasting world; of being the lords of language and the captains general of plots and characters.

"I want to be one of the greatest writers who have ever lived, don't you?"

That remark of Fitzgerald's to Edmund Wilson, made shortly after they both got out of Princeton, has been quoted many times and by Wilson first of all, in his "Thoughts on Being Bibliographed." Wilson's comment on the remark has also been quoted, but it will bear repeating once again. "Scott," he says, "had been reading Booth Tarkington, Compton Mackenzie, H. G. Wells and Swinburne; but when he later got to better writers, his standards and his achievement went sharply up, and he would always have pitted himself against the best in his own line that he knew. I thought his remark rather foolish at the time, yet it was one of the things that made me respect him, and I am sure that his intoxicated ardor represented a healthy way for a young man of talent to feel." Other young men of talent felt the same desire, at the time, to pit themselves against the best they knew. It is a feeling that casts light, for example, on Hemingway's later brag to Lillian Ross of *The New Yorker*. "I started out very quiet and I beat Mr. Turgenev," he said. "Then I trained hard and I beat Mr. de Maupassant. I've fought two draws with Mr. Stendhal, and I think I had an edge in the last one." Apparently "the last one" was not *For Whom the Bell Tolls*, in which it is hard to find a suggestion of Stendhal. My notion about *The Bell* is that he wrote it with at least a vague image in mind of *War and Peace* and that the image spurred him on to produce what is truly the best and richest of his novels. One can say that its low standing with the critical profession is a scandal, but to compare the finished book with *War and Peace* is more than Hemingway himself would dare. "Nobody," he told Miss Ross long after *The Bell* was published, "is going to get me in any ring with Mr. Tolstoy."

Now that time and men have passed, comparisons—not that one—have to be drawn and general statements, some of them negative, have to be made. Not one member of the generation carried out Fitzgerald's ambition of winning a place among "the greatest writers who have ever lived." Not one of its novelists, even Faulkner, can be set rightly beside Dostoevsky or Dickens, let alone Tolstoy, and not one of its poets ranks with Browning or Whitman, let alone with the giants of earlier times. Faulkner was its greatest man, the one most likely to remain a world figure by virtue of an imaginative power that has seldom been equaled. His place would be still more secure if *A Fable*, to which he devoted most of his energy for twelve years, had become the great novel he intended it to be; but that project of retelling the Gospels in terms of the Great War was not the one he should have undertaken. The Yoknapatawpha books are his achievement, and this in retrospect seems very deep and not so broad as we had hoped, a Grand Canyon rather than a continent.

Hemingway is out of favor, partly because of his public image and partly because his work is seldom considered as a whole. There are interconnections that make the books more impressive when taken together: for example, Robert Jordan's death at a bridge in Spain is a sequel to Frederic Henry's escape from death—and from the Italian Army—at a bridge over the Isonzo. Also it must not be forgotten that Hemingway effected a change in the style and vision of writers all over the world, including many who never acknowledged the debt. Fitzgerald seems a great man in retrospect, but his greatness has to be pieced together—from *Gatsby*, from a few of the stories, from his comments on the age, from the Rosemary section of *Tender Is the Night* (yes, and from the final chapters too)—then has to be cemented with the legend of his life. The figure he presents is that of a broken Apollo, salvaged by divers from the wreck of an Athenian galley, powerful in conception, but with fragments missing.

Those three men and several of their contemporaries were extraordinary persons, but they lacked the capacity for renewed growth after middle age that has marked some of the truly great writers. After all, that is a rare capacity: one thinks of Goethe first, then of Tolstoy (but with questions about his later work), then of

Hardy, Shaw, Thomas Mann, André Gide, but not of many others. In American literature there is only Henry James, who set out in a new direction at fifty-two after his venture into the theater had ended with a disaster. The writers of the Lost Generation, as a rule, had done their best work before they were forty-five and they had no second careers. Wilson might be an exception here, with his intellectual stamina and his lifelong rage for exploring new subjects, but even in his lonely case one feels more vigor of conception in the earlier work. Of the others who lived beyond sixty, the most one can say in this connection is that they held out, guarded their talent as best they could, and remained in a true sense incorruptible.

And what of the dream that seems to have been rejected by a new generation, to judge by its literary manifestos; I mean the dream all these writers had of bringing new masterpieces to birth? Some of these they left behind, but fewer than they had hoped. Of course the word "masterpiece" has two different and rather special connotations: it is applied either to works that are impressive in scope (without being overblown) or else to more limited works that are relatively faultless in execution. Only two works of the first type were produced by the generation: they are *U. S. A.*, which is grand in conception but often tedious in the writing, and *For Whom the Bell Tolls*, which, for all the faults that have been urged against it, is on the scale of the great nineteenth-century novels. Works of the second type are more numerous, as one might expect of a generation preoccupied with form: there are *Gatsby*, *A Farewell to Arms*, *Our Town*, *The Old Man and the Sea* . . . not to mention half a dozen books by other writers. There are also the works that are unforgettable in spite of some obvious weakness in design: *The Sound and the Fury*, *Tender Is the Night*, *The Hamlet* (my favorite among Faulkner's novels, though I wouldn't ask others to agree), and Hart Crane's cycle of poems, *The Bridge*. It may be that such works, flawed but not by any means failed, represent the generation in its essence. What I said of Fitzgerald might be true of his contemporaries as a group: that their greatness has to be pieced together.

And how do their productions compare with those of earlier times in American literature, especially with those of the 1840s and 1850s, the period that F. O. Matthiessen and others have called "the American Renaissance"? Are any of their works on the same level as *Walden*, *Moby-Dick*, *The Scarlet Letter*, or "Song of Myself"? Instinctively I distrust the question. The game of choosing Books That Will Live or Ten Books to Take to a Desert Island is one for innocents or retired professors with time on their hands. Every good work has an absolute, not a comparative, value. Still, I should say that Faulkner's story "The Bear" is as grand in its briefer fashion as *Moby-Dick,* that it may be read for as long, and that other works by members of the generation will have their place among the American classics. Beyond that I am unwilling to depose.

A more fruitful comparison might be one between the two eras, just eighty years apart, as periods of literary activity. Before the first era Emerson had prophesied, in his bold address "The American Scholar," that a new literature would soon appear on this continent. "Our day of dependence, our long apprenticeship to the learning of foreign lands, draws to a close," he said. ". . . Events, actions arise, that must be sung, that will sing themselves." Dozens of more or less talented young writers, surrounded by hundreds of cranks and come-outers, rushed to answer his call, each with the feeling that anything was possible in the new day. That same feeling of unlimited possibility prevailed in literature after the First World War. Young writers then were answering a call not from Emerson, whom they did not read, but from Joyce and Eliot (with Ezra Pound as prompter of one and promoter of both). *Ulysses* and *The Waste Land* had appeared in the same year, 1922. It seemed at the time that their authors had pushed beyond the mountains and opened territories for men of the new generation to explore. Those younger men were also heartened by the example of older American writers—Dreiser, Anderson, Cather, Mencken—who were doing some of their best work in the postwar years; and before the Second War they were being jostled ahead by still younger writers of talent. With all this growth and bustle, as in a midsummer garden, the period in American literature was clearly a second flowering.

Even after frost, the period retains an afterglow. One reason for its appeal to younger people, including those who reject most of its aims, is a gift that many of its writers possessed in common: they were almost all great spinners and weavers of legend. Most obviously the gift was shown in the legendary heroes they presented as models that would be followed, in each case, by thousands of their readers; here one thinks of the Hemingway young man like an Indian brave, the Fitzgerald young man who believed in the green light, and the Thomas Wolfe young man bent on devouring the world. Behind such heroes are larger patterns of myth, and I have discussed some of these at length, including Fitzgerald's legend of money and Faulkner's legend of the Deep South. I have failed to mention, however, Faulkner's other legend, of the dying wilderness, and the legend-become-ritual that Hemingway repeated in many contexts, of giving and receiving death. Hemingway and Faulkner most of all, but other writers as well, seemed to plunge deep into the past, or into themselves, to recover a prehistoric and prelogical fashion of looking at the world; then they looked in the same fashion at events of their own time and thereby surrounded them with a feeling of primitive magic (as Faulkner did in "The Bear" and Hemingway in "Big Two-Hearted River"). Perhaps that feeling explains the legendary quality of other stories, by these and other writers. In a sense the men of the generation were all working together to produce a cycle of myths for a new century which—so they had felt from the beginning—was to be partly a creation of their own.

Sherman, Connecticut
August 1972

Appendix:
Years of Birth

∮ In the United States as in other modern countries, we grow up by age groups, each different in its sense of life from the groups that precede and follow it. Sometimes the difference, though real, is almost imperceptible; sometimes it is as striking as that between the college class of '69, which bombinated among campus disorders, and the quietly discouraged class of '73. For those who were young at an earlier time, there was an even more striking change in mood after 1915, and its effects in the literary world are partly revealed in the list of names and years that follows. There is, however, an additional reason for making the list. This book, a sort of generational history, has dealt with a few representative figures, but they did not stand alone. It seems necessary to suggest, if only in tabular form, that they had friends, rivals, disciples, and detractors; that their books had to struggle with others for attention; and that the authors emerged from a broad background in American culture.

What follows is a list of writers born in each of the fifteen years from 1891 to 1905, greatly expanded from a similar list that appears in the revised edition of *Exile's Return*. No critical judgments are intended by either the inclusions or the omissions. This time I started with the *First Supplement* (1955) to that curious and very useful book *Twentieth Century Authors* (1942), edited by Stanley J. Kunitz and

Howard Haycraft; the supplement supplies information on half again as many authors as does the original volume. I copied down the names of those in the chosen age group and then made my own additions: first, of writers mentioned in my text (Harry Crosby, for instance); then of a few overlooked in the supplement (among them the modest poet and editor Stanley J. Kunitz); and finally of writers who have become prominent since 1955, if I could find their years of birth in *Who's Who*. Some of the women did not state their year of birth; one example is the novelist and memoirist Anaïs Nin, whose name must be, so to speak, undistributed. Some others gave the wrong year, as I happen to know, but like a gentleman (read "male chauvinist pig") I have taken their word.

There was one more step. Finding that the list had become too long and was getting too far from literature proper, I have omitted certain categories of writers. These are as follows:

> Writers of Westerns for the mass market (though I included Max Brand, more of whose books have been translated into more languages than those of any other American writer except Upton Sinclair).
>
> Mystery writers (except Dashiell Hammett, who had an effect on narrative methods, and "Ellery Queen," the trade name for a partnership that became an international industry).
>
> Popular romancers.
>
> One-book authors (unless the book was famous).
>
> Scientists, scholars, and technical writers (except those such as Crane Brinton and Margaret Mead, whose books are intended for the general reader).
>
> Children's authors, a field in which I have no competence.
>
> Official persons suspected of having their books written by hired assistants.

Even after those omissions, the list contains 385 names in all, and it seems to me a pretty impressive record of literary activity.

1891

Thurman Arnold, essayist	Marquis James, biographer
Herbert Asbury, social historian	Lloyd Lewis, biographer
Margaret Culkin Banning, novelist	Percy Marks, novelist
Samuel Flagg Bemis, historian	Henry Miller, memoirist
Octavus Roy Cohen, story writer	Elliot Paul, novelist
Richard Connell, story writer	Katherine Anne Porter, novelist
Lewis Gannett, critic	Lyle Saxon, regional writer
Maurice Hindus, reporter	Harold Stearns, journalist
Sidney Howard, playwright	John T. Winterich, bibliographer

Djuna Barnes, poet, novelist
John Peale Bishop, man of letters
Paul Blanshard, publicist
Max Brand (Frederick Schiller Faust),
  Western writer
Bessie Breuer, novelist
Pearl Buck, novelist
Robert P. Tristram Coffin, poet
Janet Flanner, journalist
Will James, regional writer
Howard Mumford Jones, historian
  of ideas
Harold Lamb, historian
R. S. Lynd, sociologist

Archibald MacLeish, poet
Dumas Malone, biographer
Edna St. Vincent Millay, poet
Edgar Ansell Mowrer, journalist
Reinhold Niebuhr, theologian
Samuel Putnam, biographer,
  translator
Burton Rascoe, journalist
Elmer Rice, playwright
James Stevens, regional writer
Ruth Suckow, novelist
Frank Sullivan, humorist
Lowell Thomas, commentator
Randolph Vance, folklorist

1893

Hamilton Fish Armstrong, publicist
Carleton Beals, traveler
S. N. Behrman, playwright
Morris Bishop, essayist
Maxwell Bodenheim, poet
Carl Carmer, regional writer
Elizabeth Coatsworth, poet, novelist
Russel Crouse, playwright
S. Foster Damon, poet, scholar
Donald Davidson, poet
Mathilde Eiker, novelist
Irving Fineman, novelist
Herbert Gorman, novelist
Ben Hecht, novelist, playwright
Stewart Holbrook, regional writer
Joseph Wood Krutch, critic
Margaret Leech, novelist, historian
Ralph Linton, anthropologist

Anita Loos, humorist
William March (William Edward
  March Campbell), novelist
John P. Marquand, novelist
Karl A. Menninger, psychiatrist
Charles Merz, journalist
Lloyd Morris, critic, social historian
F. S. C. Northrop, philosopher
Fulton Oursler, journalist
Dorothy Parker, story writer, poet
Cole Porter, lyricist
Evelyn Scott, novelist
Gilbert Seldes, critic
Thorne Smith, novelist
Hudson Strode, traveler, teacher
John W. Thomason, biographer,
  soldier
John V. A. Weaver, poet

1894

Brooks Atkinson, critic
John Bakeless, biographer
E. E. Cummings, poet
Clyde Brion Davis, novelist
George Fielding Eliot, journalist
Rachel Lyman Field, novelist
Esther Forbes, novelist, biographer
Michael Gold, journalist
Paul Green, playwright
Dashiell Hammett, novelist
Raymond Holden, poet
Rolfe Humphries, poet

Joseph Henry Jackson, critic
Eugene Jolas, poet, editor
Edison Marshall, novelist
Robert Nathan, novelist
Kenyon Nicholson, playwright
Jessica Nelson North, poet
Phelps Putnam, poet
Samuel Rogers, novelist
Agnes Smedley, China hand
Chard Powers Smith, novelist
Laurence Stallings, playwright
Donald Ogden Stewart, humorist

Genevieve Taggard, poet
Dorothy Thompson, publicist
James Thurber, humorist

Mark Van Doren, man of letters
Nelia Gardner White, novelist
Thames Williamson, novelist

1895

Ben Lucien Burman, novelist
Babette Deutsch, poet
Vardis Fisher, novelist
Buckminster Fuller, engineer
Caroline Gordon, novelist
Oscar Hammerstein 2d, librettist
Melville Herskovits, anthropologist
Robert Hillyer, poet
Susanne Langer, philosopher
John Howard Lawson, playwright
Lin Yu-t'ang, essayist

Lewis Mumford, essayist
Gardner Murphy, psychologist
Leonard Nason, novelist
Josephine Pinckney, novelist
Maurice Samuel, novelist
Nathan Schachner, biographer,
  novelist
George R. Stewart, novelist
Hans Otto Storm, novelist
Nora Waln, memoirist
Fredric Wertham, psychiatrist

Edmund Wilson, man of letters

1896

Philip Barry, playwright
Roark Bradford, story writer
Louis Bromfield, novelist
Slater Brown, essayist
Kyle Crichton, journalist
H. L. Davis, novelist, poet
John Dos Passos, novelist, traveler
Irwin Edman, essayist
Thomas Hornsby Ferril, poet
Louis Fischer, publicist
F. Scott Fitzgerald, novelist
Ramon Guthrie, poet, novelist
Henry Beetle Hough, regional writer
Bruce Lancaster, novelist

William Langer, historian
Robert McAlmon, story writer, poet
Gorham B. Munson, critic
Drew Pearson, journalist
Samson Raphaelson, playwright
Marjorie Kinnan Rawlings, novelist
Isidor Schneider, poet, novelist
Robert E. Sherwood, playwright
Grace Zaring Stone, novelist
Neil Harmon Swanson, novelist
Virgil Thomson, critic, composer
James P. Warburg, publicist
Helen C. White, novelist, scholar
George Willison, historian

1897

Joseph Auslander, poet
Stringfellow Barr, publicist
Louise Bogan, poet
Catherine Drinker Bowen, biographer
Lewis Browne, popular historian
Kenneth Burke, man of letters
Robert M. Coates, novelist
Merle Curti, historian
Bernard De Voto, critic, novelist
William Faulkner, novelist
Joseph Freeman, novelist
Paul Gallico, sportswriter, novelist
Josephine Herbst, novelist

Leslie Hotson, literary scholar
Christopher La Farge, novelist, poet
Josephine Lawrence, novelist
Eugene Lohrke, novelist
Lenore Marshall, poet, novelist
Van Wyck Mason, novelist
Dawn Powell, novelist
Fletcher Pratt, journalist
Henry Pringle, biographer
Lillian Smith, novelist, publicist
M. R. Werner, biographer
John Brooks Wheelwright, poet
Thornton Wilder, novelist, playwright

1898

Ludwig Bemelmans, novelist
Stephen Vincent Benét, poet, novelist

Thomas Boyd, novelist
Crane Brinton, historian

Malcolm Cowley, critic, poet
Eleanor Carroll Chilton, novelist
Harry Crosby, poet
Rose Franken, playwright, novelist
Horace Gregory, poet, critic
Harlan Hatcher, novelist

Walter Karig, novelist
Eugene Lyons, publicist
Donald Culross Peattie, nature writer
Henry Morton Robinson, novelist
Edward A. Weeks, Jr., critic, editor
Paul I. Wellman, novelist

1899

Léonie Adams, poet
Louis Adamic, publicist
Ralph Bates, novelist
James Warner Bellah, story writer
Archie Binns, novelist
Whit Burnett, story writer, anthologist
W. R. Burnett, novelist
Le Grand Cannon, novelist
Bruce Catton, historian
Humphrey Cobb, novelist
Hart Crane, poet
Edmund Gilligan, novelist
James Gray, novelist, critic
Anne Green, novelist

Louis M. Hacker, historian
Ernest Haycox, novelist
Ernest Hemingway, novelist
Matthew Josephson, biographer
Janet Lewis, novelist, poet
Walter Millis, historian
Vladimir Nabokov, novelist
Lynn Riggs, playwright
Vincent Sheean, personal historian
Bella and Samuel Spewack,
    playwrights
Phil Stong, novelist
Allen Tate, man of letters
Austin Warren, critic

E. B. White, essayist, poet

1900

Newton Arvin, critic
Emjo Basshe, playwright
Sally Benson, story writer
Myron Brinig, novelist
John Mason Brown, critic
Taylor Caldwell, novelist
V. F. Calverton, critic
Edward Dahlberg, novelist, critic
Foster Rhea Dulles, historian
Julian Green, novelist
Laura Z. Hobson, novelist
Quincy Howe, journalist
Cyril Hume, novelist
Ralph Ingersoll, journalist

Arthur Kober, story writer
Owen Lattimore, China hand
Richard McKeon, philosopher
Rosamond Marshall, novelist
Margaret Mitchell, novelist
Ernie Pyle, reporter
Adlai E. Stevenson, publicist
James Johnson Sweeney, art critic
Edward Wagenknecht, critic
William L. White, reporter
Oscar Williams, poet, anthologist
Yvor Winters, poet, critic
Frances Winwar, biographer
Thomas Wolfe, novelist

1901

B. A. Botkin, folklorist
Gerald Warner Brace, novelist
Virginius Dabney, journalist
John Gunther, reporter
A. B. Guthrie, novelist
Walter Havighurst, novelist
Granville Hicks, critic
Edgar Johnson, biographer
Oliver La Farge, novelist
Margaret Mead, anthropologist
Max Miller, memoirist

Theodore Morrison, poet, novelist
Louis Paul, novelist
Mario Pei, linguist
Theodore Pratt, novelist
Laura Riding, poet
Mari Sandoz, novelist, biographer
Cornelia Otis Skinner, humorist
John van Druten, playwright
Robert Wilder, novelist, scenarist
Glenway Wescott, novelist
Morton Dauwen Zabel, critic

Mortimer Adler, philosopher

Nathan Asch, novelist

Katharine Brush, novelist

Donald Barr Chidsey, novelist

Henry Steele Commager, historian

Jonathan Daniels, journalist

Kenneth Fearing, poet

Wolcott Gibbs, critic, playwright

C. Hartley Grattan, essayist

Sidney Hook, essayist

Langston Hughes, poet

Corliss Lamont, essayist

Harold D. Lasswell, political scientist

Max Lerner, publicist

Andrew Lytle, novelist

F. O. Matthiessen, critic

Ogden Nash, poet

Robert Raynolds, novelist

Quentin Reynolds, journalist

Theodore Spencer, poet

Donald A. Stauffer, critic

Christina Stead, novelist

John Steinbeck, novelist

Philip Wylie, novelist

Marya Zaturenska, poet

Hanson Baldwin, journalist

Kay Boyle, novelist

Gwen Bristow, novelist

Niven Busch, novelist, scenarist

Erskine Caldwell, novelist

John Chamberlain, critic

Marquis Childs, publicist

James Gould Cozzens, novelist

Countee Cullen, poet

Marcia Davenport, novelist

Walter D. Edmonds, novelist

Dudley Fitts, poet

Paul Horgan, novelist

Zora Neale Hurston, novelist

Charles R. Jackson, novelist

Clare Boothe Luce, playwright

Younghill Kang, novelist

Alexander Laing, novelist

Caroline Miller, novelist

Merrill Moore, poet

Louise Dickinson Rich, memoirist

Ernest J. Simmons, biographer

Irving Stone, novelist

James Street, novelist

Gerald Sykes, novelist

William York Tindall, critic

Leane Zugsmith, novelist

Hamilton Basso, novelist

Alvah Bessie, novelist

Richard P. Blackmur, critic, poet

Joseph Campbell, mythologist

Gladys Hasty Carroll, novelist

Vera Caspary, novelist

Hector Chevigny, memoirist

Clifford Dowdey, novelist

Frederick W. Dupee, critic

Richard Eberhart, poet

Stuart Engstrand, novelist

Clifton Fadiman, critic

James T. Farrell, novelist

James K. Feibleman, philosopher

Francis Ferguson, critic

George Gamow, physicist

Albert Halper, novelist

Moss Hart, playwright

Bravig Imbs, novelist

MacKinlay Kantor, novelist

George F. Kennan, publicist

Louis Kronenberger, critic

A. J. Liebling, journalist

Victoria Lincoln, novelist

Vincent McHugh, novelist

S. J. Perelman, humorist

William L. Shirer, current historian

Isaac Bashevis Singer, novelist

Charles Allen Smart, novelist

Betty Smith, novelist

Nathanael West, novelist

Christine Weston, novelist

James Burnham, publicist
Louise Field Cooper, novelist
Frederic Dannay and Manfred B. Lee
    ("Ellery Queen"), mystery writers
David Cornel De Jong, novelist
Viña Delmar, novelist
Charles G. Finney, novelist
Emily Hahn, memoirist
Lillian Hellman, playwright
Stanley J. Kunitz, poet
Meyer Levin, novelist

Phyllis McGinley, poet
Perry Miller, literary historian
Ashley Montagu, anthropologist
Herbert J. Muller, critic
John O'Hara, novelist
Ayn Rand, novelist
Kenneth Rexroth, poet
Edgar Snow, China hand
Lionel Trilling, critic
Dalton Trumbo, novelist
Mary Jane Ward, novelist

Robert Penn Warren, man of letters

The list of 385 names includes those of writers in many fields from the frivolous to the solemn. There are funny men, philosophers (mostly teachers of philosophy), speculative thinkers (Lewis Mumford, Kenneth Burke), and there is even a theologian, Reinhold Niebuhr. Some of the names gave me taxonomic troubles. How is one to classify a writer such as Henry Miller, whose books, though read as novels, are in fact candid confessions? My answer was to use the convenient term "memoirist," one that might also be applied to such younger writers as Jack Kerouac and Norman Mailer. The more or less candid confession, or "advertisement for myself," is becoming a central form of the new age.

Another question: what is the difference between a journalist and a reporter, or between a reporter and a publicist? Obviously the terms overlap, but I tried to distinguish them by applying three definitions that lexicographers might not accept. A journalist writes pieces for magazines or newspapers on miscellaneous topics. A reporter tells us, "This is how things are"; he makes a factual report that may sometimes be as long and detailed as those of John Gunther. A publicist writes "think books" in which he sets forth what he holds to be the right or the wrong policies for the nation to follow. I have classified twenty-two writers as publicists (including three "China hands," a special category), seventeen as journalists, and only two as reporters. It seems to me, however—a subjective judgment—that the quality of reporting during the age was higher than that of miscellaneous journalism and vastly higher than that of political thinking.

Some writers distinguished themselves in many fields. Bishop, Burke, Tate, Van Doren, Warren, and Wilson are all of them poets, novelists, essayists, critics, and Wilson is also reporter, memoirist, and playwright. For those six writers I have used the term "man of letters" as a token of their refusal to specialize.

Someone else working with the same material would adopt a different terminology and would certainly come up with a different list of names. Any such list, however, if carefully compiled, would lead to many of the same conclusions. One of these is that the period from 1925 to 1950, when writers of the chosen age group were most productive, was primarily an age of fiction. No less than 165 names on my own list are classified as those of novelists or story writers. If one should add to these the six men of letters, while also noting that many among the poets (59), the essayists and critics (49), and the historians and biographers (30) have each written one or more novels in their time, the emphasis on fiction would appear to be overwhelming. It was an age when many conceptions that might have been embodied in a play, an essay, a long poem, or even a short one were somehow expanded into a novel. Of course the explanation was largely economic. In those days almost all the best-selling books were novels. There were dozens of general or family magazines and each of them printed more fiction than any magazine did in later years. They offered generous rewards to those who could write to their specifications. In 1930 *The Saturday Evening Post* was paying a very few of its top authors $5000 for each story printed (Fitzgerald was paid $4000 and Faulkner only $1000 when he was lucky enough to have a story accepted, but still that would support his family for two or three months). After 1930 the magazine market for fiction became progressively smaller, and by 1960 it had nearly vanished. Critics were talking about "the decline of story telling" and "the death of the novel," but instead they might have talked about the decline and disappearance of the family-style magazine.

When fiction began to yield less certain rewards; when novelists had to be gamblers and a few of them—but only a few—made enormous killings, the others found various means to support themselves. There was a brief time in the 1930s when almost any novelist with a modest reputation could find a job in Hollywood. He could even keep the job, if he had acquired some competence in writing dialogue and in following a story line (as note the joint term "novelist and scenarist," which I might have applied to others besides Niven Busch and Robert Wilder). After World War II, there were teaching assignments open to novelists. Mass-market paperbacks partly took the place of magazines by offering small but dependable fees to "category" writers, the authors of mysteries, Westerns, medical romances, Gothic romances, and masturbatory daydreams. The present list does not include such authors, but it does reveal another development of rather more literary interest. After 1950 an increasing number of writers—some of them here classified as journalists, biographers, or social historians—produced what are known in the trade as "subject books," a few of which outsold the most popular fiction. The subjects were diverse—crimes, social movements, disasters, the life stories of picturesque rather than eminent persons—but the books were almost always novelistic in method. Though Truman Capote was first to use the term "nonfiction novel"—to describe his own book, *In Cold Blood* (1965) —it might have been applied to earlier works produced by dozens of others.

Still another conclusion from the list is that critics and essayists were becoming more prominent in the literary world. Books that publishers would have rejected in 1925 were widely praised and even read when they appeared after 1950. College English departments, as they attracted more students, were creating a substantial new audience. Women writers continued to be a minority even among novelists and poets; there are only 74 of them in my list of 385 writers, or less than 20 percent. I think there would be a much larger proportion of women in any list of writers born after 1905. Meanwhile the present list might serve as a footnote to a book that somebody else will have to write, a social history of American literature.

M.C.

Index